Oscar Satchell-Baeza

A special prize for an
outstanding Arthur Martin-Leake
essay.

June 2008

MARTIN-LEAKE
Double VC

By the same author:

Chavasse: Double VC

MARTIN-LEAKE
DOUBLE VC

by

ANN CLAYTON

with a Foreword by

The Director General Army Medical Services

LEO COOPER
LONDON

First published in Great Britain in 1994 by
LEO COOPER
an imprint of
Pen & Sword Books Ltd
47 Church Street, Barnsley, South Yorks S70 2AS

A CIP catalogue record for this book is
available from the British Library

ISBN 0 85052 397 4

Typeset by CentraCet Limited, Cambridge
Printed by Redwood Books Ltd
Trowbridge, Wilts

FOR THE SERVICE AND SACRIFICE OF
ALL MEMBERS OF
THE ROYAL ARMY MEDICAL CORPS
PAST AND PRESENT.

Contents

Maps

Acknowledgements

A book such as this depends greatly upon the goodwill and assistance of many people and institutions; without their freely-given co-operation the life of a man like Arthur Martin-Leake might easily have been obscured beyond recall. While the events that were considered newsworthy by his contemporaries were well-documented, the private side, indeed most of his seventy-nine years, were largely hidden from view – exactly as he would have wished, it must be said.

To two members of the Martin-Leake family I owe an enormous debt of gratitude. Arthur's second cousin Hugh generously made available family papers and original drawings executed by Arthur, and with his wife Sybil, extended to me the kindest of hospitality in their home, readily answering my many questions. Another second cousin, Kenneth Martin-Leake, entertained me liberally too, and gave me unlimited access to the wonderful archive of family letters, photographs and other material of which he is the custodian.

In Arthur's home village of High Cross, the present owner of Marshalls, David Webster, made me most welcome, allowing me to explore the estate freely, and introducing me to many residents of the village who were themselves most informative on the subject of High Cross's famous son. They included the Rev Hilary Sharman, Vicar of St John the Evangelist, Mrs de Ville, the late Mr 'Bumps' Wilkinson, Mrs Overton and Mrs Wilkinson. Similarly in the Essex village of Thorpe-le-Soken, the Vicar of St Michael's Church, the Rev V. R. Harrod, made time to show me round the church and graveyard, where Arthur's parents and younger brother sleep peacefully beneath the trees.

At Westminster, Arthur's old school, the librarian and archivist John Field shared his wide knowledge of the school's history with me, and allowed me to search the extensive archives; thanks are also due to Tony Money, Archivist at Radley College, Oxon, to Margaret Mardell, Recorder at Charterhouse, and to Julie Williams of University College London Medical School, for their keen interest in the project. Matthew Evans, a student of classics at the University of Oxford, kindly helped with a little Latin translation in Chapter 6.

Contacts made with a large number of libraries, museums and other institutions were unfailingly rewarded by unstinting help from their staffs. They included the Royal Engineers Museum, Chatham; the National Army Museum; the South African National Museum of Military History at Johannesburg; the Imperial War Museum; the Public Record Office at Kew; the Commonwealth War Graves Commission at Maidenhead and at Ypres; the General Medical Council; the British Red Cross; the Royal British Legion; the Royal Army Medical College at Millbank; the British Newspaper Library at Colindale. In particular I would like to thank the staffs at the Hertfordshire and Essex Record Offices for their prompt and patient assistance during the many days I spent there; the staff of the Liverpool John Moores University Library Service, particularly Pat Williams; and Peter Liddle, FRHistS, Keeper of the Liddle Collection at the University of Leeds. Others whose expertise was generously given were Lt Col Roy Eyeions of the Royal Army Medical Corps Museum at Aldershot; Shirley Dixon of the Wellcome Institute for the History of Medicine; Major Tony Astle, Archivist of the Cheshire Regiment; Hedley Sutton of the British Library (Oriental and Indian Collections); Michael Bott, Keeper of Archives and Manuscripts in the University of Reading, and Derek Crook of the Liverpool Medical Institution.

Much helpful advice was given by individuals far more expert in the Boer War and Great War periods than I, particularly Lt Col Bob Wyatt MBE, TD, Editor of the *Bulletin* of the Military Historical Society; Lt Col J. D. Sainsbury TD, FSA, Chairman of the Hertfordshire Yeomanry Trust; Denis Pillinger, Custodian of the Lummis VC and GC files on behalf of the Military Historical Society, and Chris Kempton of the Victorian Military Society.

Among many fellow-members of the Western Front Association, the help of Ray Westlake with information and Graham Maddocks with the photographs was much valued; further help and encouragement came from Trevor Pidgeon, Paul Reed, Ron Clifton, Steve Wall and the late George Wall, Colin Kilgour, Adrian Clayton, John Bailey, Derek Heaney, David Ashwin, Robin Clay, Jim and Clarice Fallon, Derek Sheard, Col T. A. Cave CBE, and G. Kingsley Ward from Canada. I was also very grateful for the enthusiastic support given by Col J. Egan and Major A. J. Tanner of 208 General Hospital (v), RAMC Liverpool, and by Major S. B. Whitmore, MBE. The editorial skills of Tom Hartman were, once again, applied in a manner that could only serve to enhance the finished product, and his knowledge and sensitive approach were greatly appreciated by the author.

In spite of the huge amount of advice and help offered by the above-named and by others, it is, of course, entirely possible that errors remain; the responsibility for them is wholly mine.

As always, my gratitude for the patience and support shown by Peter, Diane and David goes without saying, but I'd like to say it anyway.

Liverpool, July 1994

Abbreviations used in the text

AAP	Advanced Aid Post
ADMS	Assistant Director Medical Services
ADS	Advanced Dressing Station
BEF	British Expeditionary Force
BNR	Bengal-Nagpur Railway
BRCS	British Red Cross Society
CCS	Casualty Clearing Station
DGAMS	Director-General Army Medical Services
DMS	Director Medical Services
FA	Field Ambulance
FRCS	Fellowship of the Royal College of Surgeons
MAC	Motor Ambulance Convoy
MO	Medical Officer
NCO	Non-Commissioned Officer
PMO	Principal Medical Officer
RAMC	Royal Army Medical Corps
RAP	Regimental Aid Post
SAC	South African Constabulary
UCH	University College Hospital

Foreword

by

Major General F. B. Mayes QHS MB BS FRCS

Director General Army Medical Services

The Royal Army Medical Corps proudly commemorates in its VC Room the twenty-nine members of the Army Medical Services who have, over the years, received the highest award for gallantry on the field of battle available to the British Army. Among these heroic men are two medical officers who achieved the rare distinction of being awarded a Bar to the Victoria Cross. They are Noel Chavasse and Arthur Martin-Leake.

The reader will discover in Arthur Martin-Leake a man of extreme modesty, who shunned publicity, but whose spirit of adventure and patriotic fervour took him to many parts of the world in the course of his career. Thus it was that, although a qualified doctor, he first saw uniformed service in the South African Wars as a Trooper in the Imperial Yeomanry. Soon transferring to medical employment, it was initially as a Civil Surgeon, which he interestingly recorded as being financially more attractive than a commission in the newly formed Royal Army Medical Corps. Arthur's professional ambition was to become a Consultant Surgeon. It must have been deeply uspetting to him to have to eventually abandon this aim, as a consequence of a major injury sustained to his right hand in the final stages of this Campaign in which he won his first VC. Nevertheless it is clear that he continued to utilise his surgical skills to good effect whenever the opportunity presented.

Ann Clayton presents a meticulously researched and absorbing account of the life and times of this gallant man and his illustrious family, with particular emphasis on his participation in the South African Wars and the 1914–1918 War. It is an ideal companion volume to her earlier successful and equally fascinating publication *Chavasse: Double VC*.

Captain Stephen Martin = Elizabeth Hill
("Adopted" by Sir John Leake;
Name "Martin-Leake" assumed 1721)
1666-1736

(Garter King) Stephen = Anne Powell
of Thorpe Hall   of Marshalls
1702-1773

John = Mary Calvert
1739-1837

Elizabeth Hamilton (1)   =   Captain George   =   (2) Sarah Ford
1765-1807   Stephens   1781-1863
                               1760-1832

Stephen Ralph = Georgiana
1782-1865   1796-1880

Eliza = William Plunkett
1812-1845   1807-1844

Other
Issue

Susannah = Spencer Shelley   Stephen = Isabel   Rose = T. A. Stoughton   Frances   (1) C. Crespigny
of Newnham-on-Severn   1826-1893 (1859) 1835-1924   1840-1924   of Owlpen   1834-1908   (2) (1881)
                                                                  Glos.   John Russell
                                                                                                  Reynolds

Louisa Tennant = William
1831-1918

Stephen   Georgiana   William   Richard   Francis   Isabel   ARTHUR   Theodore
('Steenie')   ('Sittie')   ('Willie')   ('Dick')   ('Frank')   ('Bella')   ('Artie')   ('Theo')
1861-1940   1863-1949   1865-1947   1867-1949   1869-1928   1871-1930   1874-1953   1879-1907
                                                                                                        = (1930)
                                                                                                        Winifred Carroll
                                                                                                        1885-1932

Other
Issue

Rev. William   Hugh
Ralph   1880-1977
1865-1942   = Lois
= Jessie   Bloxham
Gann

John   Kenneth   Philip   Margery   Cecil   Hugh
d. 1973   George   k. in a.   d. 1979   Evelyn
              k. in a.   1944   1945
              1944

MARTIN-LEAKE FAMILY TREE

CHAPTER ONE

An Illustrious Inheritance

The peace and quiet of the village of High Cross in Hertfordshire is disturbed nowadays by the constant sound of traffic along the fearsomely busy trunk road, the A10, that bisects the small community. Following the line of the old Roman road called Ermine Street, a continuous stream of cars and lorries heads north towards Cambridge and south towards London. But in the centre of High Cross, leading off westwards towards Sacombe, Marshalls Lane wends its way between high hedges; at a fork in the road a sign proclaims 'Marshalls', and the house of that name is just visible amongst the trees. Here on 4 April, 1874 – Easter Sunday – was born Dr Arthur Martin-Leake, Victoria Cross and Bar, and here, seventy-nine years later, he died. From Marshalls, like his five brothers, he set off to travel the world – to India, South Africa, the Balkans, France and Flanders. But Marshalls always called him back, and from Marshalls he made his final journey, across the A10 to the little country graveyard of the church of St John the Evangelist opposite, whose tower can be glimpsed above the green canopy. One thing is certain – for this quiet, solitary man, whose experience ranged from the bazaars of Calcutta to the trenches of the Great War, and from African safari to Balkan atrocities, there was nowhere else on earth that he ever really wanted to be but in the leafy Hertfordshire countryside around Marshalls, that for him epitomized 'Home'.

Arthur Martin-Leake's ancestry on both sides included some illustrious names. The double-barrelled surname itself was assumed in circumstances that established a precise date for the origins of his father's side of the family. In the reign of Queen Anne, one Sir John Leake, who had built a career in the Navy, was elevated to the position of Commander-in-Chief of the Queen's Fleet. He was wealthy enough to purchase estates at Beddington and Oxted, straddling the North Downs in Surrey, as well as having a substantial town house at Mile End, only a mile from the Thames at Stepney, and another at Greenwich. Sir John's wife was Christian Hill, daughter of a sea captain, Richard Hill, and she bore Sir John six children. Only one, Richard, survived to adulthood, but he was a constant anxiety to his parents. Not only was he a ruthless and wilful Captain in the Queen's Navy,

1

commanding several men-of-war in such a flamboyant and headstrong way that his Rear-Admiral father was seriously embarrassed, but in affairs of the heart he would listen to no advice; his frantic father, widowed since 1709, was distraught; his sole surviving heir showed every sign of squandering the family's assets in a most profligate manner.

In 1714, when Queen Anne died, Sir John Leake found less favour with the new government, and retired. By this time he was fifty-eight, and becoming increasingly concerned about the future of his estates and fortune. Sir John's biographer, Stephen Martin-Leake, commented in 1750:

> 'All this while he had a son, Richard, his only child, but unhappily of such a natural bad disposition, that he seems to have been born to afflict him. His grandfather cast his nativity at birth, and pronounced, he would be very vicious, very fortunate, and very unhappy: that he would get a great deal of money, but squander it all away and die young. I shall only observe that this prediction was fulfilled. For being made a captain in the Navy very young, in a few years he got more by prizes than his father did in his whole life. It was an unhappy circumstance that whilst Sir John was gaining never-fading laurels, his son was counter-mining his reputation by inglorious actions; and to finish, the man married disgracefully; so that his father was discomposed by his son's repeated follies; who, by this time, having spent all, depended upon him for support.'[1]

Richard's 'disgraceful marriage' was the last straw for Sir John. The lady in question was one Martha Wells, whose fault seems to have been that she did not spring from the right sort of family. She did not provide her husband with an heir, and Sir John thus had no grandchild, not even an unsuitable one, by which to secure the family's future. In an age when property and legitimate succession were of paramount concern to anyone in 'Society', it is easy to appreciate Sir John's anguish.

He felt compelled to turn elsewhere in his search for someone to inherit his wealth and his name, and his choice fell upon his brother-in-law, Captain Stephen Martin. Here was a man after Sir John's own heart – indeed, they had served together with the Fleet for many years, beginning with the fourteen-year-old Stephen's first voyage on a ship commanded by Sir John in 1680. The older man protected Stephen and furthered his career, until he ultimately held the position of Flag-Captain to Sir John and became his closest confidant. He also had a son, who, though young, seemed already to have a promising future. Stephen knew very well the nature of Sir John's problems with his son Richard, and it cannot have been totally unexpected when, in February, 1717, his patron informed him that he had changed his will. Sir John's fortune was to be left to trustees for the use of Richard during his life; then, if he died without issue, everything was to go to Stephen. The will stated that this was 'the most public Testimony I could give, and the most grateful means whereby I might convey to Posterity this Memorial of our Friendship.'[2]

In the event Richard died in March, 1720, at the age of thirty-eight. His father, commenting to Stephen Martin that 'now we have but one son between us', allowed Richard's widow Martha to occupy the house at Mile End. Slowly his own health declined. His last request of his friend Stephen Martin was that he should assume the name of 'Leake'. Sir John died in August, 1720, only five months after his son.

Stephen did what Sir John had wanted. By Royal Warrant dated 19 December, 1721, he joined the name of Leake to his own and the Martin-Leake 'dynasty' began. The Leake Arms were incorporated into his own.

Next, Stephen set about consolidating his inheritance, which was worth a total of £30,000. He bought a country seat – Thorpe Hall near Clacton in Essex for £4,200, and spent a further £1,000 on repairs. Unfortunately he invested unwisely in what has become known as the South Sea Bubble, and when it burst towards the end of 1720 he lost £20,000. He had some enormous family expenses too. For example, he persuaded Martha Leake to leave the Mile End House in 1722, paying her the sum of £450 in compensation. He had to pay two dowries of £1,500 each for his daughters' marriages; then, in 1723, his wife died and the funeral cost £400.

He had experienced in his own family the problems caused by unsuitable marriages: his sister Hester had married 'meanly and without the consent of her father', and had been left one shilling in his will as punishment. This was not to be allowed to happen again. He decided to invest considerable effort in the future of his son Stephen, by negotiating a Treasury clerkship for him. But the post never materialized and Steven had to take the negotiator to court; it cost him £1,200. In 1727 he managed to obtain an entry for young Stephen into the Heralds' Office, but to do so he had to mortgage Thorpe Hall. Two years later his finances were so strained that he had to sell the estates at Beddington and Oxted for £4,830. Finally, as he was coming home from a concert at Ludgate Hill, he lost his 'great diamond ring', worth £500. This was a great sadness, as it had been given to Sir John Leake by Prince George of Denmark, Queen Anne's consort. The ring was never found. Stephen died in 1736 at the age of sixty-nine, considerably poorer than when he had come into Sir John's fortune.

From now on at least one son, usually the eldest, in every generation of the direct Martin-Leake line was baptized Stephen, like Captain Martin's first-born son. This Stephen caused his father no little satisfaction and pride, for he worked his way through the ranks of the College of Heralds and concluded his career as 'Garter Principal King of Arms', an appointment he held until his death. In keeping with his high office, he took part in the funeral of George II in 1760 and in the marriage and Coronation of George III in 1761. He was an avid writer and kept remarkable diaries and journals; his major work was a two-volume biography in 1750 of the family's benefactor, Sir John Leake.[3]

Stephen Martin-Leake made an excellent marriage to Anne Powell and subsequently found positions for his own sons, John and Stephen, in the Heralds' Office. Anne's father was Fletcher Powell, and he it was who owned Marshalls, the house in Hertfordshire of which Arthur and his brothers were so fond in the twentieth century. Powell had lost a great deal of money in the South Sea Bubble and had been forced to sell his Welsh estate at Downton, New Radnor. He bought the small Marshalls estate from one Samuel Dighton. Stephen and Anne spent their married lives at Thorpe Hall and when Stephen died in 1773 he was buried in the chancel of the church of St Michael in the nearby village of Thorpe-le-Soken. Fletcher Powell was also buried there when he died a few months after his son-in-law. Following this double bereavement, Anne went to live at Marshalls, thus beginning a line of Martin-Leake owners that remained unbroken until 1973. For more than a century, however, the Martin-Leakes were always buried at Thorpe.

The Garter King's second son John continued the line. He was Arthur Martin-Leake's great-grandfather. He inherited yet another house, Woodside, in Old Windsor, from a distant cousin, and spent his time between the three properties at Thorpe, Marshalls and Windsor. He too held high government office, being Chief Clerk to the Treasury and representing the King in Florida until the American War of Independence broke out in 1783. In 1811 he retired, with the magnificent pension of £2,000, and ended his days at Marshalls, where he died in 1836 of whooping cough, at the great age of ninety-seven. Like his forebears, he was buried at Thorpe.

There was certainly no shortage of colourful characters in the Martin-Leake family. One of Arthur's great-uncles, William, had a distinguished career in the Army and was present in Egypt when Napoleon's forces were defeated in 1801. In September, 1802, in company with a Mr Hamilton, who was Private Secretary to Lord Elgin, William went to Greece and hired a small boat in which to transport the Elgin Marbles to Britain. Unfortunately the vessel was wrecked, though no lives were lost, but the Marbles had to be recovered from the seabed by local sponge divers. A ship from England was sent to complete the journey, and the Marbles were placed in the British Museum, where they remain a cause of contention between Britain and Greece. In 1804 William was sent as a trusted envoy to Nelson's fleet in the Mediterranean and was received by him on board HMS *Victory*.

For many years William lived in Greece, and expended much energy in defending Greek interests, in which he had a friend in Lord Byron, whom he met many times. When he died in 1859 his collection of 10,000 coins, mostly Greek, was accepted by the Fitzwilliam Museum in Cambridge.

This was the kind of family adventure story with which Arthur grew up. His grandfather, Stephen Ralph, born in 1782 (the youngest son of John) continued the tradition of roving the world and becoming involved in somewhat hazardous undertakings. In 1815, at the age of thirty-three, he was in Paris when it was occupied by the Allies after the defeat of Napoleon. He described what he saw, in the same manner that Arthur and his brothers almost a century later would recount what happened on their travels:

> 'The streets are filled with officers and soldiers dressed in the uniforms of nearly all the nations of Europe . . . the whole city appears like one great Fair, in which the gaity [sic] of the Parisians vies with the splendour of the allied monarchs and of their armies and attendants. On the Boulevards are the stiff, formal Austrian Guards surrounding the quarters of their Emperor and looking more like machines than men; the numerous savage tribes in the service of the Emperor of Russia are seen in small parties in different parts of the city; the handsome, well-grown boys which form the Prussian Army are wandering about all the public places evidently longing for plunder and mischief, and relying more in their General, who is willing to encourage them in it, than in their king. The English are lounging hautily [sic] about the streets, holding in contempt their allies as well as their enemies and offending them both by pretending out of pure love of justice and mercy to take the part of the latter against the former; in the meantime the French are everywhere obsequious and polite, dissembling their indignation and putting the best face they can upon their unfortunate situation.'[4]

After forty-nine years with the Treasury, Stephen Ralph retired on a pension of £1,200; this was equal to his most recent salary. He inherited Thorpe Hall and Marshalls in 1862 when his brother John died without a male heir. During John's time at Thorpe Hall his eighteen-year-old niece Jessie fell from a window and was killed. Here was another tragi/romantic episode to thrill and perhaps frighten Arthur and his siblings. But Stephen Ralph only enjoyed his inheritance for a short time, dying in London in 1865. He was buried in the prestigious Victorian cemetery at Kensal Green. He left three sons and three daughters; the second son, Stephen, was Arthur's father.

Born in 1826, Stephen was educated at the Blackheath Proprietary School, then at King's College, London and St John's College, Cambridge, where he graduated Bachelor of Arts in 1848. He then decided to follow a career in the law, and was a student at the Middle Temple for five years before being called to the Bar in January, 1853. He practised on the 'Home Circuit' for a time, but was subject to a great deal of nervous strain, finding that for long periods he lacked energy and enthusiasm for his work. He lived at Maitland Park Terrace in Hampstead, but he was a studious and sensitive man and much preferred the countryside to town life; fortunately his wife shared this view, and before his father's death they were formally established at Marshalls, High Cross, Hertfordshire.

On 24 September, 1859, at Leckhampton Parish Church, Gloucestershire, Stephen had married Miss Isabel Plunkett. He was thirty-three years old, his bride was twenty-four. They were already related, in that they had a common maternal grandfather. Isabel's father was William Plunkett, Barrister-at-Law, of Lincoln's Inn but with strong Gloucestershire connections, but as he had died in 1844 there is little possibility that the bridegroom knew the bride's father professionally. At the time Isabel and Stephen met the Plunkett family was reeling under a terrible blow, the eldest son Captain John Plunkett having been killed in the Indian Mutiny of 1857–8. The sepoys (native Indian soldiers) of his regiment, the 6th Bengal Native Infantry, mutinied, and 'he, together with other officers of the Regiment, was foully murdered'.[5]

By 1865, when the couple had taken up residence at Marshalls, Stephen decided to abandon his legal career and concentrate on running the family estates and on writing legal texts. He published two works, *The Law of Property in Land* and *The Law of Contracts*, but the administration of Thorpe Hall and Marshalls, as well as his growing family, took up most of his time and energy. It seems also that he was developing a measure of hypochondria, taking the greatest of care with his health and discussing every symptom with anyone who would listen; he certainly worried constantly about his income and investments, but did find time to serve as a Justice of the Peace for Hertfordshire, as Treasurer of the Friendly Societies of High Cross and of the neighbouring village of Colliers End, and as Chairman of the Highway Board for Hadham, a few miles away.

Stephen regarded himself as particularly fortunate in his choice of Isabel Plunkett as his wife. From the day they were married she devoted herself to taking care of him and doing her utmost to relieve the burden of worry which at times threatened to overwhelm him. A small, quiet woman, with a somewhat sharp, birdlike face, she was deceptively strong when it came to running her household or bringing up her family. The epithet she applied to her quiet bespectacled husband was 'my Lovey-Dovey'; as the children grew up they always called her 'Mammy', but referred to their father as 'The

Dovey'. Her servants and her children were never in any doubt about who was in control at home, and they developed a respect for her that lasted until her death at the age of eighty-eight.

During the first twenty years of her married life Isabel was fully occupied in bearing and rearing her eight children. Stephen was born in 1861 and Georgiana in 1863, both in London. The remaining six children were all born at Marshalls: William (1865), Richard (1867), Francis (1869), Isabel (1871), Arthur (1874) and Theodore (1878).

The Marshalls estate has a history going back at least to 1337, when it was acquired by Robert Marshall (Le Mareschal) from Elizabeth de Burgh, Lady of the Manor of Standon. The house first consisted of a Saxon hall about thirty-five feet long; traces of it were discovered when Arthur's father was making alterations in 1878. When Fletcher Powell purchased it in May, 1735, there were two Marshalls tenements – one to be occupied by the new owner; the other, the farm portion of the group of buildings that huddled together on the site, was always let to a tenant farmer.[6] By the mid-nineteenth century Marshalls was at the centre of the social and econmic life of High Cross. Situated two hundred yards or so from the main thoroughfare, the house and estate were of crucial importance to the local economy. Its 259 acres brought in several hundred pounds each year in rent and provided employment for many of the local people; the total population of the village was less than 700.

Stephen's duties as a 'gentleman' involved overseeing the tenancies and tied cottages, and hiring and firing workers. In 1878, when Theodore Edward, his eighth and last child, was born, he decided that the house really could not provide satisfactory accommodation for his sizeable young family. Building works were put in train, separating 'Marshalls Farm' from the main house by moving it to the other side of the lane and constructing a new farmhouse and farm buildings. The water supply was improved. The old well near the front door was disused and covered over, though it still stands today, in a picturesque corner of the garden, and a new well was dug. A brick wall was built to surround the garden. The cost of all these improvements was almost £2,500.[7]

Now Isabel was involved in running a substantial country house. It had four reception rooms on the ground floor and six bedrooms above; of necessity, numerous servants from the village were engaged, some resident and some coming in daily. The gardens were correspondingly extensive, with lawns and shrubberies, a paddock for the children's ponies and later their hunters, an ornamental lake on which the children could play in an old rowing skiff, and a walled vegetable garden from which, Stephen hoped, the harvesting of fruit and vegetables might allow the household to be largely self-sufficient.

Social life was limited, but typical of the Victorian landed gentry. Frequent visits were paid to neighbouring families of similar social standing, the nearest being the Giles-Pullers at Youngsbury, less than a mile distant at the other side of the village. Their country house was set in parkland that was so captivating that Capability Brown himself had declared it to be 'incapable of improvement.'[8] A few miles away towards Stevenage was Bengeo Hall, seat of the Gosselin family, who were distantly related to the Martin-Leakes. Longer visits were made to Isabel's sister Rose and her husband Colonel Harrison Trent-Stoughton at Owlpen, Gloucestershire. The most flamboyant member of Isabel's family was undoubtedly her sister Frances, who was married first to Charles Crespigny, and after his death to John Russell Reynolds, Physician in Ordinary to Queen Victoria. Everyone recognized that Aunt Frances was an awful snob; when Russell Reynolds was created a Baronet in 1895 she became a 'Lady' too. Her influence on young Arthur's future was to be significant.

His ownership of Thorpe Hall gave Arthur's father constant cause for concern. It was in the Essex village of Thorpe-le-Soken, on the road between Colchester and the seaside watering-places of Frinton and Walton-on-the-Naze. Thorpe-le-Soken was a small farming community, with a population of 1365 in the 1841 Census, its name dating back to the twelfth century. The Hall was its most impressive mansion. Its estate of 354 acres brought in rents of £611, a not inconsiderable contribution to the finances of the family fifty miles away at Marshalls. The Hall that Arthur knew had been built between 1822 and 1824, on the site of a much earlier building but retaining a few of the original features. This nineteenth century house is today quite startling in design. Built of white brick, it stands square and flat-roofed, its windows arranged asymmetrically and the whole building looking out of place in its garden setting, but it has a very definite air of the Regency period in which it was built.

The gardens were supposedly renowned throughout England, though many of the finest trees had been felled in a severe winter gale in 1860.[9] Lakes covered ten acres and there were five acres of 'beautifully timbered walks'.[10] But one of Thorpe's drawbacks was its isolation, the only link with the wider world being a horse-drawn omnibus each day between Thorpe and London. By the 1860s local railway 'mania' had arrived, in the shape of the 'Mistley, Thorpe and Walton Railway Company', and Stephen agreed to sell nine acres from Thorpe Park for the construction of a line. A station was built half a mile from the Hall, and this fact was utilized to good effect whenever a new tenant was being sought.

In spite of the incursions of the railway there was enough left of the 'pleasure gardens' for them to be seen as one of the major attractions when Arthur's father was trying to find a tenant in the 1870's; he never contemplated living at Thorpe himself but needed the income from the estate. By that time the Hall needed extensive refurbishment, and Stephen spent several thousand pounds on this exercise, expenditure that added greatly to his worries back at Marshalls. Fortunately a proportion of the cost was defrayed by the sale of timber from Thorpe, but he still had to borrow £5,000 from a neighbour. After he had advertised for two years, a tenant, Lieutenant-Colonel Bridges, was found, although the Martin-Leakes retained the right to cut and collect timber and to enter and view the premises twice a year.[11] Thereafter, until the Hall was finally sold in 1913, the problems of being an absentee landlord troubled first Stephen and then his widow Isabel.

An additional responsibility was shouldered by the family in respect of St Michael's Church at Thorpe. Many Martin-Leake ancestors were already buried there, in the chancel for the most part. When the church was being rebuilt in the mid-1870s, retaining the sixteenth century red-brick tower, Arthur's father was the lay rector, and contributed a considerable sum to the £3500 cost, including a stained-glass East window to the memory of his father. The family also had an 'Obligation' to repair the Chancel roof in perpetuity; this was later transmuted into a sum of money, and a small trust fund for the purpose was set up which continues to this day.

Meanwhile in High Cross life to a large extent centred around St John's Church, which had been first consecrated in 1847; here again a family of such local standing felt it had a duty to give the church financial support, though little capital expenditure was needed until the early years of the twentieth century. The family were certainly regular churchgoers: in Victorian society this was to be expected. But there is no evidence of any real religious fervour, although Mrs Martin-Leake was always described as a 'very Christian lady'.[12] The Martin-Leakes went to church because there one made contact with one's social equals, and from one of the village's leading families regular Sunday worship was expected. It seems more likely that the children would sit through Matins in a state of suspended animation, waiting for the moment when they could run across the main street and along the lane to Marshalls, where an ever-expanding menagerie of animals awaited them, and where the fields, woods and streams of the valley of the River Bourne beckoned.

Eight children in the family meant that as far as games and friends were concerned they had little need for other playmates, and their imaginative capers were stimulated by the constant companionship of seven others, not counting the young servants invited to join in, who came from the same constant and loving background. For there can be no doubt that this was a family with extraordinary inner strength. It acted and responded as a unit, headed by devoted parents. The children all grew up with a sense of inner contentment and self-sufficiency; when the six sons went in search of adventure to the other side of the world, (and they all found it), it was a quite unusual sense of permanence and continuity, epitomized by the house, Marshalls itself, that finally drew them all back.

CHAPTER TWO

'Mammy Makes a Lovely Widow'

The education of Stephen Martin-Leake's six sons caused him no little disquiet. Dealing with the two daughters, Georgiana, known to the family as 'Sittie', and Isabel ('Bella') was much more straightforward; it was not expected that a country gentleman would send his daughters to school, and a series of governesses, together with what they could learn at their mother's knee, would very adequately suit them for whatever the future might hold. The two girls never did marry, as it turned out, but they were given a good grounding in running a home, entertaining on a modest scale, and doing 'good works' about the village. All the children were taught to ride, and participated enthusiastically in meets of the Puckeridge Hunt a couple of miles distant, and in hare-coursing with beagles at nearby Fanham's Hall. Sittie became a great help to her mother, especially after the death of the 'Dovey' in 1893; as the elder sister of the Martin-Leake boys she took upon herself the duty of writing to them during their foreign adventures, and answering any requests they might make to be sent items indispensable to life in tropical climes. Bella, six years younger, became a redoubtable horse-woman, and developed an all-absorbing interest in gardening, re-designing and replanting the Marshalls gardens several times during her lifetime.

So their father had no worries as far as the girls were concerned. The boys, especially William ('Willie') and Richard ('Dick'), were another matter, a source of great consternation to both parents. The eldest son, Stephen ('Steenie'), had from an early age been allowed to rove the woods and fields of the Marshalls estate, trapping, fishing, and ultimately shooting at wildlife and game with a shotgun in complete freedom, and the others followed suit. He and his brothers had a tutor at home during the early years, but their parents soon realized that the discipline of a public school was needed. Steenie was sent first to a small preparatory establishment, Temple Grove School, East Sheen, on the fringe of Richmond Park, Surrey. His time there was uneventful and his progress reasonably satisfactory; at any rate he obtained a place at Charterhouse, one of England's foremost public schools, which had moved from London's Smithfield to new buildings in Godalming, Surrey, in 1872. He entered the school in 'Oration Quarter' (September), 1875, at the age of thirteen. A member of the House known as

Hodgsonites, Steenie kept a fairly low profile for the next four years, not winning any prizes, or being appointed Monitor; he emerged into the limelight only very occasionally, to play in the Second Cricket Eleven. Just before he left the school in 'Cricket Quarter' (July), 1879, he shone momentarily when he took a crucial catch in an inter-house match, but unfortunately was out for a duck himself.[1] He was then accepted for a course at the Royal Engineering College, Cooper's Hill, London.

Meanwhile the second son, Willie, had followed his brother to East Sheen, with disastrous results. In July, 1878, Willie was just thirteen when his Headmaster, Mr B. F. Waterfield, who was so angry that he could not bring himself to mention Willie by name, wrote to Marshalls:

'Your boy now refuses to do any work. Mr Edgar took the class this afternoon in Arithmetic and though the work of the term has been fractions, the boy could not give the meaning of any sign used.

It is absolutely impossible for me to keep a boy in the school who behaves in this way – his example would soon be fatal to the class. No master can teach if a boy is at liberty to set them at defiance.

I am glad to avoid the necessity of inflicting punishment but this requires the withdrawal from the school of a boy who feels himself in open opposition. I have told the boy that I have no recourse but to request his removal at once. I can give him one week's further trial, but no more.'[2]

Willie's behaviour improved not at all during that final week and he left East Sheen for good in August, 1878, ninth out of eleven boys, armed with the following Report:

'He is not in my opinion stupid, and I see in him no sign of vice, but he is thoroughly idle and full of childish tricks. He is extremely careless in his work . . . thoughtlessness in addition to idleness prevents progress. . . . I cannot say that I think him in any way fit for a public school.'[3]

What happened to Willie next is not clear. Perhaps his father found a place for him at another preparatory school. But in May, 1880, he was admitted into Grant's House at Westminster School. His achievements there were unremarkable; indeed it is likely that his behaviour and attitude led to his leaving Westminster just one short year later. By this time he was sixteen years old, and his frantic father tried one last attempt to educate and civilize him. By 1883 Willie was a pupil at a school in Boulogne-sur-Mer, but he attracted trouble yet again. He wrote from the Rue Beaurepaire to his father:

> 'I can't help the row. I do not know what they have said to you but I think they have both of them behaved very badly to me. It began about talking in school. Mr Nicholson got very excited and set me some Virgil to learn and called me a 'cur' and said he would like to make my hide feel it! I told him that it was not the way to speak to a gentleman. He said he would speak to the Head about it; I said I would save him the trouble and do it myself. Then we shut up for a bit. In the evening he asked me for the Virgil. I told him I was not going to do it after the way he had spoken to me. I tried my best to explain it to the Head but Nic. had had first say and he would not hear me, he said Mr Nic. would leave if I did not leave or beg his pardon and he could not afford to lose him. I told the Head I would beg his pardon if he would retract the word 'cur'. Mr N. said he would do no such thing. The Head won't even let me play football. If the boats had suited I should have come over this morning. I am not going to stand the way the Head speaks about it.'[4]

So Willie came home in disgrace again. In desperation his father turned to an occupation that he had not hitherto considered – the Army. Its reputation as a career for gentlemen was not particularly good in the last quarter of the nineteenth century, but Willie was persuaded to seek entry via the Hertfordshire Militia, and by December, 1884, was heading for South Africa as a Trooper with the 1st Mounted Rifles, otherwise known as Methuen's Horse.

Back home the third son, Dick, was now giving his fair share of trouble. Perhaps unwisely, his father sent him to East Sheen as well, where he arrived just a year before Willie was expelled. Straightaway it was reported to Marshalls that the ten-year-old 'Leake Mi' was at least two years behind other boys of his age, and showed no intention of learning anything:

> 'In the examination he declared himself incapable of making any answer to any question and was the only boy in the school who showed up nothing. . . . Unless there is a great and speedy change, preparation for any good public school will be an impossibility.'[5]

Dick stumbled on through two more years at the school. Finally, in November, 1879, when he was twelve years old, his father had already decided to remove him when a serious complaint arrived from the Headmaster:

'My dear Sir,

I am sorry. It is never agreeable to admit a failure. This boy is sharp enough and as he grows up will probably see the folly of idleness – but we find it impossible to get work from him. Perhaps a small school may obtain a greater hold over him than we have been able to secure. I regret that I must add to my letter a complaint of serious mischief. He was sent out yesterday into Richmond Park under the care of a master. He separated himself from the master, which he is strictly forbidden to do, remained behind and was seen by the gatekeeper in the act of breaking the fences. With a thick stick he broke off the top of one paling after another. The tops of the palings were brought to me this morning and the keeper tells me that there are many more broken, split and damaged.

Had I not been known to the keeper, he could have been arrested and taken before the Magistrate at Richmond. As it is, I have arranged that the damage shall be repaired at your expense, and the annoyance of a prosecution avoided.'[6]

Dick's father immediately asked Steenie, studying at Cooper's Hill, to go down to Richmond to investigate. Steenie found that Dick had not been the only boy involved, and that far fewer palings had been damaged than the Headmaster claimed. He thought five shillings should cover the cost, not the twenty pounds being canvassed by the Head. What was more, he felt that Dick was being far too severely punished, having to do drill and lines every day until the end of term. 'I thoroughly pity him,' wrote Steenie. But Mr Martin-Leake decided to end the matter by paying the bill and withdrawing Dick from the school.[7]

Enquiries were made for another establishment, and a preparatory school nearer home, The Grange at Stevenage, was persuaded to take Dick on. This smaller school, headed by Mr Osborne Seager, seems to have been far more compatible with Dick's temperament, and there were no more accusatory letters to his father. From Stevenage Dick went on, in January, 1882, to Westminster, where he spent an undistinguished but quiet two years. In 1884 he entered King's College, London, in the footsteps of his father, and, like Steenie, studied engineering. Once they had qualified, the two brothers followed parallel careers, often working in close partnership.

Next came Francis ('Frank'), the fourth son. At the age of ten, he too was sent to Mr Seager's school at Stevenage. Early reports showed a degree of tolerance and undersanding on the part of the Headmaster:

> 'Frank is still wanting in diligence but I hope he will as time goes on improve in this respect, and he is gaining ground in his work. He is quick and has a nice temper, but is volatile at present. We must make allowances for youth and very high spirits.'[8]

At the age of thirteen, Frank had made his mind up about his future. He wanted to go to sea, and in 1882 was entered for a place on H.M. Training Ship *Worcester*. His father was delighted when he began to show a remarkable ability, winning several prizes and finally gaining a cadetship in the Royal Navy; at the same time Frank was awarded Queen Victoria's Prize of a pair of binoculars and the sum of thirty-five pounds towards the cost of his outfit. He next spent some months on board HMS *Britannia*, and in 1885 became a Midshipman on HMS *Agincourt*.

This was better news, and when Arthur started school in 1884 'The Dovey' must have realized with relief that his troubles over educating his sons were over. Arthur, known to his family always as 'Artie', also went to The Grange first, then, at the age of fourteen, to Westminster School. As it was usual for new boys to be members of the same House as their older brothers, Arthur entered Grant's, in the footsteps of Willie and Dick.

On his arrival as a full boarder on 25 September, 1888, at the beginning of 'Play' Term, Arthur was greatly impressed by his new surroundings. Westminster's history stretched back for hundreds of years; from its beginnings as part of a monastic institution it was defined as a 'grammar school' in the reign of Henry VIII, and was an integral part of the collegiate church of St Peter following the suppression of Westminster Abbey in 1540. In 1560 it was refounded with a Royal Charter by Queen Elizabeth, who, Arthur found, was still honoured as the school's official foundress. But many of its cherished customs pre-dated 1500 – traditionally prayers at dinner were said in their original medieval form, and a play in Latin was staged every December – hence, the Autumn Term was always known as 'Play Term'. Annually on Shrove Tuesday the 'Pancake Greaze' took place (and still does), where boys scrambled after a pancake tossed by a cook over a rafter in College Hall. The pupil securing the largest portion received a guinea.

Grant's, the oldest board house, was almost a school within a school, its name descending through generations of schoolboys; in the middle years of the eighteenth century, a family called Grant had run the house as a private concern, catering for a group of Westminster pupils. Boarding houses at Westminster advertised in the newspapers for boys to lodge with them, and in Arthur's time his Housemasters, firstly the Rev W. A. Heard, who left in 1890 to become Head of Fettes, and then Ralph Tanner, still administered them as a private business venture, carrying the financial risk themselves. Usually, however, running a boarding house proved to be a lucrative undertaking. Grant's was one of three substantial houses built in Little Dean's Yard in 1790 – indeed, the Yard and most of the adjoining Dean's Yard were quite surrounded by Westminster School buildings. As the boys queued for entry to 'School' they were very conscious of their proximity to national events: the twin white towers of Westminster Abbey loomed over them, and the Palace of Westminster was close by.

The sixteenth-century 'School' or 'Hall', where some meals were taken, still had many of its original features, including tables and benches, but of greatest significance for Arthur was the elephant-handled Indian silver cup, presented in 1787 by Warren Hastings and twenty-one other Old Westminsters as a tribute to their school. Over the years many pupils left the school to take part in consolidating the British Empire all over the world, and the presence of this cup on the High Table during formal meals emphasized to the three Westminster Martin-Leakes that an important potential career path lay in such countries.

Arthur was also familiar with Ashburton House in Little Dean's Yard, which the school had acquired in 1881 and where a fine library had been established on the first floor. Lessons were taken in a brand-new classroom block built next to it in 1883. He frequented the famous Westminster tuck shop – Sutcliffe's, in Great College Street, and referred wistfully to these days of buying jam and potted meat for tea in letters home from the South African War twelve years later.[9]

The nineteenth century growth of 'country' public schools such as Charterhouse and Radley meant a decline in Westminster's fortunes; fruitless efforts had been made to find a site outside central London. But it had recently recovered in size and reputation under Dr William Gunnion Rutherford, who was still Headmaster when Arthur was admitted. Dr Rutherford arrived in 1883 at the age of thirty. He had a presence and personality that could reduce boys to tears and masters to panic-stricken alarm, but he was also admired, endeavouring to build up a relationship with every boy, and keeping in touch with many of them after they had left the school. He interviewed every boy at regular intervals – a Victorian version of modern-day 'appraisal', where progress was reviewed and future paths mapped out. Rutherford made many reforms to the curriculum and to customary rituals: rowing was abolished, and participation in the annual 'Pancake Greaze' was reduced to a representative from each form, instead of the whole school of 220 boys. Arthur listened to many of the sermons for which the Head was noted, some of them taking place at Poets' Corner in nearby Westminster Abbey, but there is no evidence that he was affected any more by these religious observances than he had been at home in High Cross.

In common with all long-established public schools Westminster had a complex language of its own for new boys to learn – 'Up School' meant 'in the School building', while 'Up Fields' referred to the ten green acres in Vincent Square, a short walk to the south-west where games were played. 'Play Term' was the term of the famous annual Latin play, while a 'Play' was a whole or half holiday, granted by the Head Master on special occasions. Uniform was top hat and tails.[10] The school's historian describes what faced a new boy in the middle of the nineteenth century:

> 'A complete system of duties and obligations linked older and younger boys in a network of feudal ties. For his first two weeks in the School, each new boy (the Substance) would be assigned to a second-year boy (his Shadow) to initiate him into his new society. During that time, the Junior was exempt from all punishment. . . . Thereafter he would be a dogsbody accountable to all Senior boys, as well as being linked with one as a personal fag and appearing on a rota of specific services to the House. . . . If a Senior wished to rise early to work, the Junior called 'Light-the-Fire' would have to be up half an hour earlier, often at 3.00 or 4.00, to light a fire, boil a kettle, and call the Senior every half an hour until he chose to rise.'[11]

Arthur's contribution to the life of Westminster was a modest one. At least he did not appear once in the black ledger that served as a Punishment Book, much to his father's relief. As soon as he arrived he found his House much occupied by preparations for a performance of *Much Ado About Nothing,* so he was able to settle in quietly until that was over. He was placed in the Science Fifth, and in the end-of-year examinations came sixteenth out of twenty-one boys. Within a year he had risen to second place out of twenty-three boys, and took top place in the subject examination in Science (though he was almost bottom in Divinity). His splendid progress was the cause of much celebration at Marshalls when he took home his School Reports. He tried his hand at School sports; a game peculiar to Westminster was known as 'Yard Ties', a form of raquets played in Little Dean's Yard in teams of three, and Arthur appeared, without much success, each time a knock-out competition was organized. He played as a forward for Grant's in a football match just before Christmas, 1890. At cricket he was out for a duck in a Junior House Match in the summer of 1890, but took three catches in a match against Rigaud's, the rival boarders' House, in June, 1891. His brothers Willie and Dick are recorded as contributing ten shillings each to the Pavilion Fund in 1889, as the need for changing facilities in Vincent Square became pressing.[12]

Undoubtedly then, Westminster School had a considerable impact on young Arthur. But he was there for less than three years, and we must look elsewhere for the major and most lasting influences on the young man who was ready to leave school in July, 1891. Firstly there was his mother, to whom he wrote every week while at school, a habit he continued throughout his life whenever he was away from her and Marshalls. He always demonstrated the greatest respect for his mother and sisters, but it is highly significant that his life was dominated by masculine influences, activities and personalities. Arthur grew up with scant regard for women outside his family, particularly in areas of his life where their activities impinged upon his own. He was always of the opinion in later years that too many women, apart from his mother and sisters, and (briefly) his wife, were interfering busybodies and harmful gossips.

The principal male role-model in his childhood years was his father Stephen, who by the late 1880s was, unfortunately, in failing health, though still comparatively young. Arthur knew him as a diffident but affectionate man, absorbed in his books and constantly worrying about money and about the administration of the two family estates at Thorpe and at High Cross. The waning influence of the rather anxious and introverted 'Dovey' was easily offset, however, by the adventurous and often rash escapades of Arty's four older brothers. In the 1990s the only appropriate adjective for their activities would be 'macho'.

Willie, the first to seek his fortune in distant corners of the Empire, was sending home animated accounts of his activities in the service of 'the Great White Queen'. From Bechuanaland with Methuen's Horse he had written in the Spring of 1885:

> 'I could not manage a letter for last mail as we were on the move from Langford Camp to Barkly, a distance of 84 miles. We did all the marching early in the morning from 2 o'clock to 8 so as to escape the heat. We have been marching in small lots on account of the water which was bad and scarce. I was in the first company of the Royal Scots. Eight of us were sent off again yesterday on special duty to this place 20 miles from Barkly. We have got to ride with despatches and report on the country round about. It is not a bad place to live in as places go about here, plenty of water and a good store to get things from. We have no tent so we sleep in the open. The wet season is coming on; we had a thunderstorm last night and another this morning. It has made a most wonder-

ful change in the land; before there was hardly a blade of grass to be seen, nothing but sand; now we are green all round. I wish I had a gun here as there is lots of game – partridge, plovers, springbok.'[13]

These descriptions of foreign landscapes made the greatest of impressions on Arthur, and on his brother Theodore, five years younger. In 1887 Willie obtained a commission in the Cheshire Regiment, and his letters from now on were adorned with a large '22' – The Cheshires being the 22nd of Foot. Soon he was writing from Egypt, describing the sight of the overflowing River Nile, game shooting, and attending Church Parade in the Cairo Citadel, 'a most unpleasant proceeding and the men smelt very high'. Then came a voyage to the Andaman Islands, of which he did not think much as there was 'only a European detachment and a native regiment and the convicts'. In 1889 Willie was in the thick of the Chin Lushai campaign in Burma, and a truly *Boy's Own* spirit began to pervade his letters:

'Three days' march brought us here to Fort White; the first day began with 6 miles on the flat to what we call No. 2 Stockade, then we began climbing the Chin Hills 7 miles to No. 3, a difference of level of 3,200 feet. The men were awfully done up. . . . Fort White is very cold and damp, clouds hang about nearly all day. We have bamboo huts thatched with grass and get fresh meat pretty often, supplied by an animal called water buffalo, not very tender but very nice compared with 'bully' beef (tinned meat) . . . The Chins round here are considered the most troublesome of all the tribes. We are anxiously awaiting the arrival of some more coolies to carry our provisions, to go out and burn some villages. I am afraid I cannot get you a map of the country as it has only just been surveyed.'[14]

Other letters reached Marshalls from India, where Steenie, his course at Cooper's Hill now successfully completed, and with the letters MICE (Member of the Institute of Chartered Engineers) after his name, was an Assistant Engineer with the Bengal and North-Western Railway. In May, 1887, he was joined by Dick, also a qualified engineer and with his fence-breaking days far behind him, in the Central Provinces of India, where they were both engaged on the construction of the newly-established Bengal-Nagpur Railway. They were quartered, not always together, at various points along the line, depending on which project they were involved in, and both wrote home describing the intense heat, the incapacitating ferocity of the annual monsoon, the problems of the engineer out in the 'jungle', a term applied in India to any deserted scrubland. One of Dick's letters described an exciting encounter:

'Kodri.
We have had a visit from a panther. He came about 9 at night and caught a dog called Brandy, Willie will remember it. Brandy was just outside the verandah, it was very dark. We gave him 2 days to eat Brandy and then tied up a goat in the side verandah with a lantern hung up close to it. We broke a pane in the door to shoot through and made certain of getting him. He came the second night. I woke up and heard him kill the goat. I got up and saw him trying to pull the goat away. He was about 3 yards from the door. I fired and hit the goat in the head. We have not seen the panther since. It was a very bad shot and the panther deserves to live after giving me such a chance.'[15]

Steenie and Dick were, however, almost continuously racked by bouts of tropical fever and recurring malaria, as was apparent whenever they had leave at 'Home'; so Arthur was well aware of the daunting health hazards that faced the European in India. On the lighter side, Willie was able on occasion to visit the two engineers, whenever he could manage his annual leave in their part of the world. There was even the possibility that Frank's naval duties might take him in the direction of India. In the late 1880s he served in HMS *Sapphire* on the China Station for two years, and entered the Naval Hydrographical Service in 1891. This involved survey work in the Red Sea, the Seychelles and the East Coast of Africa, until October, 1892.[16] The impression is of the whole Martin-Leake family seeking their fortunes in the tropics and it is hardly surprising that both Arthur and Theodore were inspired to do the same. In addition, their father's brother, Uncle William, was one of Ceylon's foremost Europeans, having been employed to construct major irrigation works for the coffee planters there since 1859; he was now back in England, but regaled the family at Marshalls with tales of life in Ceylon, and of his travels in remote parts of Russia to promote the coffee trade.[17]

So these were the men whose way of life most influenced Arthur as his schooldays came to an end. There was an inborn patriotism too, an acknowledgement that the parts coloured pink on the globe in the Westminster schoolroom were rightly British, and an expectation that one could justifiably receive a comfortable living in return for protecting (or exploiting) them. At least for this family, any opprobrium formerly applied towards an Army career was rapidly losing its force. Willie, in spite of a very unpromising start in life, was actually doing very well. It was also thoroughly accepted, indeed strongly advocated, that one should invest both time and money in the exploitation of the needs and raw materials of the colonies; in the vocabulary of the day there was nothing pejorative in the use of the word 'Imperialism'.

In July, 1891, Arthur was seventeen years old. He had discussed possible careers with Dr Rutherford and with his father; a medical career was looking more and more appealing, especially after he had debated the matter with his uncle, John Russell Reynolds, second husband of Aunt Frances. Reynolds was an eminent doctor, specializing in nervous disorders and holding the post of Physician in Ordinary to Queen Victoria; he was President of the British Medical Association in 1895 and President of the Royal College of Physicians. He undertook to do what he could for his nephew, and secured for Arthur the promise of a place at University College Hospital where he was Consulting Physician. Arthur's best subject was Science, and he could confidently be expected to achieve the required entrance requirements.

Unfortunately his father's failing health and increasingly serious financial problems militated against any continuation at Westminster. Mr Martin-Leake had invested heavily in the Tunnel Portland Cement Company set up by his brother William on his return from Ceylon; the Company was not doing well, barely covering the costs of production. So in July, 1891, Arthur left school and returned to Marshalls, where he was to continue his studies with a tutor and, if necessary, attend at a 'crammer's'. By late 1892 he was sitting the examinations that would qualify him to enter medical school.

Twelve-year-old Theodore was approaching public school age, and it was felt he should have his turn, even though the expense was a cause of great worry. He was sent as a boarder to Radley College, founded in 1847 near the Thames at Abingdon, south of Oxford. His performance was only average, although he showed some aptitude for Mathematics, winning a prize in his first term.[18] But in January, 1892, the College records show him 'Absent' from school for three months. This was due to the illness and ultimate death of the Dovey.

One of the Dovey's last letters was to his eldest son Steenie in India, on 14 December, 1892:

> 'I cannot say I am any better but lately I have been much more comfortable, I think from better management. I take more opium, adding a dose at night, and I find this, together with strong drink, makes me sleep much better, till 8 or 9 o'clock, and this makes getting up much easier. . . . Arty has been through his exam and I am nearly sure has passed. His latest paper was capital; he answered nearly the whole and I can only find he made one mistake. We shall not know till January and

are now considering whether he had not better enter at once upon a regular course as a medical student at University College. They begin 3 January.'[19]

In fact such an early start was not possible. The health of Arthur's father deteriorated rapidly, and he died on Tuesday 7 March, 1893, at the age of sixty-six. His obituary prepared for *The Times*, (though not all of it was printed) stated that he had one fault; 'He was too sensitive, too delicate minded, too retiring.' But he was 'respected and loved by his neighbours and worshipped by his devoted family.'[20]

In his will, the Dovey had asked that he

'be buried *in the churchyard here* [High Cross], as being the *nearest spot* in *some quiet corner*, with *no unnecessary expense* – at the same time do as my wife wishes.'[21]

But it was decided to bury him at Thorpe with his ancestors, and the funeral took place on 11 March. Of his sons, only Theodore and Arthur were present. Bella wrote to her older brothers in India:

'Mammy has written you such a long account of Saturday. She has been most wonderful the way she has gone through it all and the beautiful way she managed everything. She was quite knocked up on Monday but was so far recovered today to be able to go to town. She had a long interview this morning with Mr Birch [family solicitor], there seems nothing to do until everything is valued. He gave £50 to carry us on, we have been very hard up as Dovey was out of money, he was going to send to the Bank on Monday, I am afraid the news must have been a great blow to you, it was to us, although we had so much notice. I am sure we ought to be thankful that the end was so quiet and without pain. Dr Willans had said so much about his having dropsy and not being able to move that one had imagined his end would be truly awful. You cannot imagine how changed everything is and how awful it was coming home Saturday night to an empty house. Except for Mammy and a lot to do I don't know how we should get on at all. There has been for a long time a good deal to do for him and taking him out in the chair, and now all that is over one does miss it terrible . . . I do wish you had all been able to come. Mammy felt so much you all being away. We had quantities of flowers and we made a large cross of our snowdrops which was fastened on the top of the coffin . . . it was a geat disappointment to the outsiders that the funeral was not here. I am so very glad it was at Thorpe. There would have been crowds here. Thorpe Church and yard are so very nice, the latter so beautifully kept. The grave is in the middle strip in a line with the East End, a very nice spot. The grave was made quite lovely, if a grave can be so, with evergreens and arum lilies and other white flowers. The day was perfect, everything very bright to look at and Mammy makes a lovely widow.'[22]

When the news reached India, Dick, Steenie and Willie were all together. Dick wrote straight back:

'Your account showed he had been going downhill rapidly and we knew it was impossible he could live much longer. It is difficult to realize what his death means out here. Perhaps it is best it happened as it did: he has been spared a long illness in bed and he must have suffered a great deal. I am very glad he is buried at Thorpe.

'Steenie came in here yesterday and has decided to go home in June. I think this a very good thing as there must be a good many things to settle which he could hardly do while out here. Willie arrived last night on 3 months' leave.'[23]

The Dovey's executors found that he had £898 in stock and £3,542 in cash, when certain items had been disposed of in accordance with his wishes. For example, he wished his law library to be sold, the proceeds to be put towards 'the advancement of Arthur and Theodore in their professions.' His wife was to have the use of Marshalls for her lifetime, but the estate was willed ultimately to each son in succession. Georgiana and Isabel received £500 each. Items from the estate of Sir John Leake, such as the Queen Anne silver gilt cup, a dress sword, and a gold snuff box, were bequeathed to the older sons. They eventually passed to Arthur, and are now in the British Museum collection.

'Ride Straight, Shoot Straight, and Keep Straight!'

Mrs Martin-Leake's time was much taken up for months afterwards with the idea of memorials to her husband. Firstly a stone had to be designed and erected over the grave; this was done, in spite of Dick writing home from India criticizing the design as 'rather straggling and it does not look very strong or lasting.'[1] Then there was the matter of a memorial in Thorpe Church. Here, an oak reredos was erected behind the altar. At High Cross, it was decided to install a stained-glass window in the church, and Mr Selwyn Image, Slade Professor of Art at Oxford, was commissioned to execute the work. Although there were numerous delays and some unpleasant wrangles about the cost, the window was finally dedicated on 28 April, 1895. It depicts Christ, the Virgin Mary and St John.

Theodore resumed his studies at Radley, demonstrating talents that would have delighted his father. He achieved a degree of prominence in football and rowing and came top of his form in 1894, his last year at the school. He had decided on a military career and entered the open competiton for a place at the Royal Military Academy, Woolwich. He was placed twenty-fifth, and went to Woolwich in 1896. Hitherto he had been given the nickname 'Mousey' by the family; from now on he was also 'The Engineer'. On 23 March, 1899, at the age of nineteen, he was gazetted Second Lieutenant, the Royal Engineers, and joined the School of Military Engineering at Chatham: a year later he moved to Aldershot with the Balloon Section.[2]

Six months after his father's death, Arthur's medical career began. He entered University College Hospital in Gower Street, London, in October, 1893, when he was nineteen years old. Against his name in the Register of Students was the entry 'Nephew of Lady Russell Reynolds' an indication of the powerful patronage exercised by Aunt Frances' husband, the consulting physician at the hospital. Arthur took up residence at No. 135 Gower Street, and enthusiastically embraced the demands of the courses in Anatomy and Biology; in April 1894 he was awarded the 'Junior Medal'. By 1895 his particular talents had been recognized by his tutors, and he was awarded the year's Silver Medal – normally a Gold Medal would have been awarded, but in that year no student quite reached the 'Gold' standard. Nevertheless, in response to a delighted letter bearing the news from Marshalls, Willie, in Madras, mistakenly hoped that 'Artie has got his Gold Medal all safe'.[3]

Arthur worked on at University College Hospital until August, 1899. During those years he was described by his teachers as 'diligent' in almost every report made about his progress. As a 'dresser' to surgeons Mr Godlee and Mr Pollard, stitching and bandaging their patients after surgery, he did 'extremely well'; as clerk to Doctors Ringer, Bradford and Blacker, he wrote up their case-notes and other records, and was said to be 'good'; and as an assistant demonstrator, showing various basic techniques to other students, he was reportedly 'very good'. He passed his first Fellowship examinations for the Royal College of Surgeons in May, 1896.[4]

Dr John Russell Reynolds, Arthur's uncle, was a well-known figure in London's medical circles in the 1890's and it must have helped the young student to have a family connection at UCH. Unfortunately Sir John died in May, 1896, leaving Arthur his British Medical Association medal – a small metal cross on a red and white ribbon – commemorating his Presidency of the BMA in 1895. At his funeral Queen Victoria was represented by Lieutenant Colonel Julian Byng, whose path was again to cross that of the Martin-Leakes twenty years later. Sir John was buried at Owlpen, Gloucestershire, near the home of Arthur's aunt, Rose Trent-Stoughton.

Also on the staff of University College Hospital was a man who was the foremost neuro-surgeon of his age. This was Victor Horsley, Professor of Pathology, then in his mid-fifties and internationally famous for his operating skill and methodology. Arthur was an observer at many of his operations on the brain and spinal chord, and was imbued with an enthusiasm for surgery that never left him. Together with a group of fellow students, he often took the short walk through the city streets to Cavendish Square where Horsley lived and had his consulting rooms; here there were casts of monkeys' brains on the mantelpieces and a well-fitted darkroom and dissecting laboratory. The great man used to advise the students that, on graduation, they should either try 'to assist a good medical practitioner for six months, or hold a Hospital appointment, or travel'.[5] Arthur certainly paid great attention to the last two parts of this advice.

In addition, Horsley displayed the greatest of concern for the comfort and well-being of his patients, never inflicting pain if it could possibly be avoided. He always insisted on anaesthesia even in the most insignificant of surgical procedures, and instructed his 'dressers' that dressings must be soaked until they came off by themselves. Arthur adopted the same practice. There is no record of Arthur's opinions about his mentor, and he would surely have disagreed with Horsley's ardent espousal of the campaigns for temperance and for female suffrage [6], but a fellow-surgeon wrote of Horsley, who was knighted in 1902:

'From his house-surgeons and students his easy simplicity, his charming sense of fun, his assumption of complete equality, won a devotion that was too deep to be disturbed by the passing agitations of the operating theatre.'[7]

Only one area of study caused Arthur difficulty. This was Midwifery, which he failed in July, 1898. Perhaps it was simply a reflection of his inability to relate to the female sex, or perhaps, because of his problems in this area, he was left with a life-long unease towards women. But he re-took the examination and passed in October. Now he qualified as a Licentiate of the Royal College of Physicians (LRCP) and achieved Membership of the Royal College of Surgeons (MRCS). He registered with the General Medical Council on 27 February, 1899.[8] From March to August that year he held the position of House Surgeon working under Dr Barlow at University College and began to look round for his next six-month contract.[9]

He obtained a locum position at the Surrey County Lunatic Asylum, Brookwood, Woking. The first extant letter from Arthur to his mother dates from this time, when he was feeling great disappointment that he had been unable to obtain a surgical post, and was both critical of and amused by the Asylum facilities:

'My dear Mammy,
It has been raining today continuously up to about 5 p.m. and coming down in torrents. The garden paths have been very much damaged by the water and part of the building flooded. The drains are in a very bad way. . . . They had the Harvest service last Friday, and a dance in the morning. It was most amusing and the patients seemed to enjoy it very much. The most annoying thing is the way my steps will not go with anyone else's.'[10]

He applied for several hospital posts in the south of England, and was finally summoned for interview at the West Hertfordshire Infirmary at Hemel Hempstead in October, 1899. He had to send home for his Certificate of Registration, which was in a tin box in the dining-room bookcase at Marshalls. 'I wonder they do not want a birth certificate as well,' remarked Arthur. [11]

The West Herts Infirmary had been established in 1827 and much enlarged during the 1830s following substantial gifts from its main benefactor, Sir John Sebright. In 1877 Princess Mary of Teck opened the hospital buildings where Arthur was to work, with fifty beds and a nursing staff of seven under the Matron, Miss C. Wilkinson. In 1899 it was one of the first hospitals in

England to install X-Ray equipment, but it relied solely on charitable donations and its Committee often reported financial difficulties.[12]

When Arthur was appointed House Surgeon in October, 1899, a good reference having been supplied by Victor Horsley, he found a gratifyingly large number of opportunities for surgery, although much of his time was occupied with the extraction of teeth, the fitting of surgical appliances, and the holding of out-patient clinics. Only one record of his surgical work survives. The patient was an eight-year-old-boy from Pinner, who was admitted on 14 November, 1899. He had a urinary tract blockage which Arthur's superior, Doctor Dove, had opened up at home. In the hospital

> 'Dr Leake deepened the incision already made and made two others, he also circumcised the child and removed a stone.'[13]

A further incision was later necessary, but after five weeks the boy had recovered and left the hospital in January, 1900. Dr Leake was not there to see him discharged; by this time Arthur was in uniform, and preparing for his first overseas exploit. He had requested leave of absence soon after the outbreak of war in South Africa and was in Watford with the Hertfordshire Company of the Imperial Yeomanry getting ready for embarkation for the Cape and some eagerly anticipated encounters with an enemy referred to already by the Hertfordshire troopers as 'Brother Boer'.

War in South Africa had been brewing for years. The Marshalls household, having three sons in uniform already, followed newspaper accounts of events with great interest, unlike the majority of the British public. Arthur's older brother Willie had been in South Africa in 1884 with Methuen's Horse and letters had reached the family describing his exploits with the British forces that were trying to contain the expansionist ambitions of President Paul Kruger of the Transvaal. Kruger's plans had been thwarted when the British annexed Bechuanaland and Zululand. As Willie described it in August, 1885:

> 'We have just had a telegram saying that Bechuanaland has been accepted as a Crown Colony. In my humble opinion it is a most dreary, good-for-nothing country. No water except for wells which soon run dry, and in some places is quite unfit to drink.'[14]

But neither the British Government nor Arthur Martin-Leake were put off by such descriptions. The long-running tension between the British and the two Dutch Boer Republics of the Transvaal and the Orange Free State had come to a head with the discovery, in 1887, of gold on the Witwatersrand (the 'Rand', a sixty-mile-long ridge running east to west south of Pretoria). The gold rush brought in a flood of prospectors, called 'Uitlanders' because of their foreign origins, whose presence was increasingly irksome to the Boers. Many Uitlanders were British, but many came from elsewhere in Europe, and from America, Canada and Australia. In arguments between them and the Boers about power and profit in South Africa, it was expected by both sides that Britain would one day step in to lend weight to the Uitlander cause. In 1895 an abortive 'raid' by Uitlanders led by Dr L. S. Jameson, friend and confidant of Cape Colony Prime Minister Cecil Rhodes, failed to shake the Boer territory of Transvaal; the Boer President Paul Kruger, convinced that Britain had supported the raid, began to prepare for conflict.

The perceived threat from Britain and the Uitlanders showed clearly that the interests of the two Boer Republics lay in concerted action. When Sir Alfred Milner arrived from London to assume responsibility as Governor of Cape Colony and High Commissioner for South Africa in May, 1897, he explored every possible scenario, but concluded that war with the Boer republics was extremely likely; although he returned to England the next year for talks with the Colonial Secretary, Joseph Chamberlain, the government was not sufficiently convinced of this to make serious preparations. A six-day conference between Milner and Kruger at Bloemfontein in the Orange Free State in May, 1899, ended abruptly with Milner's departure, and Kruger certainly began to order arms and train his men. It was now in the Boer interest to hurry the war along before Britain saw the danger, and on 9 October Kruger presented an ultimatum to London; a parallel British ultimatum had, inexplicably, been sent by sea, and was still en route to Pretoria. The Boers demanded that Britain must withdraw all her troops from the borders of the Transvaal, and must not bring in the reinforcements that had been ordered.[15] Of course the Conservative Government of Lord Salisbury could not countenance such impertinence. Colonial Secretary Joseph Chamberlain replied that 'the conditions demanded by the Government of the South African Republic are such as Her Majesty's Government deem it impossible to discuss.'[16]

When on 6 November *The Times* reported that the Boers had invaded Cape Colony, the whole Martin-Leake family shared the patriotic fervour that gripped the nation. At last, the family thought, proper concern was being shown. Reinforcements were sent and there were some early British successes at Talana and Elandslaagte, but by the beginning of November the diamond town of Kimberley, just inside Cape Colony, was besieged, as was the settlement of Ladysmith in Natal, containing a British force, and Mafeking, up near the Bechuanaland border, was about to be. As the war entered its second month, Arthur, doing his ward rounds at Hemel Hempstead, deliberated about the best way of getting out to the Cape with the utmost speed. It was felt by many that the war would be short, possibly 'over by Christmas', and he was in a state of some anxiety in case he missed the adventure. As an avid reader of the daily papers, he was soon aware that a new force, the 'Imperial Yeomanry', was to be raised by Royal Warrant dated 24 December, 1899; friends locally told him that a unit was being formed at Watford, the 42nd (Hertfordshire) Company, the Imperial Yeomanry. Recruiting began at the end of December.[17]

The doctor, encouraged by his brothers Steenie and Dick who were on leave from India, immediately applied to the Hospital managers for permission to go. They shared the patriotism that was being demonstrated everywhere else, and readily agreed, even though they had to advertise immediately for a temporary replacement for their very recently appointed houseman 'absent at the seat of war'.[18] Promising to hold his position for him until he returned, the House Committee sent Arthur a cheque for two pounds to cover arrears in his pay, and in due course received six applications for his post. He never returned to Hemel Hempstead.

By 11 January, 1900, Arthur was in lodgings with a Mrs Horton of 1 Frances Road, Watford, only thirty miles from High Cross. He was Trooper Number 5778, reporting each day to the Port Hill Drill Hall; he was too impatient to wait for the medical arrangements for the campaign to be in place, which might have allowed him to go out as a Medical Officer. In any case, the Company already had a surgeon-captain in the shape of Mr Lovell Drage.[19] Arthur described his early days in uniform:

'We were paraded in the market place with a cheering crowd all round. Captain Gilliat informed us that we were under strict military orders, and were on no account to leave the town without special leave, which would only be granted under very special circumstances. I have to pay £1 per week for a horse, which does not include grooming. Lodgings were very difficult to get.'[20]

A circular sent out by the Imperial Yeomanry Committee stipulated what clothing and equipment each officer and man should possess before sailing for South Africa;[21] the main items of uniform, jacket and breeches, were khaki, as was the slouch hat, but by early February most members of the company had service caps in the Prince of Wales's colours of purple and scarlet, paid for by each trooper.[22] However, items were obtained piecemeal, some locally and some from military suppliers elsewhere, and in the wintry weather Arthur was glad of a contribution from home:

'Thanks for the cape. It will be just the thing this weather (it has not arrived yet). They are keeping us at it hard, and have started stables at 7 a.m., 12 and 5 p.m. We are taught to groom in the military style etc. My animal is looking very well and getting on with her drill, at any rate just as fast as self. We have just had the new rifle – 'Lee Enfield' – served out. It is very heavy and goodness knows how we shall carry it. Several more officers have turned up.'[23]

His uniform was far from complete and there was considerable confusion as to what would happen next. Men were still arriving to volunteer, but not all were accepted, especially if they could not ride. Fortunately Arthur's experience of following the Puckeridge Hunt paid off:

'The latest is that we start on the 4th of February. They do not seem to know anything definite. All men that are ready by Friday [2 February] (i.e. uniformed) are to go to London to be reviewed by the Prince of Wales at Albany Barracks – no horses or rifles – I trust my clothes will *not* be here in time. The local photographer is taking all troopers free of charge and presenting each with a copy. I was taken today in uniform (lent for the occasion) also free of charge. They have chucked 10 men as a start off. One man came over from Moscow on purpose for the job. There are others to go before they have done.'[24]

As the days passed, the pace of preparations quickened; inspections were more frequent, and the local community planned to give the company an appropriately fulsome send-off. At the end of January Arthur wrote:

'Things going along much faster now; nearly all kit is served out, and seems on the whole to be good. I am sorry that I have brought so many things [from home] as everything has been given – socks, shirts, boots, etc. Mrs Horton is kindly strengthening buttons and any weak parts of the garments . . . There are dinners here on Saturday and Monday given by the Town Council and the Herts Yeomanry Officers respectively. I should like to get out of both, but I suppose for the look of things I shall have to go to one. Things at the Front seem to be very serious but the Imperial Yeomanry will put things right.'
'[1 February] We were inspected today by the General for the district. He made pretty speeches etc. and the whole proceeding was ridiculous in the extreme. We were kept waiting a very long

time in the cold wind and the horses got quite out of hand. There were many empty saddles when we were called upon to make an attack, and in spite of the large number of men who have been chucked for bad horsemanship there are still a large proportion who can scarcely ride at all. A great deal of the trouble was caused by very large and sharp spurs which have just been given out.

'Mr Dove [his horse] is now splendid and will carry out any military manoeuvre that a yeomanry horse is called upon to do. We go to London tomorrow to be looked at by Wales. Equipment is complete – the uniforms made at Hertford like mine seem to be superior to some of the others, which are already coming to bits.'[25]

Quite a stir was caused locally because considerable numbers of would-be volunteers were being turned away. The local press commented:

'The action of the War Office authorities towards many of the Volunteers who have offered themselves for service at the Front is utterly inexplicable. It seems almost as if their object was to stamp out the wave of patriotism that has spread over the whole country in the face of the difficulties of our gallant army in South Africa. However, struggle as it may, the War Office with its effete red-tapeism cannot succeed in quenching the military ardour of our local Volunteers, who have shown a most praiseworthy determination to be represented in good numbers in the fighting lines at the Cape, despite all the snubbing and humiliation that has been heaped upon them by the higher authorities.'[26]

It seems that a large number were ready to enlist when they failed a last-minute medical examination, because of a 'slight deficiency in chest measurement'.[27] This must have been most disappointing, particularly after the Church parade of 28 January, widely reported in the press, when the Vicar of Watford, the Rev R. Lee James, preached on the text:

'But thy servants will pass over, every man armed for war, before the Lord to battle.' [Numbers xxxii v.27].

He was of the opinion that

'War was sometimes absolutely necessary, and therefore was altogether justifiable, and a Christian man might – nay, he must – take his part in it.'[28]

Arthur was there, and heard the organist playing the National Anthem while a collection was taken for the town's War Fund. During the days of preparation there were numerous activities for the men, all aimed at increasing both morale and patriotic fervour. Heavy falls of snow did nothing to dampen enthusiasm for

'an assault-at-arms and smoking concert organized by the Contingent, which was held at the Clarendon Hall on Wednesday. There were some capital boxing exhibitions, fencing, and quarter-staff bouts and singing. Messrs Benson presented the Company with a silver bugle, and the Colonel hoped they would bring it back with many honourable scars after it had accompanied them on a victorious and glorious career (cheers).'[29]

The Colonel of the Yeomanry was Lord Clarendon, and his daughter Lady Edith Villiers presented each of the men in the Company with a 'keyless watch enclosed in a wristlet'. There would be no chance of wearing or adjusting a fob watch on a chain in South Africa. Then came the first of two farewell dinners to which Arthur had referred when writing to his mother; he was quite unable to avoid attending both. Over 300 men were present at the civic send-off in the Clarendon Hall on 3 February, with large numbers of ladies crowding into the gallery to observe the proceedings:

'The hall had been profusely decorated, the Yeomanry Band played at intervals, and the whole scene was most picturesque, the regimental uniforms standing out in strong contrast to the khaki of the men ordered south. The patriotic sentiments in the speeches were applauded to the echo. Mr T. F. Halsey MP said he regretted he was too old to go to South Africa with his old regiment the Hertfordshire Yeomanry, but it was some satisfaction to him to know that he was represented there by his two naval sons. One of his sons was with the guns of the *Powerful* in Ladysmith, whilst his other son was with the relieving forces. He hoped the two sons might meet as victors in the field of battle. Lord Clarendon said that never in England's history, never since Great Britain had become and remained the greatest nation upon the earth, had the Navy and the Army combined upon land to defeat an almost invisible and decidedly "slim" foe. A capital musical programme was gone through and the company broke up about 11 o'clock with the National Anthem and "Auld Lang Syne".'[30]

The menu had included turbot, fried smelts, sweetbreads, boiled turkeys, ox tongues, beef, chicken and mutton, curaçao jellies, strawberry creams, iced puddings, cheese and celery. Two days later the Herts Yeomanry Cavalry, not to be outdone, gave a second dinner 'To Bid Farewell to the Herts Company', again in the Clarendon Hall and with Lord Clarendon in the chair. The menu threatened to outshine that of the earlier civic occasion, offering crimped cod with oyster sauce, filleted soles and quenelles of lobster, turkey, ham, lamb and pheasants, champagne jellies and orange creams, and concluding with strawberry iced bombe.[31]

'The hall was comfortably draped and carpeted for the occasion, the handsome decorations were most tastefully arranged, and the intermingling of the khaki uniforms of the Imperial Yeomen with the scarlet of the comrades they are leaving behind combined to make a strikingly brilliant scene. In submitting the toast of "The Queen", Colonel the Earl of Clarendon said he had only to mention the name of Her Majesty at a gathering of this description for it to receive that acclamation, that cordial and genial response which it invariably met with. (Cheers). Profound as must be Her Majesty's grief that the declining years of her reign had been signalized with bloodshed, acute as her sorrow must be that so many of the valuable lives of her soldiers had been spent, yet he felt sure that she had the consolation that her cause was a just one, and this war a righteous one. Captain Gilliat and the men under him were now soldiers of the Queen, and there was no doubt that they would bear their share in hurling back the invader from her territory, and restoring the integrity of her dominions. His Lordship reflected with the greatest possible pleasure that those khaki-clothed warriors had sprung from the loins of the Regiment of which he had the honour of being the commanding officer (prolonged cheers).'[32]

Arthur and his fellow troopers listened, somewhat open-mouthed, as Lord Clarendon continued. Clichés flowed as he proceeded to cast aspersions upon the enemy and hand out to the Yeomanry some appropriate advice:

'Deeds, not words, are required. There must be no parleying with the enemy in the gate. Both our political and our military leaders have told us that they have put their hand to the plough and they do not, nor do you mean, to turn back until the good old Union Jack of Old England floats over the stronghold of the foe. Captain Gilliat, you and the men under your command are about to proceed to a country many thousands of miles from your native shores. The fact of your volunteering, your soldierly appearance, your rigid obedience to discipline, are, to my mind, a satisfactory proof of the stuff of which you are made. I would like to give you a few words of advice – *ride straight, shoot straight and keep straight*. In regard to the white flag which has been exhibited by our enemy of late – the white flag with the Boer means the white feather. The white feather shall never be shown; the white flag only on occasions when a truce or armistice is demanded, and anybody who exhibits the white flag for any other purpose or on any other occasion is not only a sneak but a coward. Captain Gilliat, we do not believe, either you or I or anybody here, in the man who holds the Bible in one hand and the Mauser rifle in the other. And another bit of advice I should like to give you is this – that if you met a gentleman, a somewhat aged gentleman, whose name begins with K anywhere down Pretoria way I ask you to make him sing psalms out of the wrong side of his mouth – and as for his cant, drive it down his throat with a dose of lyddite – with three inches of bayonet to keep it there. Captain Gilliat, I don't know whether you have any medical skill. I myself have no knowledge of hygienics or therapeutics, but I have always been told that for weak and fragile constitutions a recipe of iron and steel is somewhat useful. Now, the constitution of the Transvaal is both weak and corrupt. I ask you then, Captain Gilliat and your merry men, to act in the capacity of doctors to the Transvaal constitution, and either heal it of its cant and corruption or else remove it for ever from off the face of the earth. . . . I hope and believe that, on the tempestuous seas, on the rolling veldts of South Africa and under the starry canopy of heaven, around the beleaguered cities of Pretoria and Bloemfontein, round the camp fire and in the stress of battle, your minds will revert with kindly and loving memories towards the old homes, the old country, and the old friends, who from the innermost depths of deep-feeling hearts, and in all truth, faith and sincerity, wish you God speed in the prosecution of your arduous duties.'[33]

The noble Lord then stood on his chair and asked for three cheers; Arthur and everyone present were moved to stand on their chairs as well. Non-commissioned officers and officers alike were carried round the hall by their men, Captain Smith-Bosanquet shouting loudly that the men were off 'to give the Boers beans'.[34]

After this came days of waiting and uncertainty; Arthur hated inactivity and wrote to his mother on 12 February:

> 'We are almost unemployed, and I have made a few suggestions for filling up the time, but hardly like to send them to the officers. . . . They have started a regular feeding establishment in a tent – food seems good and costs 1/6 per diem – 3 meals. It looks as if we are going to stay here until the end of the war – in spite of their saying that we go somewhere about the 20th. I suppose skating is going strong? The ice here is splendid, but of course no chance of getting on it. Horses have not been out today, the roads are like ice.'[35]

By 16 February he had heard of the Relief of Kimberley and was afraid that the war was going so well that his Company would not be needed at all; 'I should not be surprised if we do not go.'[36] More good news soon arrived announcing that Mafeking had been relieved on 17 February. The popular response almost gave the impression that the war was, to all intents and purposes, over. Arthur began to hatch a plot to equip himself with a set of medical instruments, so that any possible opening for a civilian doctor to go to South Africa could be taken up quickly. Naturally, he did not want the company officers to find out about this, but on 20 February orders came that they would sail on the 28th, and each man was to have a few hours' leave, from 3 p.m. one day to 10 a.m. the next day. Arthur viewed this as a good opportunity:

> 'to go to town to see about instruments. I have plenty of money at present. The instrument case costs £4.10s. You very kindly said you would give it me so I have had it put under way. I did not think it was good policy to ask for the money at Headquarters.'[37]

However, embarkation was delayed yet again, but Arthur managed to obtain his medical instruments. Finally, at seven-thirty on the morning of Saturday, 3 March the company marched through crowded streets to Watford Junction station and fell in on the dark platform to board a special train for the Albert Dock at Tilbury, where tickets were supposed to be allocated for relatives to board the ship and bid their farewells. The men had been accompanied all the way through the town by a procession of local dignitaries alternating with the bands of the Fire Brigade, the Police and the Salvation Army. Speeches were made, and as the train moved off fog signals on the line 'furnished a salute'.[38]

Arthur had put his name down for four tickets, 'so the family can come or not as they like.'[39] Unfortunately the crowd was so great that it was decided not to allow any relatives to go on board. As the *Mercury* pointed out:

'The *Cornwall* is not a passenger ship with wide promenade decks and spacious saloons, and, as a matter of fact, all the available space was so completely occupied by the troopers alone that the gangways were jammed, and General Maurice, who came to inspect the ship, had some difficulty in making his way on shore in spite of his uniform. Had all the ladies succeeded in struggling on board they would have been exceedingly uncomfortable and would have seen nothing'.[40]

CHAPTER FOUR

'Where Do All the Boers Come From?'

The steamship *Cornwall* was filled with some six companies of Imperial Yeomanry, totalling twenty-one officers, 633 men and 190 horses. After two days at sea Arthur was settling down to a four-week long voyage:

'Up to present we have had splendid weather and the ship has hardly moved at all. The Bay (of Biscay) was smooth as glass, which according to accounts seems to be wonderful for this time of year. The ship's arrangements are just beginning to work properly; at first everything was upside-down in the kitchen and the cooks were such cissies. The food is rough but not bad. The canteen has been opened today for the first time. It quite reminds one of schooldays to go and buy jam, potted meat etc. for tea. They do not give us any drink except tea and coffee, and beer is 6d per bottle (small) so we shall soon all be teetotallers of necessity. Of course, this is a very great blow to some of the men who have been soaking for 6 weeks at Watford.'[1]

Two companies of Yeomanry from Ireland were also on board the *Cornwall*, and Arthur expressed a distaste for the Irish that lasted for most of his life. This first encounter stimulated him to comment:

'The Irish contingent are a very curious set. They are filthy, even for Tommies. Thank goodness they are at the other end of the ship so we see little of them. They spend most of the day down below learning the rudiments of musketry drill. The sergeants are at present instructing themselves, and by the end of the voyage may be fit to teach their men. . . . The health on board is good, only 1 man ill. I am especially fit. They have started a big bath on deck made of a sail, it is splendid. I take good care to be one of the first in it; it would not be too savoury after some of these Irishmen.'[2]

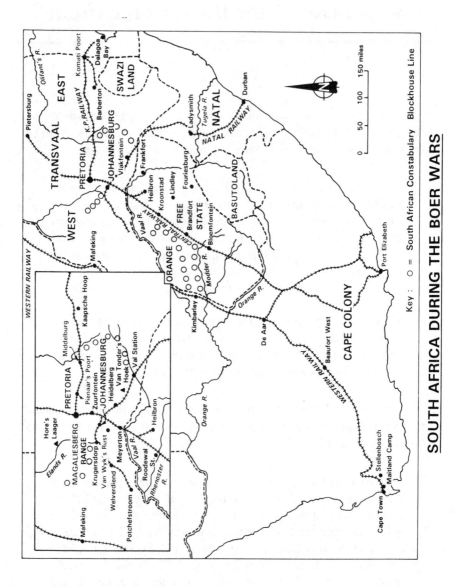

SOUTH AFRICA DURING THE BOER WARS

Key: ○ = South African Constabulary Blockhouse Line

With 190 horses on board, some were bound to suffer illness during the voyage. Arthur's oddly-named mare Mr Dove coped quite well, but others were not so fortunate:

'Weather is getting tremendously hot and the stables are beginning to stink. The Dove is very fit indeed and eats as well as ever; she also attacks her neighbours with great vigour. We have the horses out every day to be groomed and walked round, and as the ship was never meant for the job it is very awkward. Especially with the Dove who will bite at every horse she passes.'[3]

The men found the journey more and more wearisome as the days went on. Sometimes they crowded the rails to see a distant coastline pass by, counting the days before they might hope to catch a first glimpse of Cape Town. Arthur's medical skills were exercised when he was called upon to give the men lectures on 'First Aid to the Wounded', and he was pleasantly surprised to find how keen the men were to learn.[4] So the days passed quite easily for him; he always hated doing nothing. It was expected that the voyage would take twenty-eight days, ('This old tub only does between 10 and 12 knots')[5] and four days before arrival Arthur wrote:

'At last we are getting to the end of this voyage; it seems to have lasted quite a year. . . . Perhaps the whole thing is over by this time. What we are going to do when we land nobody knows, but it is probable we shall go into camp outside Cape Town for some time, especially if we are to take our own horses up country, as they are in a bad way and will require time before they are any good. 14 horses have died and nearly every animal on board has been more or less ill. The vets say they have had strangles, others say influenza etc., but they do not seem to know. Most of the deaths were pneumonia. . . . The Dove is a perfect wonder, and whilst the majority of animals are only skin and bones she is nearly as fat as when she started. I shall be very sorry if I have to leave her behind, and it is not at all unlikely as these horses may have to go into quarantine for a long time.

'P.S. arrived at Cape Town. 3 troopships waiting to be unloaded, we may have to wait some days to get off.'[6]

After waiting for a whole day at anchor in Table Bay, the Yeomanry at last landed on South African soil on 28 March. They then marched to Maitland Camp, a distance of five miles to the east of Cape Town. Arthur, already much irritated by the men from whom he had to take orders, recorded his early impressions:

> 'This is a very fine camping-ground and can hold thousands of troops. At present there are a large number of I.Y.s and a cavalry regiment. We had to learn everything by experience. Our NCOs are a very helpless and stupid set of men possessed with even more assurance and officiousness than is usually attached to that class of man. The cause of this is a huge blunder, made I believe by Lord Clarendon, who determined that all NCOs should be made from Yeomen proper. There are in the ranks a lot of old Army men, who have had stripes and know the job thoroughly. Also several men who have been in the various police forces out here, so there would have been no difficulty in finding good men who would have been really useful.'[7]

A contempt for inadequate or ineffective men senior to himself remained with Arthur for the rest of his life, whether in military uniform or as a civilian. But his mood improved when he realized:

> 'It really seems now as if we are going to see some excitement after all. . . . Camp life is delightful in this splendid climate: it is beautifully dry and not too hot, but rather chilly at nights. The great drawback of course is the company, which one gets very sick of after a bit, but of course one expected that. I always sleep in the open, the tents being very crowded (13 men in each); in fact, I have scarcely slept under cover at all since leaving England. This is much the best plan and I am now as hard as bricks and shall feel the benefit when our work begins. The dust is terrible and covers everything, food and all: it is also very trying to one's eyes.'[8]

Large numbers of ships were plying back and forth across the 6000 miles to England, taking the mails home and bringing out supplies and more horses, as it began to be increasingly realized that the Boer, fighting on his own territory, required swift action against him if he was not to have the British going round in circles. Unfortunately, a collision eighty miles from Cape Town on 5 April between the mailboat *SS Mexican* and the *Winkfield*, a troopship carrying horses, the Northumberland Yeomanry and the Yeomanry Hospital,[9] caused the loss of some of Arthur's letters to Marshalls. But the Yeomanry were glad of the fresh horses when they arrived, and the Herts Company had to acquire some Australian horses as well to make up the numbers lost through disease. Arthur liked the Australian mounts, calling them 'quiet and well-mannered'[10] but he was very concerned by the poor quality of the saddles and bridles they were having to use:

> 'The saddlery has all been condemned by General Wilson [Surgeon-General Sir W.D. Wilson, Principal Medical Officer South Africa 1899–1902]. The first time it was used in complete marching order it began to come to bits. It was bought out of the county fund and cost £16 per set, the whole lot costing about £2300. This gives you a little insight into the working of our Company. We have now got Indian saddles – they are very strong and serviceable and cost, I believe, about £5 the set.'[11]

Arthur was convinced that someone at home had deliberately sold the Company third-rate saddles, and had made a lot of money out of the deal; he thought there should be an enquiry, but there never was. Meanwhile, he managed to do some sight-seeing:

> 'I went into Cape Town and saw the Boer prisoners just outside the town, but was only allowed to see them from a distance. They look just like the pictures. . . . Yesterday I got a pass to go over Woodstock Hospital [in suburban Cape Town] from a man I know there. Lady Roberts was at the same job so I had the pleasure of seeing her. There are a large number of Boer prisoners in with typhoid; they all told the same story, that they did not want to fight and were very friendly with the English, but of course not a word to be believed. The hospital orderly tells me that the way to get them to do anything is to pinch their Bible – they will do anything to get it back. He said that they came to hospital some with scarcely any clothing at all, but every man had his Bible, generally stitched into his shirt. They are treated very well, just the same as our men.'[12]

So Arthur had caught his first glimpse of 'Brother Boer', and also of the wife of the Commander-in-Chief, Lord Roberts, who had been summoned from Ireland. Roberts' task was to take over from Redvers Buller, under whose command serious reverses had been experienced in December, 1899, giving great impetus to the recruitment of the Imperial Yeomanry of which Arthur was part. Roberts, now aged sixty-seven, arrived at the Cape on 10 January, 1900, accompanied by Lord Kitchener as his Chief of Staff, but bowed down by the news that his only son Freddy, of the 60th Rifles, had been killed at Colenso in Natal. His wife had accompanied him, along with their daughters, and thus Lady Roberts came to be inspecting hospitals in Cape Town. This formidable woman was in South Africa in direct contravention of Queen Victoria's wish that fashionable society ladies should not go out, in case they undermined the conduct of the war.[13] Arthur agreed wholeheartedly with the Queen, and expressed his views very forcefully later on.

Still in Maitland Camp nine days later, his impatience surfaced again:

'Here we are, still with no prospect of any changes. The Railway to Bloemfontein is blocked with men and transport. It is very trying to be kept here all this time when there is such a lot going on up country. We were reviewed the other day and photographed by special request of the Queen. There were between 3 and 4 thousand Yeomen on parade and the General paid us great compliments of course. Today we have had a big field day; it was most exciting. I played the part of 'Scout' and got shot several times during the day and ended up being taken prisoner. I should think the Boers would have been highly amused if they had seen the battle.

'The papers here are scarcely worth buying and we hear very little of what is going on at the Front. What a blow it must have been for Gatacre [General Sir William Gatacre, dismissed by Roberts on 11 April; in October, 1914, Arthur was to bury his son, killed in action in France] to be recalled, but it will probably do good in making some of the others buck up a bit. I should like to see some of the I.Y. people recalled before they start. Some of the junior officers are absolutely ignorant of all military matters and do not take any trouble to improve themselves. One of the regulars here, who has watched our movements since we have been here, told me that such humbugging about as we get could not go on in the Regular Army for a day.

'We have a little town called Mowbray about a mile away with shops that sell everything, and pubs which keep very good wine which is as cheap as dirt. The chief drawback to the camp is that there is not sufficient water for the great numbers of horses and sometimes when it runs short we have to take them some way to water. The weather is very unsettled – rain – the gardens and flowers are very fine, and at the proper season must be splendid.'[14]

Arthur knew that Mrs Martin-Leake would be fascinated to hear about South African gardens. The gardening season at Marshalls was just getting under way, involving much planning and hard work from Arthur's two sisters, as well as from the gardener and his boys. Steenie and Dick were on the point of returning home permanently from India, planning great improvements to the house and outbuildings. It was to be many years before the alterations were finished. The age of the combustion engine had dawned too, and the brothers were determined to be amongst the first in the county to have motorized transport.

The rest of the family were dispersed around the world. Frank was stationed with the Royal Navy in Chinese waters; Theodore had gone in March to Aldershot with the 'Balloon Campanies'. Arthur was most intrigued by the potential of balloons in war,[15] and thought it was always possible that Theo might be sent out to South Africa to help things along there. Willie, who was now serving with the 1st Battalion, the Cheshire Regiment at Trimulgherry in the Indian State of Deccan, fulminated in his letters to England about his 'rotten luck' in being 'out of the show in South Africa'.[16] He had not been home for four years, but his Regiment received an Order in May, 1900, that 'a limited number of officers can go on leave to England provided they sign a certificate that they will not go to South Africa.'[17] The Army was obviously afraid of losing regular officers to the excitement of chasing the Boers.

At the end of April the Hertfordshire Yeomanry moved at last to Stellenbosch, some thirty miles march from Maitland. It took them two days to get there and Arthur was no more contented with this camp than he had been with Maitland. Stellenbosch was the main base camp in the Cape, and its name soon entered the war vocabulary – for a commander to be 'Stellenbosched' meant that he was recalled from active service in disgrace.[18] Arthur described his new surroundings:

'There are a lot of Indian chaps here, with the horses sent over by the various Indian Princes . . . the report is that Lord Roberts has sent for us and that we are only waiting for a train. But I have long ago given up believing anything. There are several companies of irregular Horse here and some of the 'Duke of Cambridge's Own'. I am going to try and get a doctor's job in one of them but do not expect much success.

'There are any quantity of canteens all round the camp – they sell everything in the way of tinned provisions – the curious thing is that they are all in the hands of Jews of various nationalities, who must be making their fortunes out of the war. We are close to a large ostrich farm and the birds are always wandering about the camp and causing stampedes among the horses, who cannot understand them at all. I am waiting an opportunity to get some feathers.'[19]

The War Office wrote to Arthur's home address that Spring inviting him to join the Royal Army Medical Corps; the letter was forwarded, and Arthur tried to effect a transfer, but his superiors in the Yeomanry would not give him their support. He was disappointed not to be practising any medicine at all, but his spirits revived early in May when Roberts began his advance to Pretoria, 750 miles from Cape Town, and the Yeomanry followed:

'We hear that the Boers are in full retreat everywhere and that Lord Roberts has begun his great move. We all expected to be in this and imagined ourselves first into Pretoria. I have had to give up The Dove and have another horse. I hope the Balloonist is getting on with his job; tell him South Africa and the war is not what we think it at home. Officers are much wanted, especially in the Yeomanry. We lost one of ours (transferred) and have got such a *funny little thing* [sic] in his place – a girls' school at home would have been more in his line.'[20]

Lord Roberts had indeed developed a strategy which he hoped would end the war; Bloemfontein, 300 miles south of Pretoria, had been taken on 13 March, and a six-week pause had been necessary to re-equip the Army and clear the Central and Western railway lines down to Cape Town. In mid-May Roberts began his advance on Pretoria, with a force of 100,000 men. The Yeomanry followed, taking three days by train to reach Bloemfontein, climbing steadily towards the high ground of the Rand some 5,600 feet above sea level, passing sites of earlier battles and a blown-up bridge over the Orange River. Arthur noted the fearful number of enteric fever (typhoid) cases in the town. This disease, highly infectious and causing severe intestinal symptoms, was to become the scourge of both sides:

'Hundreds of sick are coming in daily, nearly all enteric etc. The water supply here when the Boers held the waterworks was, I believe, something shocking; they put all their dead horses into the water. . . . We hear that Roberts is going as hard as he can and taking all before him. The camp here extends for miles around and is a wonderful sight, they say there are 25,000 men here. For general news concerning a Tommy's life out here I refer you to their letters which are published in the papers, but you must not believe anything in them. Every man nearly is trying to send home the best stories.'[21]

By 25 May the troopers had reached Brandfort on the way to Kroonstad.

1. 'In the reign of Queen Anne Sir John Leake was elevated to the position of Commander-in-Chief of the Queen's Fleet' (p.1).

3. 'Stephen [Arthur's father]…was subject to a great deal of nervous strain' (p.6).

2. 'Stephen… concluded his career as "Garter Principal King of Arms"' (p.4.)

4. 'Stephen regarded himself as particularly fortunate in his choice of Isabel Plunkett as his wife' (p.6).

5. The family at Marshalls, c 1877. Left to right (standing) Stephen, Sittie, Steenie; left to right (sitting) Willie, Isabel, Arthur, Bella, Dick, Frank.

6. Steenie and Sittie play in the garden at Marshalls, c. 1864. (The old mulberry tree may be seen on the left.)

7. 'He bought a country seat — Thorpe Hall, near Clacton in Essex' (p.3). This photograph was taken c. 1890.

8. 'In July, 1913, General the Hon. Julian Byng bought Thorpe Hall' (p.116). The 'Byng' extension may be seen on the right.

9. A picnic after an afternoon's snipe-shooting at Marshalls, c. 1895.

10. Marshalls from the kitchen garden, 1994. The walls and arches were constructed by Steenie and Dick in 1912.

They had to march from now on, and had to rely on stubborn mules for transporting supplies:

'If we have to march all the way to Kroonstad I should think we may get there in time for the *next* Boer war. We are marching by the same road that Lord Roberts advanced by. It is strewn with soldiers' stuff of all kinds and any quantity of dead horses, so you can imagine the stink . . . miles and miles of flat land without a tree or animal of any kind on it. The extraordinary thing is, where do all the Boers come from to fight? We had tremendous excitement yesterday while on the march. A large force was reported to be advancing on us by the scouts; we were formed up in battle array and advanced to meet the attack, but our enemy turned out to be cattle. You can imagine our disappointment. I am glad to say the scouting was not being done by the 42nd. I have got The Dove back, and I am in excellent health and enjoying the life.'[22]

On 8 June Lord Roberts entered Pretoria. Arthur and his fellow troopers followed four days' march behind. Now the Boer guerrilla attacks, by swiftly-moving 'Commando' units, began to occur on the major lines of communication, particularly the railways. The Boer leader in the area north-east of Kroonstad in the Vaal River area was Christiaan De Wet, who soon developed a phantom-like persona in the eyes of his British antagonists, so easily did he come and go across the veldt. From Roodewal Station near the Rhenoster River Arthur wrote in the middle of June:

'We marched up as far as the Vaal River and were on the way to Pretoria, about four days behind Lord Roberts. When we got to the Vaal De Wet started his little games in this neighbourhood so we turned round and have been after him ever since. Lords Kitchener and Methuen are here with 5 or 6 thousand men, and mean to settle De Wet soon, but so far he has been too much for them. We have had a lively time of it for the last 3 days, after the Boers nearly all the time – a big fight last Monday about 3 miles from here – we had a very hot corner but the Boer shooting was so bad that we only had one man hit (an officer of the Suffolks) and a few horses. De Wet is supposed to have about 4,000 men with him and 4 guns. He shelled us from 4 different directions at once the other day, but very few shells burst and no harm was done, but to the uninitiated it was distinctly unpleasant. The exciting times that we are in at present make up well for our past troubles. I am in the very best of health and enjoying the fun. You of course know the terrible disaster which happened to the Derbyshires at this place.'[23]

The Derbyshire Militia had suffered a grievous blow on 4 June at the railway station where Arthur now found himself. De Wet had attacked an inexperienced battalion guarding a bridge; 500 men had been taken prisoner, ammunition was captured, and the line at that point was destroyed.[24] The Yeomanry were only too aware that the same thing might happen to them. Consequently they were very 'jumpy' and suspicious, and Arthur reported to his mother that

> 'the station-master and 2 or 3 others are prisoners in our camp and are going to be tried, they gave the Boers information which led to the disaster.'[25]

By mid-July the 42nd Company was attached to General Broadwood's 2nd Brigade of cavalry, chasing De Wet. On 20 July they were rushing after him as a 'flying column' to stop him joining up with General Louis Botha, leader of the Transvaal Boers. Within days at least six large columns of men were after De Wet but with no sign of success. Arthur thought this was to some extent due to the Boer cattle and horses being able to move faster on the veldt. From Heilbron Arthur wrote in some dismay about the decline of the Hertfordshire Company, and again expressed a wish to obtain a medical posting:

> 'The Company is now only 40 strong – some are prisoners, some are ill. Also, our horses have given out. There is a large hospital here and I have applied today for an exchange onto the Medical Department and think I shall get it. The Colonel said he would be very glad to take me over but the difficulty is that I have no proof at all of qualification. I have to go and see him again tomorrow. He is a very nice old chap and I expect the transfer can be arranged.'[26]

Later narratives of Arthur's exploits have maintained that he was present at the surrender of Boer leader Marthinus Prinsloo at Fouriesburg in the Orange Free State on 29 July, 1900, but there is no evidence that either Arthur or the Hertfordshire Yeomanry were anywhere near this place. At the time of Prinsloo's surrender they were involved in the pursuit of De Wet in the area of Pretoria.

Then came news of another possibility. The Boxer Rising in China had broken out, with the British and other Legations at Peking being besieged since 20 June, in a frenzy of anti-foreign hatred. An international force of 20,000 men and seventy guns was being hastily assembled at Tientsin, and Arthur was delighted to hear that his brother Frank had been appointed Commander of HMS *Bramble*, a recently completed gunboat. Together with the *Britomart*, also commissioned at Devonport, Frank's ship left for China on 1 July. The 4th Balloon Section from Aldershot to which Theodore belonged was also sent out. Arthur thought he might try for China too:

> 'We hear that the war in China is going strong; is that so? Directly I can get down country I shall try to get out there as a Doctor. They must want them badly out there; how exciting the papers must be just now. Give Frank my best congratulations and tell him I expect to hear of great things done by HMS *Bramble*. If war by sea is anything like this, there is ample opportunity for a good commander with some dash. I am trying to send a wire to you to get me on the Medical Department for China but have not yet been able to get one off. If you get this letter before the wire and things are not yet over, will you please get Aunt Frances on the job? What a state of corruption the Chinese government must be in. . . . What a grand thing for the Balloonist, but I hope he will be able to keep the indisciplined creatures (i.e. the balloons) under control. Their transport seems to be the great difficulty and prevents them from being used more out here. What a pity Willie cannot come in for a job out here; he must be much disappointed. I would like to see him, as there are lots of questions on things concerning war to ask him. The whole thing is a mystery to me.'[27]

Arthur's own sector of the war was thrust into the limelight on 16 August. De Wet escaped pursuit through Olifant's Nek, a pass in the Magaliesberg Range north-west of Johannesburg. Arthur was more than a little dispirited when he wrote home from Pretoria:

> 'We crawled in here yesterday, tired, dirty, ragged, lousy and foot-sore, and worst of all heart-broken, because De Wet is still at large. We have chased the man now for over 3 months and never hardly been more than a few hours behind him. He has been surrounded time and time again and yet still got away. He is certainly a wonderful chap but I think largely over-estimated. Our generals move so slowly and will always stick to such huge amounts of baggage that he finds it easy to get away. It was not till

lately that Methuen and Ridley began to press him at all. For the last fortnight we have been marching night and day. We left De Wet hotly pursued by Baden-Powell and others. We left the chase a short time back with Ridley's column to go and relieve Colonel Hore [commanding Mafeking's Protectorate Regiment of 500 Australians and Rhodesians] who was surrounded at Brakfontein on the Eland's River. There was no fight as De La Rey had cleared off when he heard we were coming. The camp was well worth seeing; they had been shelled for 12 days hard, it was indeed a plucky stand. The Bushmen (Australians) could not say anything bad enough about Colonel Hore. He never showed himself once during the seige and would like to have surrendered if allowed.'[28]

This became known as 'The Relief of Hore's Laager' (camp). Arthur's contempt for a commander who seemed weak or cowardly had become more and more apparent as the war went on. He would very much have liked to get away to some other sphere of action, such as China, but that disturbance was, unfortunately for him, very shortlived. The Legations were relieved on 15 August and even Theo had arrived in China after the fighting was over. Balloon ascents were made, however, and the British contingent compared well with balloonists (or 'balloonatics') from the other nations represented there.[29] After this, most of the Balloon Section was sent off to India, but Theo went back to Aldershot.

Early in September the remnants of the Yeomanry were at Welverdiend, west of Johannesburg, under the command of Irishman General Arthur Fitzroy Hart, of whom Arthur said:

'Hart is the most awful terror that we have met out here yet. Everything has to be done as if we were on parade at home, and he has stopped all looting. So we get no farm produce, chicken, ducks etc. I enjoy the simple distinction of having been pulled out of bed by him the other day, for still being asleep when he rode round. He is quite off his nut on the subject of marching. His great weakness is night marching and at this form of amusement he is a perfect devil. He is an extremely miserable looking man and I am sure must be a serious case of insomnia. We call him the 'Midnight Walker'. But he gives the men extra rum if he thinks they deserve it. . . .

His method of pacifying the district is to march all over the place firing the 4.7 at Boers miles off who don't care a D---, and the only effect it seems to have is to make birds wild and kill our horses.'[30]

Willie, rejoicing in much more military experience, wrote to Marshalls from India, sympathizing with Arthur over being part of Hart's column:

> 'I am very sorry for Artie as he, like all others, must be very sick of the proceedings. I also know General Hart well by reputation. His brother is now commanding Quetta [North-West Frontier]. They are both well-known as men of most extraordinary energy and are never content unless doing something or worrying someone. They think men are machines and horses are made of iron. General Gatacre was the same stamp of soldier and hence his failure. On active service the most successful generals are those who pay most attention to feeding and resting their men.'[31]

Willie also wrote directly to South Africa from time to time, and Arthur was most amused by his likening De Wet to a flea. The Boer leader was still proving to be very elusive, but Arthur now believed that basically the Boers had 'simply been playing a cowardly runaway game which anyone could do in a country so exactly suited to it as this, and with any amount of cattle at their disposal'.[32] The town of Potchefstroom, for example, had been hastily evacuated by the British in July; when Hart's column returned to it two months later it was easy to reoccupy as the Boers had disappeared into the veldt.

By now (early October) there were hardly any of the 42nd Company left; a reinforcement draft sent out never reached the Hertfordshire Company.[33] There was a Yeomanry Hospital at Krugersdorp which was so comfortable and so easy for the men to get into that only some twenty remained 'fit for duty'. Arthur thought many of the men were 'shirkers', and that allowing them to get away with it was one of the greatest failings of the Army authorities. He was going to try, yet again, to obtain a 'medical job'. This time he had three days' leave in Pretoria, and was armed with a letter of introduction to the Principal Medical Officer from Captain Hart, the General's son.[34] Arthur obtained a position as a dispenser in one of the Pretoria hospitals while he waited for a reply.

The Army Medical Department had been transformed into the Royal Army Medical Corps by Royal Warrant dated 23 June, 1898, effective from 1 July. The then Secretary of State for War, Lord Lansdowne, had indicated that, before the RAMC was formed, Army doctors had not always been treated with the respect they deserved, but that was now to change. Officer ranks in the RAMC would lose the prefix 'Surgeon' and Medical Officers would now hold the same commissions and would be treated with regard to pay and promotion exactly as fighting officers.[35]

Arthur clearly believed that a transfer to the new Corps would be to his advantage. He had taken leave of the Yeomanry at Krugersdorp on 18 October not appreciating that he would not return. Almost before he knew it, he was attached to the RAMC as a 'Civil Surgeon' with pay and uniform corresponding to the rank of captain, and was sent to a military hospital at Pienaar's Poort, some twelve miles east of Pretoria.

CHAPTER FIVE

'The Hat and Legging Brigade'

On arrival at Pienaar's Poort, Arthur realized on reflection that a complete transfer to the RAMC would not be desirable for financial and professional reasons. He wrote home:

> 'They sent me at once to a hospital here, where I found a major in charge (Major Curtis, RAMC, attached to the Connaught Rangers), an Irishman, nice chap, but more soldier than doctor. He has handed over the hospital to my care and says he does not care what happens as long as it is in military order. This is quite in keeping with what one knows of the RAMC. I was very glad to be taken on as Civil Surgeon as they might have made me join the RAMC when I should only have got lieutenant's pay. As things are now I get £1 plus extras per diem. I got refitted at Pretoria and also some of the outward and visible signs of an officer attached. The change was very sudden and I was considerably upset by the first Tommy who saluted. The fact of having eaten humble pie to volunteer officers for so long made me forget that I was anything but a Tommy. This place is about 15 miles east of Pretoria on the Komati Poort Railway and is held by the Connaught Rangers and some Artillery. There is some prospect of being attacked by Boers, as they are in some force about 5 miles off. I shall not be sorry if it comes off as there is very little work at present.'[1]

The boredom of inactivity only served to increase Arthur's impatience with his superior officers. A few days later he described how 'all the bad cases are put on the train and sent into Pretoria. The Major is determined not to have his returns spoiled by a high mortality, so he likes somebody else to do the killing.'[2] Two weeks later the hospital was visited by the Principal Medical Officer for the district, who reported very favourably on the hospital, but Arthur thought he could see through the 'bull':

'This was not in any way due to the treatment or comfort of the patients, but to stones set in geometrical patterns about the place and whitewashed, the grass brushed the right way and flags flying.'[3]

Telling Arthur that he only had to ask, Major Curtis was trying to persuade him to seek a commission in the RAMC, but Arthur was very reluctant to take such a step. He felt that, while he would be 'settled for life' if he joined the Corps, and would have a pension of £350 a year after twenty years, (an amount almost impossible to obtain in civilian medical practice), yet it could mean that the final qualification of Fellow of the Royal College of Surgeons would be put out of his reach for ever. The *Times* historian of the war agreed:

'(In the RAMC) opportunities for gaining useful experience were very limited; few facilities for study were provided, and ambitious officers had usually to find them at their own expense and in their periods of leave. Promotion was almost wholly by seniority, independent of scientific merit.'[4]

Above all, Arthur told his mother, 'the Army is extremely distasteful to me.'[5] Major Curtis even put in a recommendation to the PMO for Arthur's commission. Arthur persistently refused to apply. But at the end of December, when he went to the Pay Office in Pretoria to collect his salary, he found he was not allowed to draw anything at all, because his name had been mistakenly 'omitted from Army Orders'. When the error was corrected, he was still only allowed to draw basic pay, and complained that he had been 'done out of all allowances, amounting to 5/- per day, and will have no gratuity at the end of service and no passage home. This is because they employed me on the spot and not from England.'[6] Greatly disgruntled, he applied to the PMO to be sent out 'on commando again, having had quite enough of this most luxurious and inactive life'. The PMO told him to be ready to move at very short notice, so he occupied his time in doing post-mortems on the many horses that were dying of disease, and in treating civilians and soldiers in the vicinity of Pienaar's Poort. He travelled several miles to see patients and was often paid in kind, receiving figs, apricots, eggs, chickens, and once the skin of a springbok and an offer of lessons in Dutch.[7]

During the last weeks of 1900 the Pretoria region was battered by heavy and frequent storms and the army's tents were in danger of being blown away. Arthur had his own solution to the problem:

'I am building a hut to live in. My house is going to be the finest mansion in Pienaar's Poort. It is 6 feet by 13 feet, has a verandah along the front, a door (with hinges) and one, perhaps two, windows. My black boy is going to make a floor out of ant heaps, which set as hard as cement when pounded hard with water. I am also going to make some chairs and tables. Enclosed is a rough outline of the advertisement I am going to put in the paper when leaving –

THE PIENAAR'S POORT MANSION
This charming Residence to let, situated on the slope of a picturesque kopje and overlooked by 2 imposing 15-pounders and carefully guarded at night by numerous piquets. One-storey Hall, Dining and Sitting Room facing north and overlooking an extensive and beautiful view of the veldt with the whisky factory of Eerstefabrieken in the distance. . . . The whole finely decorated inside with limewash, as supplied by Government, and well furnished with bed, chair and table.

The amusements in the neighbourhood are many and varied – the Circuses of Botha and De Wet are often within easy reach and can be seen performing in the vicinity and much can be learned from them. The Sanitary Arrangements are excellent and have been passed by the highest officials.'[8]

At Christmas that year Arthur received a large package containing tobacco from his mother, which he shared with his colleagues. Puddings and beer were obtained from the regimental canteen of the Cornwalls, but he regarded Christmas Day as 'a great nuisance, the men are determined to get tight if they possibly can. . . . I shall be glad when it is all over.'[9]

Letters from home, containing details of developments at Marshalls, were of constant interest. Steenie and Dick, described by their brothers as 'The Engineers' or 'The Nabobs', had arrived home from India, having decided that they had suffered enough from the vagaries of disease and climate while working for the Bengal-Nagpur Railway. Worse still, their latest project, a bridge over the Roopnarayan River north-west of Calcutta, had sapped their energy for years; with seven major spans and four minor side arches, built over a tidal river with fearsome shoals and currents, it had been a tremendous undertaking.[10] Now, they complained, the Directors of the Bengal-Nagpur Railway headed by Sir Trevredyn Wynne, had not paid them the amount agreed in their original contract. The whole family fumed and fulminated to each other about this by letter, but no further payment was made and a sense of injustice stayed with Steenie and Dick for many years. They now set about making changes at home, leading Arthur to comment:

> 'Improvements at Marshalls of a substantial nature seem to be going ahead fast. It is difficult to believe that at last the door into the pantry is under way. It makes me think that possibly even De Wet may be caught and the war come to an end if the world lasts long enough. What an addition the conservatory will be. An ancient and decrepit family will be able to sit and discuss its grievances surrounded by the splendours of tropical vegetation, illuminated by the brilliant rays of the acetylene lamp.'[11]

Frank, now at Singapore with HMS *Bramble*, also liked the idea of Marshalls being endowed with an acetylene gas lighting system:

> 'This is, I should think, the very thing, although I know nothing more than one sees in the advertisements. Electric light is, of course, out of the question, and so also is the tallow candle. Your comfort when these things are finished should be great. Do not burn the house down – often an accompaniment to a change of lighting system.'[12]

Frank was less enthusiastic about the new driveway being constructed by 'The Nabobs', wishing that 'both gates could be blocked and ourselves live inside undisturbed'.[13] He was reflecting the family love of privacy and seclusion, but the resurfacing was necessary as Steenie and Dick were planning to purchase High Cross's first motor car, and Mrs Martin-Leake asked Arthur whether she should not sell the Marshalls horses, now that none of her sons were at home. Arthur replied that she should; there was no point in keeping a horse for his sole use as 'I may not be at home for a long time.'[14] Some horses were retained, so that Bella and Sittie could continue to hunt, but the stable block at the back of the house was partially adapted to provide garaging for the car, a wonderful Model D three-horsepowered De Dion Bouton with handwheel gearchange and steering handle; Bella photographed Steenie and Dick proudly driving it up and down outside the house, leading Arthur to comment:

> 'Last mail brought the astonishing news that a motor-car was parading up and down the drive. Has the family become more sociable? It certainly seems that the new century is going to see a great change at Marshalls. In fact it is "undergoing the process of discovery", as Frank would say.'[15]

On 22 January, 1901, Queen Victoria died, to the stupefaction of the British Empire. The news came as a great shock to Arthur, as his hospital only received first news of her illness the day before. From Quetta, Willie wrote:

'The proclamation of King Edward VII has been read out at 5pm all over India. The poor old Queen's death was so sudden that one can scarcely realize that she has gone. Her strong will and influence will be missed all the world over.'[16]

Mrs Martin-Leake was moved to send a letter of condolence to the new King, and Arthur remarked:

'No wonder you must have a new carriage-drive and all modern improvements to your mansion. No doubt if you keep up the correspondence he will appoint you Maid-in-Waiting to some article of his furniture. You might mention a few of my grievances to him next time you write (most brave and patriotic volunteer in South Africa, etc). It is difficult to realize what things can be like without such an old institution as the Queen. What a lot of Royal ceremonies you must be having now'[17]

Frank suggested that their mother should have added a postscript to her letter to the King, telling him 'how badly we were treated when Queen Anne died,'[18] a reference to Sir John Leake's fall from favour in 1714.

At the same time Arthur was annoyed to learn that his old hospital at Hemel Hempstead had appointed Dr Arthur Whitehead as his permanent replacement, although the Committee had promised to keep his job open for him until he returned:

'They have broken their agreement, but what does it matter? They are but a poor feeble set of old muddlers who meet once a week to have a sociable afternoon and do their best to make mountains out of nothing.'[19]

Early in the New Year a new impetus was felt in the war. Kitchener had arrived and, according to Arthur, 'has started with great vigour'. Rumours were circulating that reinforcements were being sent out for the Yeomanry, which surprised him:

'They wouldn't get me as a Yeoman next time. . . . I shouldn't think men would be so easily caught now as they were. My little trip with the Imperial Yeomanry meant a loss of something like

3 or 4 hundred pounds, and what is worse I have to suffer for it as long as I am out here in the way of loss of pay.'[20]

By mid-January he had been sent to Kaapsche Hoop, some twelve miles from the Delagoa Bay railway line, a small village with a garrison of 400 men. A fresh policy had been enthusiastically espoused by the new Commander-in-Chief, the main objective of which was to bring Boers and their families together in camps, sweeping them from the veldt by the concentrated efforts of the British forces in a series of lines and blockhouses. The Boer commandos were to be deprived of food and shelter by the systematic burning of their homesteads, and surrender was encouraged by the promise that any who gave themselves up would not be sent out of South Africa. At Kaapsche Hoop Arthur saw the early results:

'The Boers have been collected from the neighbourhood and brought in and are living in tents, wagons etc. So the place is very overcrowded. There is a lot of illness amongst the civilians, and with their dirty little ways, I have plenty to do. . . . Brother Boer is dancing round us day and night as usual, but has had a rather more successful week than usual, he has had 4 wagons with provisions, oxen, mules etc., and yesterday got all my wordly possessions as well, except the clothes I had on; fortunately he did not get me. I am now living on charity as regards clothes. The only things of any value they got were my case of surgical instruments and medical books. Our columns in these parts do nothing at all, directly Boers are reported to them, they always have important business in the opposite direction. Two columns have been caught in front of the line for almost a month and have only moved occasionally for a short distance to get away from the Boers. People at home can have little idea of how things are being carried on out here – one long-headed old Boer is worth any number of these column leaders.'[21]

A bout of fever in the second week of February put Arthur into hospital at Middelburg, further west along the Delagoa Bay Railway, and with good food and medical attention he made a speedy recovery, but hoped to 'go on the trek from here. It is a much more healthy life and suits me much better.'[22] Within a few days he was sent east again to the hill town of Barberton, where he hoped to start a 'paying practice', as he had heard that it was a large and flourishing settlement. If the Principal Medical Officer still refused to allow him to go on the trek, 'I shall threaten to go back to the Yeomanry. But everyone is sick of the war and hopes it will soon end.'[23]

Reinforcements were being sent to South Africa from all over the Empire, including India. On 21 January Willie had received a War Office telegram at Quetta, ordering him to leave the 1st Cheshires and proceed to South Africa to join the second battalion. 'No reason given,' he wrote, 'but I don't think it is to relieve Lord Kitchener.' Via Durban and Johannesburg he arrived at Potchefstroom in the Transvaal in March, and thereafter made a number of long treks,[24] but he and Arthur never met up with one another until Arthur was on the point of being invalided home a year later.

At Barberton Arthur found himself attached to the 1st Yorkshires, and could see no opportunity at all for starting a civilian practice. His impatience increased to breaking point:

'I am thinking very seriously of giving a fortnight's notice to the authorities and taking my discharge, which I can do as I was employed locally. I could then rejoin again as a Civil Surgeon in London if I wanted to and the home pay would more than make up for the passage home – at present I am making a great loss.'[25]

Perhaps he knew that eminent consultant surgeons like Frederick Traves were being paid £5,000 per annum by the British government for their services in South Africa, because they had

'left lucrative work at home in order to give the hospitals in South Africa the benefit of their experience and skill.'[26]

Three weeks later Arthur acted. Threatening resignation, he wrote to the Principal Medical Officer demanding to do medical work on a homeward bound ship, and received the PMO's agreement. Now all he had to do was wait for a ship. It seemed likely that he would sail from Durban.

Then, quite unexpectedly, he heard of a new force being set up, a force which promised an end to his boredom and might even provide him with some trekking. The unit was being called the 'Baden-Powell Police', but its proper title was the 'South African Constabulary' (SAC). It was being raised under Lord Roberts' Proclamation Number 24 of 22 October, 1900, whereby Major-General R.S. Baden-Powell was required to draw up a scheme for a Constabulary Force of 6000, increased in December 1900 to 10,000 men. The force had to be ready for service by June, 1901, and was originally, as its name suggested, to have a policing function, but, as the war showed no signs of coming to an end, the SAC was employed as a military force under the direction of British Army commanders. It was constantly engaged in trekking, and on the blockhouse lines.[27]

Many members of the SAC were recruited from Britain and around the

Empire, single men only and aged between twenty and thirty-five. Testimonials as to their good character were required, and riding and shooting skills would give a man preference. A daily sum of five shillings was paid during the three-year minimum contract. Baden-Powell made it plain that

> 'promotion will be by merit and commissions will be obtainable from the ranks.'[28]

Baden-Powell designed the uniform of the force, which some commentators called 'B-P's Own'[29] and others, less charitably, called 'De Wet's Own', when their efforts to apprehend the elusive Boer leader failed. The first recruits were kitted out in Stetson hats from Canada, 'stove-pipe' leggings (which few wore and all regarded as uncomfortable and unsightly), khaki serge Army pattern jackets and riding breeches. Ribbons and stripes were in dark green.[30]

Medical care was a priority. Attached to each Troop of one hundred men was a Medical Corporal who carried out basic first aid, and a doctor was allocated to each area where several Troops might be stationed. Wounded or sick men were sent to Imperial Military Hospitals at first; later, SAC hospitals were established at Divisional Headquarters.[31]

From Pretoria Arthur wrote home on 17 May:

> 'I start tomorrow morning to Zuurfontein [a few miles north-east of Johannesburg] to see about a job in the police. They want doctors badly. Terms £510 per annum, 2 horses and servant and grub. Rather better than the Civil Surgeon's pay from home, and considerably better than mine. As far as I know at present there is a 3-month's trial to begin with. I think I shall very likely try it but do not know enough about it yet.'[32]

By 24 May he had joined the SAC. From Krugersdorp he described the new corps:

> 'I have joined this show for 3 months' trial and am stationed at the hospital here, but shall probably be moved soon. The corps is quite in its infancy at present, many of the men having no kit yet and there are only a few horses; the hospital arrangements are in much the same condition, nothing to doctor with and no accommodation but no doubt things will improve in time. However, all the deficiencies of the Force are amply made up for by the great display of B.P. hats and leggings. The Corps is built round these, in fact they are the foundation of the whole thing.

The title of South African Constabulary is entirely a misnomer; they should be called the 'Hat and Legging Brigade'. This division (A) is chiefly made up of Canadians, good chaps some of them but very much the colonial. They have just come out and of course are very smart as regards uniform, which is a very important part of the game, especially as "Our smiling B.P." designed it himself. I am off to J'burg one of these days to try and scrape together some green ribbons etc. to endeavour to carry out the "great self-advertiser's" idea of what a policeman should be like. I now hold the rank of captain. This is a bit of a knock, rather too sudden a rise from nothing. Willie will be much amused when we meet and he sees two stars up. You will very likely see me home at the end of August. The Army and its funny little ways have nearly chafed all my epidermis off. . . . Hoping you are all well and have not yet been killed by the motor car.'[33]

This letter was signed 'Arthur M-L, Capt S.A.C., by the grace of B.P. etc'. The sarcasm applied by Arthur to the SAC Inspector-General was to be repeated often in his letters, but it was no worse than the scorn he frequently felt for anyone in authority, either military or civilian. The basic cause seems to have been Arthur's impatience with inaction and superficiality, and he could never accept that those placed in positions of responsibility might know best. Indeed, he suspected that they were often promoted simply because they were incompetent fools. 'Perhaps if a little intelligence instead of smart appearance had been the qualification for such posts the war might be over by this time.'[34] He had criticized the Imperial Yeomanry, the RAMC, and now the SAC; soon he found another great source of unease when female nurses began to arrive at the Krugersdorp hospital to assist the SAC doctors:

'We are desperately short of medical instruments. I am moving to Swartkop (near Johannesburg) which is held by the SAC. Nurses have arrived here, so I am delighted to go.'[35]

A week later, on 7 June, he complained

'There is no peace in this show; it is neither one thing nor the other, and as they have started nursing sisters of the worst description, I shall give it the chuck as soon as possible.'[36]

In the middle of July Baden-Powell was on his way to England, and Arthur wrote scathingly:

'Our "Smiling Comedian" is on his way home on sick leave, in truth, I think, to satisfy his vanity with a great reception. Do not let him turn your heads. An empty rum cask makes more noise than a full one. This show is in a bad muddle. It is perfectly scandalous to see human life played with in this fashion. I can get nothing here, except fancy things to make a show, and have to use convalescent patients to nurse others dangerously ill. After writing many times for surgical instruments they send me a few knives wrapped up in paper and an instrument used for a certain operation peculiar to women. . . . Have had to run in my hospital sergeant. Court-martial to follow. Rum led to port wine, then a little more port, then a great deal more, next day most mysterious illness. I am very lucky to have found him out so soon.'[37]

Newly arrived at the SAC Hospital at Meyerton to the south of Johannesburg, he found his problems were increasing:

'I am going one better than the Israelites. I am making hospital equipment out of less than straw. I left Krugersdorp with mattresses and opening medicine and come here to find bedsteads and closing medicine. This makes treatment a little bit puzzling. In fact, the cases have to be sent to the military hospitals where they charge 4/- per diem for every SAC man. Thousands have already been spent on the hospitals and the thing was started nearly a year ago. Poor miserable taxpayer, if he only knew. But it should be some comfort to him to know that leggings and hats look very nice and that polo is a good game.'[38]

When his three months' trial with the SAC was up in August, Arthur decided to stay on, partly because he had made a few good friends, but mostly because he saw prospects of doing some surgery. In September he took on the duties of doctor to the employees of a coal mine near to Van Wyk's Rust, eighteen miles south-west of Johannesburg, where his division was stationed, and was paid ten guineas to vaccinate all the 'natives' against enteric fever. He also received five guineas monthly as a retainer, and hoped the position might lead to other work. He then 'started a tent for natives, the only qualification for entry being surgical cases willing to have an operation.'[39]

Boer attacks were still occurring along the line of posts and blockhouses manned by the SAC, De Wet in particular being a great nuisance. Again, Arthur's view was that the 'show' could have been brought to a satisfactory conclusion with better leadership and more commitment from the troops. In October he transferred to the SAC's 'C' Division, stationed at Cyferfontein between Val Station and Heidelberg, and described the system of block-houses across the veldt:

'The plan is that the SAC will go on driving the Boers in front of them, till they get to the coast. Brother Boer will then be drowned in the sea and the war will be over. B.P.'s great work (which the papers say is three-quarters finished) will be completed. He will then return to England and the band will play. At present the line of posts has blockhouses about every 2000 yards. But of course the Boers can get through any night they like. There are several Boer commandos in front of us which will have to shift soon. The Proclamation does not seem to have produced much result. The pen may be mightier than the sword but the rifle takes the cake.'[40]

The 'Proclamation' issued by Kitchener on 7 August, 1901, had stated that all Boers who did not surrender by 15 September would be punished by being forced to pay the cost of keeping their families in the 'concentration camps', while their leaders would be subject to 'perpetual banishment' from South Africa. The concentration camps were by now receiving vociferous criticism from a small group in England, a criticism fuelled by the findings of Emily Hobhouse and of the 'Ladies' Commission' led by Mrs Millicent Fawcett.[41] Arthur passed no comment on the camps, but Willie had strong views:

'I think that transportation of every male we catch is the only way. These refugee camps are all humbug and most expensive. . . . A strong press censor is required in England to burn all the papers which criticize the action of the Government or the Army authorities while settling this country.'[42]

As 1901 came to an end, Arthur was in camp at Val Station, where

'They have made me into a travelling M.O. with about 50 miles of line to look after. I like the job, carry a shotgun and have lots of good duck shooting. But it is not doctoring, simply a sort of forwarding agent for sick men. Your question about my future is a difficult one to answer as I have no idea myself what to do.

Money is slowly accumulating, and when I have enough to carry on with for a bit at home I shall chuck this and return, but I don't much like leaving till the war is over.'[43]

His impatience with the medical provision increased during January, 1902:

'The SAC hospitals are full to overflowing, and there is nowhere to send sick men. Here there are 80 bad cases with 1 orderly to do all the work, cooking included. This I consider is a perfect scandal and our P.M.O. and the authorities should be Stellenbosched. They have had lots of warning and plenty of time to prepare and knew quite well that there would be a lot of sickness at this time of the year. It seems to me that these people are worse than useless; they never learn anything from experience and have absolutely no idea of organization. In fact the only thing they do understand is dress and how to have a good time. I cannot understand how we can ever expect the war to come to an end when these 'fancy articles' are put to run the show; no wonder the Boers can walk all round us. The line of blockhouses is moving forward shortly. This line is a perfect farce; the country behind, which is supposed to be clear, is full of Boers.'[44]

His words were prophetic. He was soon to be engaged in a fierce action with the enemy, an action that brought disaster to the troop with whom he served and almost resulted in his own death, in the precise circumstances he had described – a body of Boers attacking from an unexpected direction. The series of events began in the early days of February, as Arthur's troop was moved further out into 'the high veldt'; his last letter from 'the SAC line of Blockhouses' before the attack was again full of anger and frustration:

'I wonder how long we shall go on fooling ourselves like this. We must have captured and killed, during the last year, more Boers than ever existed, but yet their numbers in the field seem to increase rather than diminish. Their supply of food and horses was supposed to be exhausted more than a year ago, but still they are splendidly remounted and apparently well-satisfied with their diet. And last but not least, their army as an organized force ceased to exist when "Bobs", our greatest soldier, went home but yet we hear now that De Wet has 5000 men and guns in the Free State.

'What does all this show? We have had ample proof that the army is quite unable to use any tactical skill and is unfit to be matched against an enemy who thinks about his movements at all. But why should we persistently go on? I fear it indicates a decaying Empire brought on by Red Coats, Gold Lace and the "Dontcha know" manner.'[45]

CHAPTER SIX

'And Then He Refused Water'

Four days later Arthur's part in the South African War was over. Before daylight on Friday 8 February, a mounted party consisting of 150 men drawn from three SAC troops left Val Station under the command of Captain Wessex Capell and headed out into the veldt. No definite reason for the expedition had been given to the men, but the talk amongst the survivors afterwards was that the objective of the sortie had been to find out the strength of a body of Boers operating in that sector.[1] The men were right. A post-action report by Colonel J.S. Nicolson, Chief Staff Officer, stated that

> 'Previous reports made by the SAC of the presence of the enemy at this point had been discredited, and the Commander-in-Chief ordered a forward move of the line of posts of 'C' Division. Major J. Fair, commanding the Division, very properly sent Capt. Capell with a detachment to reconnoitre previous to making such a move, and thereby saved what would otherwise have probably been a disaster.'[2]

The party took up a position in the area of Cyferfontein[3] overlooking Van Tonder's Hoek. As dawn broke, American Trooper George Cullis later recalled, a group of Boers could be seen at a distance of 140 yards, apparently 'all set and waiting for us'. Fighting continued for some three or four hours, as the sun blazed down and drinking water began to run out. A party of some forty Boers advanced and succeeded in rushing the SAC's left flank which was commanded by Lieutenant Thomas O.P. Abraham, approaching unseen under cover of a *donga* (the dried-up bed of a stream); here, amid scenes of great confusion, Arthur responded to the cries for help from the wounded, and went from one to another applying dressings as best he could. Trooper Robertson saw a Sergeant Waller, severely hit in the leg, being attended by Arthur who lay flat on the ground, all the while under heavy fire at close range. Sergeant Waller was heard to advise the doctor to stay out of sight, but then Abraham was wounded, and Arthur went over to him. He found the Lieutenant mortally wounded and in terrible pain, so tried to place him in a more comfortable position. A volley of shots caught the little group, Arthur sustaining wounds to his right hand and left thigh.[4] At one point George Cullis was sent from the centre to bring Captain Leake over to tend wounded there:

'I did not know Captain Leake was a surgeon attached to us so had to follow along the firing line enquiring for him. This I did, after crawling back to get my horse which was probably a quarter of a mile behind us. Eventually I found him. Then I knew he was a doctor as he was taking care of the wounded on the left flank. He said, "Get me a horse and remain mounted." This I did and went back to him and found that he was out of action wounded.'[5]

Captain Capell managed to withdraw the left flank, but had to leave the dead and wounded where they lay. They were soon overrun by the Boers, who seemed to have no wish to take prisoners and left them there, but expressed their great regret at having shot the doctor; they said they had had no alternative when he rushed forward.[6] As the wounded lay among the dead for hours until they could be taken back, Arthur refused to partake of their precious water supply, saying he would wait until the others were taken care of.

Meanwhile, Capell sent a message to Lieutenant Swinburne who was holding the right flank, ordering him to withdraw too. Unfortunately the orderly carrying the message was shot and the message never reached Swinburne, who stayed at his post, even when the Boers sent him a signal telling him either to surrender or 'expect no quarter'. Capell's men fought skirmishes all the way back to the line of blockhouses seven miles distant, and when night fell Swinburne managed to escape as well, bringing in their casualties. Captain Capell said in his report of the action:

'I cannot speak too highly of every officer and man, the latter being cool and splendid when in the firing-line.'[7]

The SAC losses were heavy: two officers, Lieutenants Abraham and Algernon C.B. Blackett, and six were killed; there were seven serious injuries, including Arthur, and three slightly wounded. Twenty-four horses were killed or missing. This was the largest number of SAC casualties in any single day.[8] Arthur was removed without delay to the SAC Hospital at Heidelberg, where his thigh injury responded to the treatment, but very great concern was felt about the wound to his right hand. The wound was 'dressed antiseptically', and it healed during the next four weeks, but an examination and case conference held by a Medical Board on 12 March found

> 'Complete paralysis of muscles supplied by ulnar nerve with atrophy, loss of sensation and power over area of distribution.'[9]

The Board decided that Arthur should be granted six months' sick leave in England. At present, his 'capacity for earning a livelihood is totally impaired, and is likely to be permanent unless an operation for the reunion of the severed nerve proves successful.'

His family were naturally alarmed to hear of his wounds, which were described as 'severe' in the newspapers.[10] but he soon wrote (using his left hand!) to reassure them:

> 'Getting on well, wounds healing. The only doubtful thing is the nerve to the inner part of the hand which I am afraid is divided. Have to go and look for fingers when I want them. This is, however, a small matter and can be put right by an operation. Hope you got wire all right; did not send one at first as I thought the report had stated 'slight'. If they don't give me leave I shall take it. It will be very nice to see you all again, and you can be sure that my departure from this place will be expedited as far as is within my power. Hope you think my left hand is improving and will be able to read this scrawl.'[11]

Frank, in Hongkong with HMS *Bramble*, was angry that his brother was wounded, and wished he could bring his ship's guns to bear upon the Boers.[12] As Arthur prepared to depart for home, Willie hastened to meet him at Heath's Hotel in Johannesburg on 12 March. He sent their mother the news that

> 'He is quite mended and gets about as if he was none the worse, but his right arm is still suffering from the effects of the wound; not much power in his right hand. The SAC authorities have made a most stupid mistake about his passage. A berth had been booked for him for the 9th and they wired to him that he was to sail on the 19th; he has consequently missed his passage, but of course he will soon get another. The SAC and the military authorities don't seem to pull well together which is very unfortunate. You will be glad to get him home again. He has done well out here and seems to be popular and very well thought of by those he has served with.'[13]

In the event Arthur sailed from Durban on board the *Orcana* on 23 March and arrived home at Marshalls on 16 April. Willie was convinced that Arthur should receive the highest award for bravery:

> 'I hope Arthur will get a VC, but I fear the SAC have not gone the right way to work to get much out of the military authorities. Many VCs have been given for far less and he certainly deserves one.'[14]

A total of seventy-eight Victoria Crosses was awarded in the war, fifty-nine of them British.[15] At SAC Headquarters it seems to have been realized straight away that Arthur's actions should be recommended for just such an award. On 12 February Major Fair ordered that a Board of Officers should be convened in order to collect evidence of what had happened, and all the survivors were interviewed, particularly Sergeant Waller who was in the same hospital as Arthur. The men were unanimous in their praise for the doctor, leading Baden-Powell, on 3 March, to send the Board's evidence to Lord Kitchener, the Commander-in-Chief in South Africa:

> 'I have the honour to forward and strongly recommend for the favourable consideration of the General Officer Commanding-in-Chief, the enclosed evidence of gallantry in action on the part of Surgeon Captain Leake SAC, as being a case possibly deserving of recommendation for the Victoria Cross.'[16]

The recommendation was challenged at the highest level. On 17 March all the documentary evidence was sent by Lieutenant-Colonel W.N. Congreve VC, Private Secretary to Kitchener, to Surgeon General W. Wilson, Principal Medical Officer at Pretoria, together with a request:

> 'Will you please inform me if you consider that in this case Captain Leake was doing anything more than his duty.'[17]

Wilson replied two days later:

> 'I have read over the enclosed and I consider that Captain Leake has done well (and I trust that the majority at least of the medical officers would have tried to have done the same if they had the opportunity). Captain Leake had the chance of distinguishing himself and he availed himself of it. He could, I consider, have been more careful of his own personal safety and not have

incurred censure for doing so. I consider him well worthy of recognition for his services.

I consider your question "was he doing anything more than his duty" would exclude everyone for the Victoria Cross, for it is everyone's duty to do his very best.'[18]

Kitchener was still not satisfied. On 24 March he sent the following to the War Office:

'I have the honour to forward herewith a recommendation for the Victoria Cross in the case of Surgeon Captain Leake, South African Constabulary. I am of the opinion that, though the Officer in question undoubtedly showed great devotion to duty, he at the same time was only carrying out his manifest duty, and I therefore consider that the bestowal of the DSO would be more appropriate than the VC, and I therefore recommend him for the former.'[19]

On 23 April, in London, the Commander-in-Chief, Lord Roberts agreed with Kitchener, and recommended the Distinguished Service Order to the Secretary of State for War, St John Broderick. Broderick, however, disagreed with them both:

'C in C
This would almost have seemed to me a case for the V.C.
St. J. B.'[20]

An unsigned 'Minute Sheet' accompanying Kitchener's recommendation, had seemed to come down firmly in favour of the Victoria Cross:

'The Regulations respecting the Victoria Cross were amended in 1881, so as to admit of the decoration being conferred in cases of marked gallantry in the *performance* of duty. . . . A modification was introduced by the Royal Warrant of 23 April 1881 defining the qualification as "conspicuous bravery or devotion to the country in the presence of the enemy" which was intended to include marked gallantry in the performance of duty.'[21]

Roberts gave in. A final laconic note was sent to his Military Secretary:

'Submit to the King for the V.C.'[22]

The award was approved by Edward VII on 8 May, and the announcement appeared in the *London Gazette* five days later, together with the following citation:

'Arthur Martin-Leake, Surgeon Captain, South African Constabulary. For great devotion to duty and self-sacrifice at Vlakfontein, 8th February, 1902, when he went out into the firing line to dress a wounded man under very heavy fire from about 40 Boers 40 yards off. When he had done all he could for him, he went over to a badly wounded officer, and while trying to place him in a more comfortable position he was shot 3 times. He only gave up when thoroughly exhausted, and then he refused water until other wounded men had been served.'[23]

[The exact location of the action has been obscured by the fact that the place name included in the citation, i.e. Vlakfontein, occurs at least three times in the Transvaal and Orange Free State. The author is convinced, as a result of collating SAC and 'Official History' accounts with Martin-Leake's own letters, that the location is as indicated on the map on page 38, i.e. some thirty-five miles to the south-east of Johannesburg.]

Arthur had been at home in High Cross for just four weeks when his Victoria Cross was gazetted. The *Hertfordshire Mercury* reported it in glowing terms:

'We are glad to chronicle such heroic conduct on the part of Captain Martin-Leake, and trust the gallant officer will soon be completely restored to health. All will congratulate him on so worthily deserving such a high distinction. He has the true traits of an English officer, conspicuous bravery and tender humility.'[24]

The People declared, somewhat inaccurately:

'Captain Leake comes from a good old fighting stock, and has had four brothers fighting at the Front, so there is no small element of patriotism in the family.'[25]

The injury to his hand prevented him from visiting friends and relations; his major single excursion was to University College Hospital, where he discussed the possibility of an operation. The chosen surgeon was his former tutor Victor Horsley, the leading neurologist, who had recently been knighted. Horsley was in the habit of not charging fees to fellow medical men,[26] and this was a consideration to be taken very seriously by the Martin-

Leakes, for whom there were still perennial financial problems. It was planned that the operation to repair the damage should take place in June. Meanwhile, the family had large numbers of congratulatory letters to deal with, and Arthur himself was deluged with invitations.

Family letters arrived from near and far. The *London Illustrated News*[27] likened Arthur's deed to that of Sir Philip Sidney who in 1586 had been mortally wounded at Zutphen in the war against the Dutch, and had passed a cup of water to a dying soldier with the words 'Thy need is greater than mine'. This certainly struck a chord with Uncle William home from Ceylon, who wrote to his sister-in-law:

> 'Though full of business I cannot let the post go without sending a line of congratulation on the achieved V.C. The narrative of the gallant deed makes one's heart beat quick – Philip Sidney isn't in it – he only gave a drink first to *one* wounded comrade. I am getting congratulations all round, which though in no way earned are much to be enjoyed.'[28]

He asked Arthur to

> 'accept my hearty congratulations on your hardly earned honour. I shed tears of joy as I read about it this morning – they were sending off a telegram to you as I left home which I hope was couched in terms befitting the occasion. As one meets men in the street they ask, is the hero your son? One asked through the telephone, is he your brother? Life becomes most exhilarating! I hope that the hand gets better.'[29]

Aunt Frances, Lady Russell Reynolds, on holiday in County Kerry, was quite carried away by the reflected glory:

> 'My Dear Arthur,
> I must write to tell you how rejoiced I am at this recognition by the King, and those you have served, of what you did to help and save others on 8th February, at the risk of your own life, which thank God was spared. You must not mind the publicity of your reward, for you have set the best example, which may help many other fellows in such moments of danger in carrying out duty and care for others. I am proud that your name brings another distinction and honour to University College Hospital and I know how well pleased Uncle Russell would have been on your account – we are all delighted.

I hope H.M. will confer it on you himself. Have you any uniform? I trust your hand is beginning to improve . . .
Your very affectionate aunt, Frances Russell Reynolds.'[30]

Cousin William Ralph, Headmaster of Dulwich Preparatory School, said he could imagine 'no one better than yourself grimly sticking to his post'. He went on:

'May only the hand get right so that there may be nothing left to mar the backward gaze. My congratulations too to the proudest of mothers who must find some solace now for all the anxieties and war's alarms. High Cross will be *en grande fête*, I suppose, to celebrate the triumphant warrior. Hip, hip!'[31]

From Willie, still 'leading the same old Blockhouse existence' in South Africa, came

'My very best congratulations on your well-earned V.C. I had a telephone message from our Headquarters on the 15th to say it was announced in the Summary. When given, it has generally been well-deserved; it certainly was in your case. May you live long to wear it. I expect by this time you have had to get that smart kit with green piping and had an interview with H.M. to receive the Cross. What a pity B.P. was not at home. He would have designed a special kit for the occasion. How is the arm getting on? I hope it is not giving trouble. Mind you BOOM your V.C. well. You will find it a much better advertisement than a dozen other letters after your name and worth many scientific gold medals. If treated with judgement you ought to find yourself on the King's Household before long, at least by the time you become an old grey-headed gentleman like myself.
'Don't bother to answer this but tell anyone who is writing to send me latest reports on the arm.'[32]

Theo and Steenie were still at home and were able to express their feelings in person, but from Dick, staying with friends in Essex, came a heartfelt note:

'My dear Artie,
Most – most Congratulations.
R.M.L.'[33]

Frank, with HMS *Bramble* on the China Station, told his mother he had seen the news in a despatch from Kitchener:

'I congratulate Artie and think we should have his picture painted. It is splendid. One's feelings are of the greatest satisfaction and I rejoice to think what great pleasure it must afford you who so well deserve it. Such an honourable fillip cannot fail to have far-reaching and beneficial effects on the family. Willie, I suppose, will soon be home, so I congratulate you on getting your sons back from the wars with nearly whole skins; make them build the conservatory. I will subscribe £5 and more when I join Steenie and Dick and get the pickings customary for the office-boy.'[34]

Letters flooded in from family friends like the Joys who lived in Swanage:

'My dear Mrs Leake,
  I was looking at Cyril's sweet peas in the garden, with him, when the girls came leaping down the walk in the greatest excitement, shouting and laughing and waving the *Daily Graphic*. "News, news, good news – guess!" "Peace?" said I. "No, no, about someone we know! Artie Leake". (Forgive this seeming irreverence, do we not drop the Mr before the names we honour most?) "Artie Leake has got the V.C." Then it was my turn to cheer and shout. Indeed we are all very glad and happy at this recognition of your brave, unselfish and modest son, and we rejoice with you, dear Mrs Leake. The account of his heroism in the *D. Graphic* brought the tears to my eyes. He is another Sir Philip Sidney.'[35]

Mr T. F. Halsey, Chairman of the 'feeble set of old muddlers' at the West Hertfordshire Infirmary, offered the 'sincere congratulations of the Committee', (but did not offer Arthur his old position back).[36] The (un-named) Captain of Westminster School, presenting his compliments,

'begs to inform Mr Leake that the School would feel greatly honoured if he would come down to ask for a Play (day's holiday) on the occasion of his obtaining the Victoria Cross.'[37]

James Gow, Headmaster of Westminster, wrote to Arthur's mother:

'Please allow me, on behalf of all Westminster School, to offer to
you and your son our heartiest congratulations on yesterday's
happy news. It must be a great joy and consolation to you. I am
a little late in writing because I wished to speak to the boys on
the matter before doing so.'[38]

Later in the year the Prologue to Westminster's Latin Play contained the
line *'Partem doloris habuit, partem gloriae'*. The first phrase – 'For some there
was pain' – signified the fact that seventy Old Westminsters had served in
the Boer War and six were killed; the second phrase – 'for others Honour' –
referred to Arthur's VC and the decorations for gallantry awarded to two
others, Rawson and Vyvyan.[39]

On behalf of the Hertfordshire Company of the Imperial Yeomanry,
Abel H. Smith MP told Arthur of his delight at hearing of the award,
and invited him to come and visit the Company while they were in camp.
And among many letters from former student colleagues at University
College Hospital was one from Mr Laurence Fuller informing Arthur that
'Horsley still makes bold incisions'.[40] This may have been a well-intentioned
attempt to reassure the wounded hero, who was awaiting surgery at Horsley's
hands.

But Arthur's operation was still a few weeks off. Meanwhile, he heard
from Windsor Castle that the King would present the Cross in person on
Monday, 2 June, and speedy preparations had to be made to obtain the
appropriate full-dress SAC uniform. On 31 May a Peace Conference at
Vereeniging brought an end to the war in South Africa. So at the first post-
war ceremony for the presentation of awards, Arthur met the King at St
James's Palace and received his decoration. He shunned publicity about it,
as he was to do for the rest of his life. A photographer was engaged to take a
formal picture after the audience; Arthur's right hand was still splinted and
bandaged, and it can be seen that the photographer thought it best to 'touch
in' the hand rather than allow the wound to be too obvious.

Arthur stayed in London and within a few days was operated on by Sir
Victor Horsley. Senior staff at University College Hospital visited him in his
room – men like Dr C. Bolton, who said he was 'highly honoured that you
should have been my dresser'.[41] The outcome was not an unqualified success:
Arthur had a permanent loss of flexibility, which was naturally a great worry
to a man who hoped to become a surgeon in private practice. As Willie
pointed out,

'If Artie's hand is not quite sound he ought to get heavy damages
out of the SAC for their neglect.'[42]

73

Returning home to Marshalls to convalesce, Arthur decided to study for the examination that would qualify him for Fellowship of the Royal College of Surgeons, while he waited to see how well his hand would heal. He was given a series of exercises to do each day, and contented himself with reading and enjoying the gardens, just coming to their seasonal best. He enjoyed the company of his youngest brother Theodore, but 'Mousey' was soon sent out to Malta with his Royal Engineers Balloon Section. The King's Coronation was due to take place on 25 June, but had to be postponed when he was taken ill with appendicitis. Arthur was interested to see that the surgeon who performed the operation at Buckingham Palace was none other than Sir Frederick Treves, who had made quite a name for himself during the Boer War. It was even more interesting to see, on the guest list for the rescheduled Coronation of 9 August, that invitations to attend had been accepted by Boer leaders Botha, De Wet and De La Rey. On 17 August the three Generals were introduced by Lord Kitchener to the King on board the Royal Yacht.[43] There was something very ironic in these developments. In due course Arthur received the two medals to which he was entitled for his part in the South African Wars – the Queen's South Africa Medal (with clasps for Wittebergen, Cape Colony and Transvaal), and the King's South Africa medal (with clasps for 1901 and 1902).[44]

Arthur sat for the FRCS in October, 1902, but did not pass. In February, 1903, he was awarded Disability and Wounds Pensions of one hundred pounds per annum each, to be paid from SAC funds. These amounts were regarded by all as highly satisfactory. He retook the examination that spring, and this time was successful, being admitted to the Fellowship of the Royal College of Surgeons on 11 June, 1903. By some means he had managed to convince the examiners that the performance of his right hand was at least adequate.

In spite of this success he was very concerned about his future career, quite certain that the specialism in surgery on which he had set his heart was out of reach because of his war wound. But then Steenie and Dick put forward a proposition. They had heard that the Bengal-Nagpur Railway (BNR) needed a doctor, and they suggested that Arthur should apply. The work would be demanding, but only a limited amount of surgery would be required. Given the doubts about Arthur's hand, this seemed an ideal solution. In June he was interviewed by Mr Robert Miller, the Managing Director, at the Railway's London offices in Old Broad Street, and was offered the post of 'Chief Medical Officer of the Company In India'.[45] His starting salary was 1000 rupees per month, there being about fifteen rupees to the pound sterling. Arthur's BNR contract stated that he would proceed directly to Calcutta, a first class passage to be provided by the company, and his contract would last for three years in the first instance. The BNR Agent would direct him where to live, and he could only undertake private practice with the Railway's permission. Like all European employees, he would have to become 'an efficient member of the Bengal-Nagpur Railway Volunteer Corps.'[46] His employment would start on 6 January 1904.

The pay was not, in Arthur's opinion, princely, and when he was later informed by the Colonial Office that his disability pension was to be discontinued, 'as your disability is not equal to the loss of a limb, and you have obtained employment at a fair remuneration'[47] and that his wounds pension was to be reduced to fifty pounds per annum, he was moved to write to the Under-Secretary in the following terms:

'I wish to state that I am leaving England to take up my appointment on the Bengal-Nagpur Railway on 6 January, 1904. I wish to appeal for an alteration in the decision arrived at about my pension of £100 per annum. I underwent an operation for nerve suture 18 months ago, and am now able to say that the operation has not been a success, as was hoped. The condition of my right hand is extremely unsatisfactory, there being much deformity and loss of power.

'I am a Fellow of the Royal College of Surgeons of England, and have held many resident appointments in Hospitals; I therefore had every prospect of success as a Consulting Surgeon at home, but now, owing to my inability to operate, I have to take a purely administrative post in India, with a very moderate salary, and no further prospects or pension.

'I consider that a wound pension of only £50 per annum is quite inadequate to meet my case, when taking into consideration the large sum of money expended, and the time taken in education, to obtain the Fellowship of the College of Surgeons. I can no longer hope to carry on my profession as an operative surgeon with my seriously damaged right hand and consider that the loss is inestimable. I shall be much obliged if you will reconsider the matter, or let me appear before a Medical Board for their decision.'[48]

Only after Arthur had lived in India for almost a year were there any developments. On 7 November, 1904, he was summoned to appear before a Medical Board in Calcutta, which found that

'There is a loss of power and sensation in the muscles of the right hand supplied by the ulnar nerve which was severed at the time the injury was received. There is also some contraction of the little and ring fingers which has a tendency to increase as time goes on in spite of dumb bell exercise and massage.'

The Board certified that he would be 'permanently incapacitated for military duty,'[49] but said nothing about his abilities as a doctor. Consequently the final decision, reached in 1905, was that he would receive one pension of one hundred pounds per annum. This was made permanent in October, 1908, and Arthur received this sum annually for the rest of his life.

But in January, 1904, he set off for a new life in India, his Victoria Cross in his pocket.

11. 'Arthur... went..., at the age of fourteen, to Westminster School' (p.15).

12. Arthur as a trooper in the 42nd (Hertfordshire) Company, Imperial Yeomanry, 24 January, 1900, in a borrowed uniform (see p.29).

13. The family at Marshalls, 1902. Rear: Willie, Theo, Bella, Arthur, Dick. Front: Sittie, Steenie, Isabel, Frank.

14. 'A wonderful Model D three-horsepowered De Dion Bouton…; Bella photographed Steenie and Dick proudly driving it up and down outside the house' (p.54).

15. 'I have shot my first tiger' (p.84). Arthur is on the right.

16. Arthur's drawing of the rogue elephant shot by him in 1908 (see pp. 90-93)

17. A warship of the French Fleet at Malta, August, 1914, photographed by Arthur (see p. 117).

18. Arthur in the uniform of the Royal Army Medical Corps, September, 1914.

CHAPTER SEVEN

'The City of Dreadful Night'

The first leg of the journey to Calcutta was overland to Marseilles via Paris. Mrs Martin-Leake was very upset to see Arthur go, and sent him an emotionally charged farewell letter. He replied:

'My dear Mammy,

Got your letter this morning in Paris. It is myself who should thank you, for being the best Mama in the world, and not the other way about. After all, what does it matter if we are separated by a few paltry miles? The pen can always bridge them over.

I had what I consider to be a most perilous sea-voyage – Willie is quite right, sea-going is not safe and should not be undertaken. The great drawback to this country seems to be these jabbering, baggy-trousered apes, who cannot apparently understand anything. I have, however, found out that "vin ordinaire" produces something to drink.'[1]

He then proceeded to Marseilles by train, and embarked on the Peninsular and Oriental Steamship *Marmora* for the onward journey. The first-class cabin provided by his new employer undoubtedly entitled him to feel 'POSH' – the epithet just coming into common usage to describe superior accommodation on the voyage to India: 'Port Out, Starboard Home'. As the *Marmora* steamed through the Mediterranean, he came to the conclusion that he was

'quite a good sailor – at any rate, have not been absent from a single meal yet. The passengers are extraordinary, nearly all are globetrotters going up the Nile with Mr Thomas Cook for 3 or 4 weeks. They are a wonderful collection – old spinsters, broken-down City men, Germans and Yanks. At present they seem rather cantankerous and inclined to quarrel. If the "Old Maids" of Marshalls [Sittie and Bella] ever think of taking a Cook's Tour, remind them of this – no amount of Pyramids, Sphinxes, Dams etc. could possibly compensate for the presence of the "globe trotters". I thought of Mousey and drank his health as we passed Malta the other day. Saw some Russian warships.'[2]

The warships were no doubt proceeding towards anticipated encounters with the Japanese Navy in the forthcoming Russo-Japanese War. By the time the *Marmora* reached Aden on 17 January, Arthur was complaining that

'I have passed the time in eating and sleeping, and am getting into a beastly state for want of exercise. I expect to make an attack on the first tree I meet in Bombay and dig it up.'[3]

From Aden it was only three days' voyage before the lights of Bombay were seen on the horizon as the ship approached at dusk – 'Queen Victoria's necklace' these lights were called by seasoned travellers. The passengers disembarked into launches which took them in small groups to the Apollo Bunder where the passenger landing quays were situated. Arthur was then taken in a cart with his luggage across half a mile of the south-eastern quarter of the city to the Victoria railway terminus, a massively pinnacled and turreted monument to the Raj. His first introduction to Indian railways was as a passenger in a first-class compartment of a Great Indian Peninsula Railway train, which carried him east for 500 miles to Nagpur, in an area noted for its oranges; Nagpur was the capital of the Central Provinces. Arthur noticed that Indian railway stations were never empty. In the middle of the night there were always people sleeping, sitting or lying on the platforms, waiting for something; a distraction from their poverty perhaps, or for company, or maybe just for shelter. One of Arthur's colleagues noted a few years later:

'In no other land does the railway seem to play so great a part in the welfare of the nation. . . . In India a railway takes you by the hand and shows you the different people of a vast Empire at their various tasks.'[4]

Nagpur was the western terminus of the Bengal-Nagpur Railway (BNR). Here Arthur boarded one of the trains on which most of his working life for the next thirty years would be spent. The route was through typical Bengal scenery:

'Water tanks by the hundred, palm trees and banana plants by the millions, jute and rice in the water-covered fields; mud huts, goats and pariah dogs are among the principal features of the landscape. The moist climate, the perpetual presence of water –

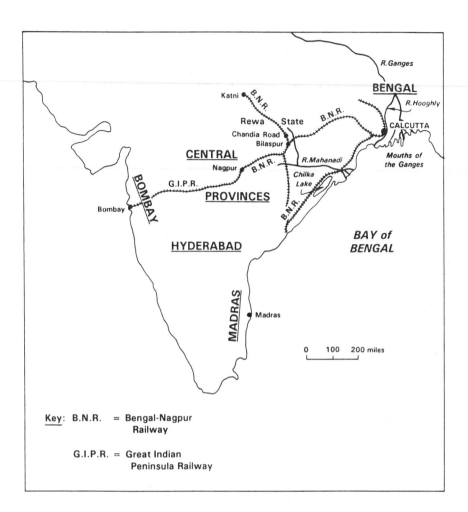

INDIA

most of the country is submerged for the greater part of the year
– serves to keep the countryside green and pleasant-looking, and
Bengal is often almost beautiful. . . . Bengal scenery will long be
remembered.'[5]

The journey to Calcutta was not straightforward on this occasion, however,
as he recounted to his mother on 27 January:

'Have arrived at Calcutta at last. Should have got here about 4
days ago, but had many interruptions on the way. First of all,
met the BNR Volunteers out for their training at a station named

Jharsuguda. Stopped with them for 2 days, and was able to make the acquaintance of most of the officers of the line, a large number of whom know Steenie and Dick, and were most anxious to know what they are doing. As usual, there was a Field Day. It seemed to be of the ordinary Volunteer kind, a great noise, much confusion, half the companies lost, and universal satisfaction to end up with.

Then I went to visit a hysterical Mrs Sanders – she and husband certain that an infant is coming but don't seem to know quite whose job it is to produce it, or whether they will each have one. Have sent them a nurse.'[6]

As for every other new arrival in Calcutta, called 'Queen of the East' by many, but 'The City of Dreadful Night' by Kipling, Arthur's first impressions were of a noisy, smelly, incredibly crowded city. It was sixty-five miles from the sea on the River Hooghly, the westernmost tributary of the Ganges. The BNR terminus was at the Howrah Station on the north bank of the River Hooghly; from there it was a *tikka-ghari* (horse-drawn carriage) ride of some three miles to the Headquarters of the railway at Garden Reach. On the way Arthur passed through shanty-filled areas of the poorest type, but also through gracious tree-lined streets and open spaces that showed how strong had been the British influence when parts of the city were being planned. The people of Calcutta seemed not to care what the British did; one anonymous observer called it the 'city of four million bystanders'. Calcutta in 1904 was, of course, the Imperial capital of all India, a status only lost in 1911. In the meantime the Governor-General had his residence here, on the edge of the Maidan, an enormous open space reclaimed from a swamp; one wonders if Arthur recalled that other Old Westminster, Warren Hastings, who had been the first Governor-General in 1773. Also in this central area was Fort William, the nucleus of the original British settlement, overlooking the grassy Maidan where, in Eden Gardens, Indian cricket first began in 1804, when a match was played between Old Etonians of the East India Company and 'Calcutta'.[7] There was also space on it for military parades, golf, football, tennis, riding and polo, and it was fashionable to drive back and forth along the roads that criss-crossed it.

Garden Reach was rather inappropriately named. It is true that the BNR offices were housed in a palatial building embellished with balustrades at roof level and exotic trees at its entrance; but the district was enclosed on the south-east side by enormous dock undertakings at Kidderpore, and by the somewhat unsavoury River Hooghly to the north. A series of bungalows and larger houses divided into flats in Garden Reach were set aside for the use of BNR employees. When Arthur first arrived he stayed for a few days with an official called Clark and his wife, while he waited for his first flat at 16 Garden Reach Road to be made ready:

> 'The Clarks have looked after me splendidly, and Mrs Clark has taught me much about how to go on in India. She has got me some servants and furniture. I shall try to get someone to share it as it is much bigger than I want.'[8]

Soon he was receiving large numbers of visiting cards; this was the custom when newcomers arrived. The correct procedure within the British community was to return the call and leave one's own card, and then accept the ensuing invitations to dinner. As might be expected, Arthur's patience soon gave out. He complained that he was 'getting no peace at all', and berated Steenie and Dick for 'letting me in for such a place'.[9] At the root of the problem seem to have been the 'Railway Wives', particularly one Mrs Bess Beckett, wife of the Chief Engineer and Acting Agent (Chief Executive) William Beckett. Arthur was not well-disposed to the Becketts from the start, because the whole Martin-Leake family felt that the Agent had been party to the raw deal experienced by Steenie and Dick over their bridge-building costs. As soon as the Doctor began his work in earnest, his unease began to surface. He may have had his own private saloon whenever he took a train along the line, and every kind of servant to carry out his wishes, but, as ever, women were the bane of his life:

> 'I am out along the line. This job is really only fit for 3 years. The Medical Department used to be at Khargpur but is now moving to Garden Reach, apparently for the express purpose of looking after the officers' wives who have complained bitterly because they have no medical attendance and had to send into Calcutta when ill. They are an awful set of creatures who have carried the science and art of gossip to the highest pitch. . . . I now understand Steenie and Dick's extreme adversity to the matrimonial state, and most fully agree. [Dick had often written home declaring his intention never to marry.] Railway men seem to be able to find the most extraordinary wives and I cannot imagine where they get them from. This line is completely a one-horse show; the married men spend all their time trying to keep in with authority and there is much ill-feeling accordingly. I do not wonder that S. and D. had to clear out.'[10]

The 'one horse' was undoubtedly Bess Beckett, described by Arthur variously as 'massive' and 'The Manageress'. It seemed that everyone was afraid of her, and she had tremendous influence over her husband. While Arthur spent his early weeks inspecting small 'hospitals' and dispensaries along the line, all in a poor and neglected state, Bess Beckett had other plans; she wanted to set up a 'Nursing Institute' to provide nursing care for officers and their families. It would cost 28,000 Rupees and would be quite useless in his opinion, just another of Bess's drawing-room schemes. Although he was the Chief Medical Officer, she had not bothered to inquire as to his views. He thought the money would be better spent on improving the medical care of the railway's employees. But Bess was very powerful, and soon he was obliged to agree to be Secretary of the proposed Nursing Institute.

He was fortunate in that he arrived in Calcutta during the Cold Weather which lasted from October to March. Average daily temperatures were only around 70 degrees Fahrenheit, and these months were treasured as the only time when English flowers could be grown, a reminder of Home. ('Home' was always written with a capital letter, and would have been spoken with one too, if that were possible.) The British in India usually grew their plants in pots to facilitate watering and to enable precious specimens like geraniums and chrysanthemums to move with the household at short notice; Arthur would soon have become familiar with the sight of paths and driveways tightly lined with every shape and size of clay plant pot, although his own interest in gardening only blossomed during the First World War. But as the Hot Weather approached and the temperature rose into the eighties, only the arrival of the monsoon in July could bring any relief. For the hottest months of the year the Government left Calcutta and made for the hills at Simla, where a duplicate Residence and government buildings had grown up, as well as a whole township of houses suitable for the wives and families of Raj officials.

In Calcutta the Railway wives became more irritating as the weather got hotter:

> 'The women of this Railway are the trial of one's life, in fact this would be a splendid job in their absence. They are quite 5th rate ladies, they take offence at nothing, they gossip worse than a set of villagers and will scandalise and wreck a man in about 2 minutes. The wicked scandal that these railway women spend their time in making and spreading is not to be equalled by anything ever done at home. Mrs Clark is the only exception. Fortunately Bess goes to the hills in the Hot Weather.'[11]

Mrs Beckett wanted Arthur to begin to work on a contract system, whereby each family would pay a single fee and could then send for him as many times as they liked. Arthur refused pointblank, saying he would get no peace at all under that system. He had managed to obtain a little private practice but found that Calcutta was over-endowed with medical people and there was less scope than he had hoped for. He was getting to do a little surgery on Sundays (his day off), but was rather dismissive of his skills and called it 'butchery'. He was summoned to treat a European and his two servants who had been mauled by a panther and were suffering from blood-poisoning, but fee-paying cases like that were rare. He now got around Garden Reach in his own pony and trap, and Sittie had sent him a bicycle. He soon learnt to play 'bicycle polo'. It was also quite the thing to have a motor cycle, and three Garden Reach employees could be heard noisily coming and going. News from Marshalls told Arthur that Frank had bought one for getting about the lanes around High Cross; this was to be a lifelong passion. Mrs Martin-Leake often had a critical servant problem at home, but in Calcutta servants were so numerous that her son was embarrassed about them; they attached themselves to him whether he liked it or not.[12] He had to sack his 'Head Man' and told his mother:

> 'The native is the most irritating beast I have ever come across, and if the climatic conditions were not against it, I should become a violent servant-beater. The Indian servant is the plague of my life; for craft and roguery, there can scarcely be his equal in this world.'[13]

With Bess away in the hills life quietened down, and Arthur proudly reported an operation he was going to perform:

> 'I am going to hunt for stones in a man's kidney. If successful I expect to get lots of cases – already they are coming in faster.'[14]

The operation was a success, Arthur describing with relish how he 'took the chap's kidney out, opened and cleaned it and put it back'.

As the weather grew hotter, the trials of life in Calcutta increased. Arthur's flat had electric fans, so there was no need for him to employ the services of a 'punkah-wallah' to move a fan suspended from the ceiling as in so many other dwellings. Quantities of ice were also available at a price from the railway. But Arthur was most troubled by the biting of mosquitoes at night, especially as his two brothers had almost had their careers in India ruined by bouts of malaria. He described Garden Reach as

> 'a foul place, being nothing but a mass of railway concessions, lines, locomotive trucks, offices and noise, situated on the banks

of the Hooghly, which is crammed full of big steamers and craft of all kinds, and is little better than a huge sewer; in the immediate neighbourhood are lots of factories and jute mills with huge chimneys, which smoke, and in the evenings we are generally in a sort of London fog, but much more smelly. To get to Calcutta it is necessary to pass through about 2 miles of very low-class bazaars, and cross over two dock bridges, which are as often as not open, delaying about half an hour, very awkward for dining in Calcutta.'[15]

Nevertheless, he did join the Bengal Club in the city, and here he often dined and discussed polo and the other sports played on the Maidan. Here he also met men for whom the real bonus of living in India was hunting the teeming wildlife out in the area known as 'jungle'. Mile after mile of sparse vegetation, largely unexploited by man, meant that the opportunities for 'shikar', as it was called, were endless. In May he 'bagged' his first bear, and was bringing its head home to be mounted when it was stolen by jackals during the night. But, as he said, 'the skin was not much good – at this time of year they are rather scabby.'[16] A few weeks later he went on a tiger shoot with a man who had thirty-seven of the beasts to his credit, but none were seen on this expedition. Every European's ambition in India seems to have been to shoot a tiger and Arthur commented in later years:

'For some reason the very mention of India appears to be associated with Tiger, and if you happen to have served in that country the success or otherwise of your service is often, in the opinion of many at Home, summed up in the number of tawny-coated animals with the black stripes which you may have brought to bag.'[17]

Ideas about conservation of wild animals were in their infancy; some Maharajahs laid on specially contrived tiger shoots for distinguished guests, including the Governor-General and visiting royalty. Riding on the backs of elephants, a 'bag' of dozens in a day was not unusual.

In his early months in India Arthur too had an ambition to 'bag' a tiger, and achieved his objective during his first summer:

'I have shot my first tiger. It gave me much satisfaction. We were out in camp for a week and had an excellent time. There were three tigers about and we had very bad luck in not bagging another. I have handed the skin over to the Army and Navy

Stores in Calcutta and they are going to take the necessary steps here, and then send it Home to be mounted and forwarded to you. I have asked for the head to be mounted but perhaps you would prefer it flat. I am sending the claws next week accompanied by a cheque. Also 2 bones from the shoulder which are much prized by sportsmen but I don't know why. It is a Hot Weather skin, that is to say the fur is very fine and short, but well-marked. It is somewhat damaged by bullet-holes – I was afraid of the beast mauling the beaters who were close by, so continued firing until she was dead.'[18]

The finished tiger skin arrived at Marshalls in January, 1905, and graced the hall floor for decades. Towards the end of Arthur's life it was draped over a sofa in his study, and when he died it was presented with other skins to the RAMC. At first he simply went hunting with a gun over his shoulder and dried apricots for sustenance stuffed into his pockets, but he was to become an expert in the sport and published a book about *shikar* during his final tour of duty in India in the 1930s.

In 1904 in Calcutta there was a less pleasant game afoot. Again, women were involved:

'I have had a frightful row with the nurses, and they took the opportunity to go on strike. The European hospital has no operating theatre so we had to take a case to the native hospital for an operation. They refused to come and help as they consider a native hospital is not good enough for them. The 3 Assistant Medical Officers were present so we did not care a D--N and carried on without them. I cannot tackle irate females myself and have handed over the whole thing to Beckett, expect there will be a Committee meeting.

It is extremely interesting to watch the various husbands. It is difficult to imagine in some of the cases where the wives have gone up-country that the changes could have been so rapid and complete. Poor, melancholy individuals, who used to sit at home and mind the infants, have now become the leaders of all kinds of gaiety – oh, wives, if you only knew! Railway wives are a separate species. A term of years in this country is necessary for their manufacture. But the female department of this Railway does not cause me any worry. I let them alone as I would a hot cinder, and am going to raise my fees so that they will go elsewhere for their gossip and pills.'[19]

He rather despised the wives' vanity too; he noted in 1905, when the Prince and Princess of Wales were to visit Calcutta, that 'the ladies are going Home in great numbers, so that they can come out with good complexions for the occasion.'[20] On the other hand, at least one of the nurses found an ally in the doctor. She wanted to get married, but such a step was expressly in breach of the terms of nurses' contracts, and if discovered she would be sent Home. Arthur agreed to act as one of her witnesses at a secret ceremony, an opportunity for thumbing his nose at the authorities which he greatly relished.[21] In the event, he won the dispute with the nurses and they apologized, but it took almost a year.

By the end of that first June the break of the monsoon approached, regular as clockwork. It normally hit the southern states of India about a week before it reached Calcutta, so the inhabitants knew what was coming. While they waited in eager anticipation (because the monsoon heralded the end of the Hot Weather), Arthur noted the tremendous humidity in the air; how people stayed in their flats and bungalows with the shutters closed, and the Club became important as a place of evening escape from the gloom. On the trains, huge blocks of ice would be placed on tin trays in the middle of the first class compartments, on which passengers rested their feet until it melted away.[22] When the rains arrived, they lasted for six weeks, increasing the humidity and causing papers, boots and clothes to turn green with mould. Calcutta was one of the worst places in India for heat combined with humidity. Insect life increased, as did illness, and Arthur had to treat people for malaria, typhoid, cholera sometimes, and a multitude of skin complaints like prickly heat, impetigo and 'dhobi itch' – this last probably caused by the residue of starch left in clothes by native launderers.

The monsoon might bring thirteen inches of rain each month from July to September; Arthur described his first experience of it:

> 'Absolute depression has spread over Garden Reach. Work is suspended and offices are closed. It has rained pretty constantly for the last week, but this morning has started coming down in sheets and the whole place is more or less under water. Drainage is very bad and water can only escape when the tide in the Hooghly is very low. This will go on until the end of September.'[23]

Obviously in a busy railway company work could never cease altogether, but it resumed properly with the onset of cooler weather in October. People began to return from the hills, or to come out from Home. The 'Fishing Fleet' arrived – girls from England with impeccable breeding and education, looking for a husband during the Indian 'Season'; those who failed went back Home, unkindly dubbed 'Returned Empties'.[24] But there was never any gossip about Arthur being preyed upon by the young ladies, as he continued his practice of firmly refusing invitations to dances or other social occasions. He was glad to report that Sir Trevredyn Wynne was coming out again to resume his duties as BNR Agent, removing Beckett and the 'massive' Bess.[25] Wynne was greeted with great enthusiasm by all, and, said Arthur,

'He paid people's back pay and listened to their grievances, so that the whole tone of the Railway has changed.'[26]

But Wynne only stayed long enough to tidy his desk; he then took up an appointment with the Indian Railways Board. The inclusion in Arthur's letters of every minute detail of life at Garden Reach indicates the pervading introspection of life among the British community in India, which was beginning to infect even him; he was far more comfortable away from people, on *shikar* or alone in his railway carriage travelling down the line to dispense medical advice to the BNR's more distant outposts. He certainly was not at all impressed by the pomp and ceremony put on in Calcutta for the arrival of Lord Curzon, the Viceroy, in December, 1904. Nor did he make any comment on the hot political potatoes of the day, like Curzon's plan to partition the state of Bengal in 1905, causing much native unrest.

Inexplicably, after 1905 Arthur's letters home were not kept by his mother. Consequently, little evidence survives of his reaction to a family tragedy in 1907. His twenty-eight-year-old brother Theo had returned from Malta, in December, 1906, and was stationed at Aldershot with the Royal Engineers Balloon Section. Early in 1907 a new Commanding Officer arrived, Colonel J E Capper, a man with unrivalled experience in military ballooning. He found in Lieutenant Martin-Leake a young 'balloonatic' who was one of the most competent on the establishment, having made flights in China and in Malta, as well as over most of southern England. He had been an observer of many experimental flights in 'heavier-than-air-craft', i.e. aeroplanes for military purposes, and had a promising future in the field. But, as Willie noted, when he wrote up Theo's story in the 1930s, 'it was written otherwise in the Book of Fate'.[27]

Balloons were of great interest to King Edward VII, and he chose the Aldershot Balloon Factory of the Royal Engineers as the location for a Royal Visit on 28 May, 1907. He was accompanied by His Imperial Highness Prince Fushimi of Japan, and a highlight of the tour was to witness a 'free run' in the 'War Balloon' *Thrasher* by Theo and a colleague, Lieutenant William Caulfeild. The two balloonists were introduced to the King's party, and at 4.40 pm the balloon was released and ascended over Aldershot, Theo and Caulfeild standing up in the basket, saluting.

The *Thrasher* was one of the smaller War Department balloons, covered with gold-beater's skin (a fine membrane derived from calf-skin) and inflated with hydrogen, its gas capacity being 10,000 cubic feet. Beneath was hung the 'car', in which the men stood; they were able to ascend and descend by operating a valve to let gas escape, or by jettisoning bags of ballast slung round their basket. A compass and thermometer were carried and the car was equipped with an anchor rope some 120 feet long, with a grapnel at the end. If travelling close to the ground in a 'free run', the grapnel could be used to catch in a tree or hedge, and thus stop the balloon. It was quite possible, in the right conditions of temperature and altitude, for a balloon to stay up for several days, but normally they were not advised to stay up at night. Theo and his colleague were instructed to send a telegram as soon as they landed anywhere and to 'stable' the balloon overnight before going on.

The Royal Party watched until *Thrasher* was out of sight to the southwest. No news of it was heard that night or next morning, but there was no real concern for its safety – balloons often landed in out-of-the-way places. but by the evening of 29 May Colonel Capper became sufficiently anxious to ask the Admiralty for assistance in tracing it. Messages were sent to all the coastguard stations along the south coast, and in the afternoon of 30 May a telegram was received from the Receiver of Wrecks at Brixham, Devon, that the balloon had been picked up at sea by a fishing smack, the *Skylark*, eight miles off Exmouth, and that the two officers were not in it. The balloon was still partially inflated and was floating twelve feet above the surface of the sea, the basket being under the water. Further conflicting messages during the day did nothing to lessen the anxiety of the family waiting at home in High Cross.

The balloon was landed at Brixham and Colonel Capper immediately went down to inspect it. He found everything in order, even the handwritten log of the flight was complete but gave no hint of any problems. Meanwhile, the search for the two men continued for a few days, but was abandoned when it was felt there was no more hope. Even Aunt Frances mobilized her friends in the area of the search to ask local people if they had seen anything. The Japanese Embassy sent the sympathy of Prince Fushimi, and a letter of condolence from the King's Private Secretary arrived at Marshalls on 7 June:

> 'I am commanded by the King to convey to you the expression of his Majesty's sincere regret and sympathy with you in your great sorrow. His Majesty is the more shocked at the sad occurrence owing to the fact that he was present and spoke to your son and Lieutenant Caulfeild just before the ascent.'[28]

Colonel Capper gathered what evidence he could for an Inquiry into the disaster. Two farmers near Winterbourne Abbas had seen the balloon travelling low over the fields, and had heard the two officers shout, asking them to catch hold of the rope, but they had not been able to reach it. It flew over an inn, the 'Coach and Horses' at Winterbourne Abbas, and the officers asked people outside for the location; then it was last seen going out to sea at Abbotsbury, and was lost to sight.[29]

No explanation was ever found for the accident. A memorial service, attended by Sir John French and many more was held at St George's Garrison Church at Aldershot on 7 June, and one for Theo at High Cross on 12 June. No sign of the bodies was found until 23 June when Caulfeild was recovered from the sea. The 'badly decomposed' body of Theodore was found in the sea near Bridport on 29 June. At the inquest, attended by Steenie and Willie, it was decided that one of the officers must have let go and the other was pulled out of the basket trying to save him, and a verdict of 'Accidental Death by Drowning' was returned by the Coroner's Jury.[30]

The family decided that Theo should be buried at Thorpe in the same grave as his father, and a full military funeral was provided by his fellow-officers, some of whom carried the coffin. All of his brothers and sisters except Arthur, and his mother and Aunt Frances, were present. The Last Post and Reveille were sounded over the grave by a bugler of the Royal Engineers. Subsequently a plaque was placed in the church at High Cross, and another in the church at Thorpe. In 1908 a stained-glass window to the memory of the two balloonists was unveiled in St George's Church, Aldershot, and the sum of one hundred pounds was given in Theo's name to the Union Jack Club in London, to provide a bedroom in the Club for the use of visiting Royal Engineers. Artie did of course write to his mother, and his sister described the letter as 'greatly touching',[31] but the original does not survive.

Arthur's own life in uniform continued in a minor way from 1905 onwards, when he joined the BNR Volunteer Rifle Corps, as directed in his contract of employment. The Corps had been raised in 1888, and when Arthur arrived in Calcutta it consisted of two battalions, each with about 600 other ranks and thirty officers. It was under the command of the Commander-in-Chief, India, but was mostly used to protect the railway when required. Arthur was put in the first battalion based at Khargpur for operational purposes, while the second battalion was centred on Nagpur. The battalions were divided into detachments that were situated at twenty-eight stations along the line. When Arthur joined on 28 April, 1905, he was classed as 'Staff' and was given the rank of Surgeon-Captain, the same rank he had held when he left South Africa. His two brothers had been members too, in the 1890s, Steenie as a captain and Dick as a second lieutenant. Now, the

Honorary Colonel was Sir Trevredyn Wynne, while the Commanding Officer was Lieutenant Colonel William Beckett, husband of the infamous Bess.[32]

Arthur's first camp with the Volunteers, early in January 1905, was held at Khargpur, and he criticized the organisation of it from the beginning – 'I am a mounted infantryman but don't do much or anything except display ribbons.'[33] There was a forty-one-strong band, but little real action for someone like Arthur. Railways throughout India were often threatened by robbers – 'dacoits' – and the occasional train crash required uniformed assistance from time to time, but basically the Corps proved to be more of a social gathering for the British officials, rather than a serious military force. However, urged on by their wives, most railway employees from Garden Reach participated with an eye to promotion in the company.

As the years of his contract passed, Arthur took to the life of the British sahib as if it were second nature. Christmas was traditionally the time when Europeans went out into the 'jungle' for a few days' shooting, and Arthur was no exception. In India there was little point anyway in trying to recreate a typically English Christmas, and especially not for Arthur, who never had cared much for such festivities. So a *shikar* would be planned and a few native bearers would carry the provisions, tent and equipment. The railway was ideally placed to deliver the hunter right into the heart of the central Indian plain. The shoot in 1905 was moderately successful and Arthur was able to send home a huge bison's head for his mother's birthday. He also shot another tiger, the head of which he decided to send to Sir Victor Horsley – 'he might like it'.[34]

Tame elephants known as 'koonkies' were ridden by the huntsmen, but wild elephants were fair game for their guns. Arthur went in pursuit of one such animal, a rogue male, in December, 1908, and described what happened in detail for the benefit of the family at Marshalls:

'I spent Christmas with the manager, a man named Wood. On the 28th I moved on to a village 12 miles further and pitched my camp there. The object I was in pursuit of was a rogue elephant. This beast had been in these parts for years, and as he was such a bad character there was no difficulty in getting his death warrant. A few days before I arrived at the place he had killed a man, and the damage he used to do to the crops was something enormous. However, he has now gone to the place of perpetual sugar cane and buns, so we will speak no further ill of him. You will be somewhat surprised to hear of this as I have not mentioned the subject before because I always thought the chance of getting him was very small. I have, however, been making preparations for a long time past. A policeman who had shot at an elephant in

Burma once, and was consequently quite an authority on the subject, was to have come with me, but owing to the recent attempt to blow up a train he could not get away. I was quite glad he could not come, as his health is very bad and he would probably have cracked up. The following is an extract from the letter I am sending to Horsley, and it will save writing the account over again:

I arrived at camp about midday and spent the afternoon in trying to get all the information about the animal from the surrounding villages. He had not been heard of for about 4 days and I was rather afraid that he had made off to some other district, as his hunting ground was by no means small. However, orders were given for news to be brought into camp directly he was heard of anywhere. Twelve o'clock at night I was called by some excited natives who said he was in a sugar cane field close to the village. I was soon ready and set out for the patch of cane which was only about a quarter of a mile away. It was a small patch about 50 by 40 yards and rectangular. There was no doubt that the elephant was inside – he was crushing it down in a wholesale fashion and having a fine old meal. The river was 150 yards away on one side, and the jungle on the other, and the river bank was the only chance of cover. There was a prickly hedge about 4 feet from the cane all round the sugar. The moon rose just as I was starting out.

The most likely place for the beast to come out was on the jungle side, so I took up my position there. The cane was very high, about 10 feet, and I could only follow him by the noise. He showed not the slightest inclination to come out and continued trampling down and munching the cane. At last after some hours he began to work towards one corner as if he had had enough and meant to come out. I got round the corner, and in a few minutes he poked out his head, twelve paces from the corner (measured afterwards). This was most excellent, and after munching a little more sugar he began to pull down the hedge with his trunk. Directly he was out far enough to expose his shoulders I gave him both barrels as quickly in succession as I could. He turned back and went crashing through the cane; it was an exciting moment as I did not know which direction he was taking. However, luckily for me, he went out the other side and away to the jungle. He trumpeted three times in his retreat and I knew he must be badly hit. On reaching the tent it was 3.30, so the beast had been in the sugar cane over three hours.

The night was jolly cold and I was glad to get between blankets again.

At dawn I started off with five natives and my servants, the latter to carry some food and water, spare ammunition and camera. The tracking was very easy at first as there was a lot of blood and the jungle was thick; the beast had fallen down after going a short distance. After a time we got into open jungle with gravelly soil and the tracking became difficult and slow; the bleeding had ceased some time back, and we lost the track completely at one time. The natives began to get very tired of the whole affair and one by one disappeared, till I only had 2 left. These chaps are not at all keen sportsmen and are not good trackers. I had to do most of the work, and the two men between them carried the 8-bore. At last we came up to the beast; the men bolted and I only just got hold of the gun in time to prevent it going with them. The noise of these chaps going off excited the old beast and he pricked up his ears and looked remarkably truculent. I got to within 25 yards and gave him a shot behind the shoulders, and had made up my mind that he must have the other barrel in the head if he charged. Much to my relief he staggered round to make off, so I gave him the second shot in the shoulders. He went off for all the world like a skidding motor-bus and collapsed after going a short distance. I think one of the shots must have got him in the heart.

The next thing to do was to collect my scattered following and get some food. After much shouting and when they were quite certain the beast was dead, they began to return. The time when he fell was 1.30 (6½ hours' tracking). He had the appearance of being very old and had no tusks. There were large cavities where the tusks had been, and a very foul discharge was coming from them. He measured 5 feet 3 inches round the foot which would give his height as 10 feet 6 inches. This is very large indeed I believe, but I do not know much about the height of elephants and have got to look up the subject.

Next morning an early start was made with the apparatus for cutting off his head and removing the brain. The following was the outfit:

Twenty coolies; rope and tackle; large stew pot with cover; axes, choppers, saws, chisels of various kinds, two amputating knives, small instruments for dissection, stone and file for sharpening tools, two large steel hooks; tin, rubber tubing, and various sizes of glass cannulae for injecting the brain. One gallon of 10% formalin and 2% bichromate solution ready mixed, and some formalin and bichromate in case more solution was required.

Work started at 8 a.m. as follows: a band of skin 12 inches broad was removed as far round the neck as could be managed. The muscles were divided for a similar extent, and by means of the hooks and rope were got away in several large masses. The exposed ligaments were divided and the rope was attached to the trunk and the head pulled backwards by 20 coolies; the intervertebral ligament went with a snap, and the head was free with the exception of the muscles and skin on the underside; these were cut from within outwards without difficulty. Time taken 3 hours. The head was then turned over and the vertebral arteries found. A cannula was tied in on one side, and the other artery ligatured. The brain was then injected with about 5 feet of pressure. The fluid came out freely through the carotids and after it had flowed for a little while these were dissected and tied. The fluid was left on under pressure for about 1 hour while the base and occipital region was being cleaned. The skull cavity was opened, first in the occipital region where the bone is quite thin, then by means of saw and chisel the base was gradually removed; this was a somewhat difficult matter as the bone in these parts is very dense and hard. The dura mater which is very thick and strong separated easily from the bone, except in the anterior fossae, where it was very adherent and it was torn somewhat in trying to separate it. The result of this was that the lower surfaces of the frontal lobes have been damaged, as the brain matter was very soft and friable and would not stand any manipulation. On removal the brain was put into a large enamel iron stew pan, packed round with tow, and covered with 10% formalin. This was just completed by dusk and the whole thing had taken 9 hours, with the exception of a quarter hour off for tiffin [lunch].

The whole performance was watched by a large collection of natives who looked on in blank amazement. I could get very little assistance of any use and had to do practically the whole thing myself.'[35]

One hopes that Arthur's mother appreciated this long description, and that Sir Victor Horsley was grateful when he received the elephant's brain to display alongside his collection of monkeys' brains. The rest of the elephant was undoubtedly secured as trophies also – the feet for use as flower pots or umbrella stands, or as a receptacle for glasses and decanter. At least two eventually stood in the hall at Marshalls, along with Arthur's first tiger-skin. On his Home leaves, which came round every two or three years, Arthur could see for himself how the house was enhanced by his trophies. He could also observe the improvements being made to the gardens, now that 'the Engineers' were at home. They had demolished and rebuilt a whole new wing, built a new greenhouse and potting shed in 1908 (the date was inscribed into the stone lintel), an apple house and a woodshed, and a new wall and archway to the vegetable garden (1912). The gardens had been tended by Sittie and Bella, working alongside their brothers, and the family was virtually self-sufficient in fruit and vegetables. Across the road, the church in High Cross was embellished with a new tower in 1906, at a cost of £1155,[36] for which funds had been enthusiastically raised by Sittie and Bella.

In many ways the family had enjoyed more consecutive years of stability since the turn of the century than they had enjoyed in the previous half-century. But when Arthur arrived home on leave during the Hot Weather in 1912, the first signs of conflict in Europe were apparent, ultimately to change the world for ever. Trouble was brewing in the Balkans and, when it erupted, Arthur could not resist the urge, once again, to go and see things for himself.

CHAPTER EIGHT

'Quite the Worst Country that I Have Ever Seen'

Montenegro, the Land of the Black Mountain, was not a name that tripped lightly off the tongues of most Edwardian gentlemen in 1912. Newspaper accounts of events in the Balkans had brought the area into public consciousness from time to time for the past fifty years. Fairly localized squabbles were usually the reason, triggered by the declining fortunes of the two Powers, Austria-Hungary and Turkey, whose spheres of influence were in contention between the Black Sea and the Adriatic. In 1876 both Montenegro and her neighbour Serbia had taken their opportunity and declared war on Turkey, the 'Sick Man of Europe', and the Congress of Berlin in 1878 had demonstrated the willingness of the European Great Powers to intervene in Balkan affairs.

Unfortunately, as far as Montenegro was concerned, the Congress had been a great disappointment when it placed the two provinces on her northern border, Bosnia and Herzegovina, under the Austrian heel. The seeds of future trouble were sown when the Congress recognized independent Bulgaria. All the Balkan states, stimulated by a rising tide of nationalism, were manoeuvring for position as Turkey and Austria-Hungary loosened their grip. Montenegro's ruler, Prince Nicholas, who was in power from 1860 until he was deposed in 1918, was determined to wrest more territory from the crumbling Ottoman Empire, and the Austro-Hungarian annexation of Bosnia-Herzegovina in 1908 only strengthened his resolve. He declared himself King of Montenegro in 1910. The next year an opportunity arose for King Nicholas to stir up trouble between his southern neighbour Albania and Turkey, and he supported an Albanian uprising against their common enemy.

The tension reached breaking point in the spring and summer of 1912; by September Montenegro was in alliance with Serbia, Bulgaria and Greece in opposition to Turkey. Nicholas was determined to use this show of unity to break Turkey once and for all. On 6 October he broke off diplomatic relations, and two days later began hostilities, calling it a 'Holy War'. Serbia, Bulgaria and Greece joined in the fray on 17 October.

As the crisis developed, the British newspapers began to take increasing notice. The European Balance of Power, and peace between the Great Powers, the principles at the heart of Whitehall's foreign policy, were at stake here. Arthur read with interest Foreign Secretary Sir Edward Grey's statement to the House on 7 October:

> 'A very critical state of affairs exists in the Balkans and gives rise to grave apprehension. The Great Powers are taking what steps they can to prevent a breach of the peace. There is the strongest desire between the Great European Powers who are most directly interested in the Balkans and whose frontiers would be most affected by war in that region to see peace preserved, and this is, I trust, a guarantee that if the peace is broken in the Balkans, none of the Great European Powers would be involved in the war.'[1]

The *Times* commented that the conflict 'threatens to be the fiercest the world has seen for many decades.'[2] Grave concern was expressed about the lack of medical provision for the large numbers of Balkan soldiers likely to be wounded in the conflict, but the first appeal for help was apparently made in a message from the Crown Princess of Greece (Princess Sophia, sister of Kaiser Wilhelm II) to Queen Alexandra, Consort of Edward VII: 'Cannot your people do something for the sick and wounded?'[3] The Queen passed this on the Council of the British Red Cross who decided to send medical teams out. Permission had to be obtained from the Foreign Office and from the Balkan states involved in the fighting, but this was readily given.

A large sum of money would be needed to fund the Red Cross Mission and a letter was published in several newspapers on 17 October, signed by Lord Rothschild, Chairman of the Council of the British Red Cross Society (BRCS), setting out the suffering that was already occurring and would certainly increase during the coming winter in the war zone:

> 'It is difficult to bring home to the public of this country the appalling suffering involved in a winter war in the Balkans. Communications are difficult, the cold is intense, and even rudimentary transport is a matter of extreme difficulty; moreover, the fighting in this particular war is likely to be of a specially bitter and severe character, while, on the other hand, the medical organization available is quite inadequate to cope with large numbers of wounded.
>
> In order to mitigate, in some measure, the terrible suffering entailed by such a winter campaign, the British Red Cross Society is preparing to despatch expeditions to the belligerent countries.

The invested funds of this Society are only applicable to wars in which British troops are engaged. A Special Fund, therefore, is necessary. The services of the Society will be rendered impartially to all the combatants concerned, but it is, of course, open to any subscriber to earmark a donation for the special assistance of one or other of the belligerent parties, and any instructions to that effect will be strictly observed.'[4]

As *The Times* pointed out on the same day,

'The Balkan peoples have always thought much about rifles, and give little thought to doctors and nurses.'

The Fund, to be known as 'The British Red Cross Balkan Fund', soon received a flood of donations – £41,000 within a few days; promises of much more, unfortunately, did not materialize, and the BRCS bemoaned the poor public response. Nevertheless, large donations by private individuals allowed the planned number of units to be sent out one by one.

So a Medical Relief Committee was set up by the Red Cross, and plans were made for three separate units to be sent to three different areas. The first was to cover Bulgaria, Montenegro and Serbia, the second Greece, and the third Turkey. An 'on-the-spot' Director was appointed to supervise each area.[5]

Arthur Martin-Leake, reading reports of all the preparations, wrote at once to the BRCS to volunteer. On 16 October a telegram had been received at the Foreign Office from Cettinje, the Montenegrin capital, that severe fighting had taken place and that relief was urgently needed. So the first BRC Unit was hastily put together. Arthur received a telegram at Marshalls, ordering him to report to Headquarters at 9 Victoria Street, Westminster, without delay. He called at the London offices of the Bengal-Nagpur Railway in Old Broad Street to obtain approval for what might turn out to be a prolonged period of leave, and then presented himself to Sir Frederick Treves, Chairman of the Red Cross Medical Relief Committee – the same Treves of whom Arthur had been aware during the South African War. Now Treves was a household name, having saved King Edward's life on the eve of his Coronation in 1902. He had earlier come to public attention through his involvement with the famous 'Elephant Man' in the 1880s.

The Unit to which Arthur was attached was the first to go, and was directed to Montenegro. Each Unit had three doctors; Arthur's colleagues were Drs A. Bradford and F. Goldsmith. There were also three dressers, who were fourth and fifth year medical students. The six nursing orderlies were ex-soldiers of the Royal Army Medical Corps, who had left the Corps with 'a good character', and the five general duty orderlies were either ex-soldiers or members of the recently-formed Voluntary Aid Detachments. A cook completed the Unit. Arthur would have been relieved to hear that it was not intended to send out any women, at least not to start with. All members wore khaki uniform with the Red Cross armband, and their equipment was purchased with money from the Balkan Fund or by public donation. The BRCS was receiving hundreds of enquiries from the public about what gifts would be most suitable, and large quantities of winter clothing and bedding were pouring in.[6]

As ever, matters moved far too slowly for Arthur. Bureaucracy and delay never failed to cause him great irritation and he wrote home from London on 19 October:

> 'These people are too bad for words. We don't start until tomorrow evening and they might as well have let me know. I used some awful language in the office when I got there.'[7]

The *Daily Telegraph* was perhaps a little more objective:

> 'In the work of preparing for the sending out of this detachment, the society's office at Westminster was one of the busiest places in London. Throughout the day the committee and officials were busily engaged in dealing with applications from men willing to proceed to the scene of operations. Even to a superficial observer it was obvious that these would-be candidates for the errand of mercy were, as far as the bulk of them were concerned, men holding good positions in life. There were doctors of good standing in their profession, ready to abandon temporarily their practices and devote their skill to the scars of the wounded. Clean-limbed, athletic young medical students, who wanted to go out as dressers, and members of other professions, University men many of them, who were "willing to do whatever is wanted".'[8]

As last-minute preparations were made, Sir Frederick Treves commented:

> 'The public will be interested to hear that we are getting an exceptional class of men, many of them familiar, as medical men, with campaigns. The three surgeons who are going out on Sunday, for instance, are all first-class civil surgeons, but they all saw service in the South African War, and one of them won the Victoria Cross in that campaign. They are men who could do

anything. They are, in fact, picked men, and practically all of them can ride, and can speak French. The work seems to have appealed to the adventurous spirits of the medical and other professions. We have men offering to help who have done the most extraordinary things. They are giving up everything to go, and it is interesting to see that there is the same spirit of adventure now as there was in the time of Elizabeth.'[9]

Carrying only medical equipment and a supply of drugs and bandages, the first Unit set out from Victoria Station on Sunday, 20 October. Frank was there to see Arthur off on the ten o'clock train that evening. The party embarked on the Royal Mail night boat for the Dutch port of Vlissingen, and then travelled by train through Germany and Austria to Trieste, which was reached forty-eight hours after leaving London. Accompanying the party was the reporter from the *Daily Telegraph*, R. M. McGuire, who, according to Arthur, was 'going to make as much as he can of it, and raise funds at home.'[10] The Red Cross Director for Bulgaria, Montenegro and Serbia was also travelling with them. This was Surgeon General G. D. Bourke CB, who had until recently been Principal Medical Officer in the Irish Command. Arthur was not very enthusiastic about his fellow-doctors:

'The two other doctors, who both come from Australia, appear to be rather given to the common fault of colonials – Dick can hold forth upon this.'[11]

Disappointingly, Dick's views on 'colonials' are unknown.

At Trieste, after stocking up with essentials like candles, knapsacks, waterproofs, clasp knives and celluloid watch-covers,[12] the party went on board an Austrian Lloyd Line ship, the *Carnatic Sea*, and the same day proceeded south along the Dalmatian coast, calling at ports here and there and 'island-hopping'. Arthur and his colleagues spent a whole day inoculating everyone against enteric fever, reputed to be rife in the war zone; many of the personnel had an adverse reaction and were ill for a day or two. Russia was also sending out a Red Cross unit, which had arrived at Trieste at the same time, but this group was sailing by a later boat. The Russians had three female nurses with them, and Arthur, surprisingly, told his mother he hoped they might be acquired for the British unit. He hoped that more equipment might be obtained from a Red Crescent party, which was aiming to get through to Scutari in Albania; the British had heard that Scutari was surrounded, and expected the Red Crescent staff to join up with their unit.

A rather interesting memoir of Arthur survives from this journey. It was written anonymously during the early months of 1915 and was published in response to the award of the Bar to Arthur's Victoria Cross. Perhaps it was written by one of the 'colonials' already referred to:

'It was on the journey which we both chanced to be making to Montenegro together, during the Balkan War in October, 1912, that I first met Dr Martin-Leake. . . . I was at once struck by the reticence, the modesty – I had almost said the shyness – of the man, for I knew – thought not from himself – that he possessed the great decoration "For Valour" which it is the ambition of every man in His Majesty's forces to gain. Somehow I associated with the possession of the VC stalwart physique, overflowing animal spirits, volatile energy. Lt Leake, RAMC, as he now is, justified not one of these descriptions. He is a thin, spare man, well under the medium height, with fair hair, a light, fair moustache, a complexion tanned by the Indian sun, and cheeks thinned, as I fancy, by visitations of malaria. For Dr Leake, as I then gathered, had spent a good deal of time in India. . . .

'I have suggested that he was quiet in demeanour almost to the point of shyness. But there was nothing morose or gloomy about the man. His, on the contrary, was one of those sunny, imperturbable natures which nothing seems to be able to ruffle. I can scarcely imagine Dr Leake losing his temper about anything or anybody. Around the thin lips a genial smile was always playing. The mouth, that indicated swift decision, never curled in a sneer; the light-blue eyes always smiled in sympathy with the lips. A pleasant and lovable companion, Dr Leake, if ever there was one; simple, and absolutely unaffected in his conversation, free as a sweet-tempered schoolboy from anything in the shape of guile; one of those men, all too seldom met in this hustling age, who will talk on any subject but themselves.

'The combined knowledge of the entire party at that time only supplied the haziest notion of the act of gallantry by which he won the Victoria Cross in the South African War, and wild horses could not drag the details from himself. When, as I remember, the subject was mooted – for it is not every day one has the honour of rubbing shoulders with a "VC" hero – he only smiled, and the smile, somehow, ended the matter.

'But a man of action, nevertheless – a handy, resourceful man – a man who did everything he had to do without fuss, and still more without murmur. I can recall the workmanlike way in which, on the voyage down the Adriatic, he set about inoculating us all against the typhoid. While one of the other doctors of the expedition prepared our arms, Dr Leake, with his shirt-sleeves well-rolled up, sat behind a little spirit lamp preparing the injection. Then, as we were ready, one after another, he would rise from the table – and the thing was done. A few days later, too, I can remember how energetically he worked with the other members of the expedition in adapting to the purposes of a hospital the tobacco factory which had been placed at the disposal of the mission at Antivari. It was navvy's work, most of it, but he toiled as hard as the humblest orderly in the party.

'That I take to be the secret of Dr Leake's character; he performs the task that comes to hand without the slightest thought of self. The path of duty is the only road he knows. From what I saw of him, I should think that anything like personal, physical fear is absolutely unknown to him when there is duty to be done.'[13]

Was this the same Dr Leake whose acerbic remarks were even then being discussed across the Marshalls breakfast-table? Of course, this appreciation was written in the 1915 euphoria following the award of the Bar to Arthur's VC, and its style and content are in keeping with other contemporary descriptions of military heroes, but one cannot help speculating about the impact that sight of his letters home might have had on such a piece. Perhaps the safety valve of private letters, in which he could 'let off steam' about people and issues that annoyed him, enabled Arthur to present a serene countenance to the outside world. However, the description certainly emphasizes a reticence about his Victoria Crosses that many observers noticed.

When the expedition reached Cattaro (now Kotor) on 25 October, it was directed to go further south to Antivari (now known as Bar), a few more hours' sailing down the coast. But Arthur had time to take some photographs, and to write home:

'We only receive rumours but they seem to be going at it hammer and tongs all along the line. Cattaro is the most wonderful place I have ever seen; it is tucked away in the hills which come down to the water's edge on each side of this kind of inland sea. . . . Don't worry about me, you can be quite sure that I am not going to get into any danger.'[14]

Next day they arrived at Antivari. This small port was connected to the interior of Montenegro by narrow gauge railway as far as the western end of

THE BALKANS 1912 - 1919

Lake Scutari, and was therefore usefully placed when convoys of wounded were being removed from areas of fighting. One of its main industries was tobacco-growing and processing, and the BRC unit was offered a tobacco factory to use as a base hospital. The building was large enough to house a hundred patients, and cookhouses and other facilities were soon put up. Arthur observed to his mother:

> 'There are a few Montenegrins left here and they don't seem to be at all fond of work. The Italians are developing this place [harbour and railway work]. This is fortunate because we have been able to get hold of plenty of wood and other materials for

102

building. The British Minister from Scutari met us at Cattaro, and came on here to help us start – he is quite a nice chap, Count de Salis by name and an Irishman. The "Count" part is something to do with his Montenegrin splendour. I believe he had something to do with us coming here, so we should be quite independent of the Red Cross people from other nations. We are quite on our own here and likely to remain so. We are living in quite a good hotel and in fact are doing war in the greatest of style and comfort. The hotel is crammed with reporters of every nationality, and they are the most unhappy lot you could possibly imagine. They find they cannot go any further. Our own pet reporter [from the *Daily Telegraph*] has been playing about the hospital today and has been sadly in the way.

'I start tomorrow with the Surgeon-General [Bourke] for the army, if we can get there. We are going up to see about a field hospital and to find out if there are any means of getting the wounded down. Don't know if I shall be able to take any photographs; these people seem to be frightfully particular about this kind of thing. Of course, we have not got nearly enough stuff to run a hospital but are living in hopes of getting some sent out. Please ask Willie to send me 100 Wills Three Castle cigarettes about once a fortnight.'[15]

The next day Arthur saw the front line. The offensive was being directed by General Martinovitch, Montenegro's Prime Minister and War Minister. Arthur had great respect for Martinovitch, calling him 'a fine chap' and 'the only one who is any good'. He described, particularly for Willie's experienced eyes, what was happening:

'The military situation is very interesting. The Turks are in a very strong position [the fort of Tarabosh] on the high range of hills which command Scutari. They are said to have been fortifying this place for some years past. The Montenegrins are more or less round them except on the Scutari side. We only saw one Montenegrin position but it seems to have been the main one as their Headquarters are there. They are pounding away with big guns, not doing much harm – the Turks seem to be quite good gunners and every day the Montenegrins are having a certain number of casualties from shell fire. We were on the top with the General and his staff when the Turks spotted us and made us skedaddle very quick. What the Montenegrin does with his guns I don't know, but he seems to be quite happy and goes on popping off all day long.

'The Montenegrin Army from behind is very amusing and we had a fine chance of seeing it. There seems to be little or no system and we passed men straggling in all day. I fancy they work much in the same way as the Boers, and each district has its commandant and each village its lieutenant. The old men have to be sent back and given jobs behind. We passed any number of these poor old things, who call themselves the "Special Reserve". One could not help thinking of Haldane's Special Reserve at home. Every pony, mule and donkey is being used to take up food and ammunition, and it is impossible to get hold of anything with four legs for ourselves. We are fed by the Army. They seem to have quite good rations, bread (coarse but good), and meat, which the country seems to have in plenty, is quite good.

'We passed several hospitals on the way up. A Montenegrin doctor informed us that he is the only Montenegrin medical man. Their extemporized hospitals are not half as bad as one might have expected, and they are fairly well supplied with dressings and instruments. The patients are very keen to get out and fight again. Fighting is everything to these people, and the wounded are quite a secondary consideration.'[16]

A week later he was beginning to chafe against inactivity; the railway was of no use as yet, the Montenegrin authorities were unhelpful to say the least, and the Red Cross was becoming more irritating:

'Not much news. The hospital is filling up, but nothing of interest in it; only simple bullet wounds and local sick people. A motorboat was to be used for bringing wounded down the river, but it is broken down. There are large numbers of wounded up at the front but no hospital and no transport to transfer them. I quite believe that the Government, if you can call it such, want to keep us out of sight as much as possible. If we are to be any good, we have got to get ourselves up and shall receive no help from the authorities. The old General [Bourke] is not at all pushing and is afraid of spending money. Dr Bradford is only intent on making as big a show here as possible and getting out lots of nurses. It does not seem very hopeful, and mind you don't give any money to the Red Cross! These semi-civilized people only want to be left alone and have their fight to themselves.

There is no doubt that the Montenegrin is a tremendous fighter and will stick at nothing.'[17]

He even had time for bathing in the sea, determined to keep fit even though the water was becoming very cold as winter approached. One of the few recreations available was to give the press correspondents misinformation, and Arthur warned his family not to believe anything they read in the papers. The elderly King Nicholas of Montenegro had passed through Antivari on his way to the front line and a meeting with General Martinovitch and had promised to do something about the unit's transport. They had a car, but it kept breaking down due, according to Arthur, to the poor quality Italian petrol they were having to use. Dr Bradford, technically in charge of the unit (although the *Daily Graphic* on 6 November printed a photograph of the medical team with Arthur designated as being the senior member. Had the reporter been deliberately misled?), had wired London requesting that six female nurses be sent out; Arthur was not getting along at all well with Bradford, and criticized the move:

'This is, I think, a mistake, because we don't know yet quite what use we will be. My own belief is that this Red Cross business has been forced on Montenegro, when they do not really want it at all. They could not refuse to have us because of public opinion.'[18]

At the beginning of November Arthur was detailed to move to Pentari just inside Albania, where Montenegrin forces were attempting to hold the Turks at bay to the south of Lake Scutari. With two dressers he was to set up a Field Hospital. His letters described the experience:

'Started from Antivari on Monday [4 November] at 4 p.m. in a boat taken from the Turks a few days before at Scutari; the boat is driven by an oil engine but also has sails and is about 50 tons. A very amusing voyage and well entertained by the Montenegrin Captain, who would insist upon our drinking more wine than was good for us. Stopped the night at Dulcigno where there are three Russian hospitals. We lodged in one of these in a ward; there were no patients and they have not yet had any. The hospital is very well equipped and puts us altogether in the shade. We left before daylight and did not see the Russian doctors as they were out the evening before. Reached the mouth of the River Boyana in about two hours and shortly after entering it some Turks were seen to the South, but they did not fire upon

us. Arrived at Pentari at midday. The Turks had only been
cleared out from the river a day or two before and they had
shelled the boat on the way down; one shell had gone through
the deck but not done much damage. We had on board about 20
Montenegrin soldiers going up to the Front, and some supplies
of pork and biscuits. The salt pork was very popular and was
much looted all the way up. These soldiers at any rate had all
they wanted during the voyage. The Captain took us below for a
feed and we had to eat raw pork and drink more wine. Thank
goodness I have a strong stomach, but I am wondering what sort
of parasites I shall be full of presently. There was a very cold
wind blowing all the way and the hills in the distance were
covered with snow.'[19]

At Pentari Arthur found a building to convert into a hospital. It was filthy,
having been previously occupied by farm animals, and there was a great deal
of cleaning-up to do. His impressions of the local people were not favourable:

'This country is peopled chiefly by Albanians, and they are quite
the filthiest people I have met so far. They are an indolent lazy
lot, and only work enough to produce just the food they require.
Just now they have lots of cattle and sheep which they are said to
have stolen from the retreating Turks. The Albanian has joined
in with the Montenegrin, having bargained for his own terms
with the King first. The Montenegrin has the most supreme
contempt for the Albanian as a fighting man, and thinks him
quite useless in every way. We are living in the house of an
Albanian priest, he is an awful brute and requires watching. We
can't get any help from these Albanians. We have only just got
enough food for the wounded, and it is difficult to understand. I
don't see why the Albanian should have quite his own way here,
as he is the absolute scum of the earth.'[20]

Wounded men soon began to arrive at the improvised hospital. Many were
in a very serious condition, as they had been brought over many miles of
rough and mountainous terrain, often dragged along the ground on makeshift
travois pulled by men or mules. Arthur hoped to send numbers of wounded
down the river by boat to the Russian hospital at Dulcigno, but heavy rain
made the river impassable. His hospital had to take over some more nearby
rooms, but still the wounded kept coming and the accommodation for them
was very cramped. General Martinovitch came to look round and promised
better supplies of food, and Arthur was gratified to learn from the orderlies

that he had kept his promise. Biscuits, rice and a sack of pork arrived, causing great rejoicing among the patients. Martinovitch was becoming quite a friend of Arthur's, even supplying him with an elderly English-speaking Montenegrin as an interpreter.

Several ladies of various nationalities had turned up in the area, offering to help in the relief effort. Knowing his views on the subject, Arthur's family must have been taken aback to hear that he almost approved of one of them.

> 'There is a French lady here and she has attached herself to our hospital. She has been in this country before for some years and knows all about the people and speaks their language. She came out about three weeks ago and obtained a pass from the Government to go where she pleased, and has been wandering about trying to do something. She is a wonderful woman and is doing splendid work in the hospital. She has been cooking, nursing and making herself generally useful and has been a tremendous help. My dresser talks French quite well so we get on like anything.'[21]

He was interested also to come across several Montenegrins who spoke a little English but with strong American accents. These were men who had emigrated to the United States as part of the huge tide of East Europeans that had headed for the New World and its promises in the previous twenty or so years; now they had come back to help their native country in its apparent hour of need.

The Red Cross instructions were that the wounded must be sent all the way back to the base hospital at Antivari, where Dr Bradshaw was still in charge. But Arthur considered it more efficient to send them just as far as the Russian Hospital at Dulcigno, until it was full. He was of the opinion that there were quite enough hospitals and medical personnel in Montenegro and Albania for immediate needs, and indeed no more were sent out from London. Units were still being got ready for other areas, however, particularly for Greece and Turkey. The British Red Cross was trying very hard to be even-handed in its efforts. Not for the first time, however, Arthur was aware of the value of a properly organized medical aid system in a war zone:

> 'The complete absence of organization is felt up here near the fighting, and now, if the weather remains bad, we are practically cut off from the base hospitals. These Montenegrins get themselves along in a wonderful way, even when badly wounded, and it is quite surprising to me to see some of the cases riding down on mules from the front. If a man is quite knocked out, his friends and relatives bring him down on a stretcher, so a badly

hit man means the loss of at least four more from the fighting line
– not sound from the General's point of view. One cannot watch
this sort of thing going on without seeing the importance of an
organized Medical Corps for an Army, and if the War goes on
long enough there is sure to be a great deal of sickness and it will
become still more obvious.'[22]

The weather was now worsening every day – constant rain on the lower
slopes and deep snow on the upper. The Turks were dug in on Tarabosh
Mountain and their fortress could be easily seen from Pentari. Sporadic
gunfire was heard all day, as the Montenegrin Army tried desperately to
capture Scutari. Rumours flew round that the war was almost over, that
Constantinople was being shelled, and that the Turks were in full retreat.
Meanwhile, Arthur's hospital was filled to overflowing and no casualties
could be taken away by boat owing to the bad weather. Badly wounded
patients began to die, many of them arriving from the front with wounds
already gangrenous. Arthur described the scene in one of the 'wards':

'Imagine the cowshed [at Marshalls Farm] and the whole 50
percent dirtier, and you will be able to get a sort of idea of the
place. Wounded are packed all round touching one another and
a wood fire burns on the floor and fills the place with smoke so
that you can't see across. I think the smoke is perhaps good; at
any rate it covers some of the smells. Expect to have to take off
an arm and a leg in a day or two if the cases can't be sent to the
Russians. I am not looking forward to this under such
conditions.'[23]

Reporters were still around. One from *The Times* seemed genuine enough,
but another turned out to be 'a military chap' just out to have a look round.
He was speedily recalled to England.[24] Some Italian doctors appeared at the
hospital, and began to take over, quite ignoring Arthur's presence:

'I quickly sent them about their business, and perhaps on
afterthoughts it was as well that this had to be done through an
interpreter, as I lost all my recently acquired Continental polite-
ness. It was a bit of a blow to them, especially as they thought
they were quite the people up here.'[25]

He even began to lose his earlier enthusiasm for 'the French lady', who
seemed to have become less energetic altogether:

19. 'Arthur spent almost three weeks out in the Salient... finishing up at a location near Zonnebeke' (p.133).

20. 'Their Advanced Dressing Station was in a large house known as the "White House"' (p. 133).

21. 'On 12 November the "White House" was hit by a shell' (p. 135.) (Both photographs taken by Arthur).

22. 'I am sending some photos. Several are of the Bishop of Khartoum'
(p.150). Arthur in centre, the Bishop on right. (See also p.156).

23. Arthur's mother in declining health, 1915.

24. The four brothers on leave at Marshalls, 1915. Left to right Willie, Steenie, Arthur, Dick.

'She seems to be showing signs of moving on somewhere else. She has probably caught this from the Montenegrins who always have much business elsewhere when there is a job of work. The people in this part of the world are all talk and promises and you cannot catch them anyhow for work. They are far worse than the native of India, who does work sometimes when it is to his own interests. A Montenegrin official has been sent to specially look after us and arrange the food supplies. He is called "The Director". He spends his time munching huge chunks of raw pork and biscuits and wears a red cross. The whole thing is most amusing and it is very difficult to understand how the Army gets along at all. I suppose it is because every man is so keen to get at the Turks and is bent on being in the fight. There is much looting going on and in a little while there will be no stores to be taken over.'[26]

On 10 November the weather lifted and the boat was at last able to depart for Antivari. The Frenchwoman was on board, saying she would return but Arthur had his doubts.[27] (A month later his mother enquired with some interest about his relationship with the mademoiselle, to which he replied that his dealings with her had been 'very brief', and he had no idea where she had gone.) Two more Italians arrived, having been travelling around the area with 'a cinematograph machine'. They had been filming 'The Guns In Action', but, as Arthur pointed out, 'the pictures won't be of any interest as there is nothing doing in these parts now.'[28] A few days later he had another encounter with this prototype media circus:

'Found the Italians still here, as they had not succeeded in getting any transport to take them down. They have been amusing themselves during the day by getting up a sham fight between the Montenegrin guard who look after the bridge and some Albanians. They say this will be a splendid picture for show because people will not understand that it is a sham. I don't think they really know themselves that the Albanian is helping the Montenegrin. They also got hold of my staff here and arranged a show at the hospital. Men were brought in and bandaged up in all kinds of ways and a great display was made. I pointed out that this would not do at all and that it was not the wish of the Red Cross to appear at the Music Halls. The film has now been destroyed. I rather believe that one of the orderlies instigated the whole thing. He is an old Tommy and it is quite the sort of thing an old Tommy would do. The dresser should have known better.'[29]

Going out to the firing line at a strongpoint called Suka Dajtchit, Arthur saw the opposing sides sitting on hilltops looking at one another. The Montenegrins had no guns at that position, and were becoming daily more frustrated, but General Martinovitch told the doctor that he had orders to do nothing that might incur great losses. Crown Prince Danilo, the Montenegrin Commander-in-Chief, was on the other side of Scutari with a battalion, but could not move due to a rain-induced quagmire in the way. Martinovitch's aim was to take the port of St Giovanni di Medua – 'very important to these people because they think they will keep it after the war and it will be one of their plums.'[30] Arthur continued to take photographs of everything, and brought dozens of films back to England with him at the end of the war. The tiny negatives and prints are still in the possession of his family. As he told his mother,

'These people like to parade for their pictures if they can put on all their trappings but don't like being taken without preparation.'[31]

Next day, he went out to see another part of the line called Murichau in the Tarabosh area. The Montenegrins had eleven guns there, mostly Russian, but some Italian:

'This Army is run by the Russians entirely, and their ammunition and most of the supplies come from Russia. We are living upon Russian biscuits, and wherever I go they think I am a Russian. The Turks, who are apparently trained and run by the Germans as far as one can learn, are doing some very good shooting. They have given the Montenegrin batteries rather a hammering but in spite of this have not done any real harm. Eleven men have been killed after three weeks' shelling. The Montenegrin gunners like to think they have knocked hell out of the Turkish batteries. The Montenegrins have made very poor fortifications, considering the time they have been up here. They might have been almost without casualties in their batteries if they had made proper sunkpits, at least so one would imagine from the few casualties they have had even with the most meagre fortifications. There is an idea here that the Bulgarians are doing so well that the Turks must give in and that Scutari will be demanded in the terms for peace. The weather has been very fine for the last two days and the country looking its best. Though the hills are covered with snow, it is quite warm in the valleys and has been just like spring today. It is a very fertile country and even the Albanians cannot help having good crops.'[32]

On 12 November the war seemed to be reaching some kind of turning point:

'There is some important movement on today. The troops have been withdrawn from their positions at Suka Dajtchit. Something like 3000 men passed through here on their way to the Turkish left flank. Rumour has it that they are going to try to get to St Giovanni di Medua. Prince Danilo's Army is also said to be working round in that direction. It is a very interesting sight to see this large body of Montenegrin soldiers on the march. They are a curious-looking lot, old and young and wearing every kind of costume, for the most part in rags, but some in new clothing which has just been issued to them. They are mostly fine men and look very hard and capable of putting up with any hardships. Their transport is practically nil as they only take along what stuff they can carry and the meat is driven. The men are all over the place and sleeping in every corner where there is any shelter, as it is pouring with rain now.'[33]

Arthur made plans to move on with the troops and set up an Aid Post nearer to the anticipated site of the fighting. He and some of his men moved on down the line with General Martinovitch's forces, and heard on 18 November that Scutari was surrounded and completely isolated. The city, important to the Montenegrins because it had been in Turkish hands for 400 years and was larger, with 30,000 inhabitants, than any Montenegrin town, was the object now of a long winter campaign, but it was impossible to take Scutari without first being in control of Tarabosh, a strong modern fortress perched on a steep, bare rock. The BRCS unit's relief contribution in the deadly battle was a considerable one.

On 17 November news reached them that St Giovanni di Medua had been taken by Martinovitch and Arthur was asked to accompany a boatload of wounded back to the base hospital at Antivari. For three days he had been the only medical man available to deal with the needs of 5000 men and reached Antivari in an exhausted state, but felt he had helped the Montenegrins who

'seem to like to have an English doctor with them just for the show of the thing. We found a shop here with lots of lager beer, and you can imagine things got very merry and much entente passed between us. I have had a pretty rough time living in Albanian houses and feeding with these people. The Albanian is without doubt the filthiest animal, except perhaps the Turk.'[34]

At the Antivari hospital the six female nurses requested by Dr Bradford had arrived, much to Arthur's annoyance:

'There are six nurses here. I wish they were mules, then I could get my stuff along. Have done quite an interesting operation this morning, mending a man's face which was more or less blown to pieces. All the reporters have now cleared off. Turkey seems to be about finished and we hear many rumours about the war ceasing. I should like to be home by Christmas.'[35]

After gathering together a stock of medical supplies and food, Arthur returned to St Giovanni di Medua. He was accompanied by Dr Goldsmith, the other member of the Red Cross unit, who was to set up a temporary base hospital there. They were not impressed with the countryside round Medua:

'This is such a dirty hole, and it is getting quite unbearable with the filth of this rabble army. It is quite the worst country I have ever seen, nothing but huge heaps of stones topped with swamps. Can't imagine anybody thinking it worth troubling about. It is, however, good enough for such people as inhabit this part of the world.'[36]

He found the morale of the Montenegrin army to be good, due to the large numbers of Americans who had returned for the war. But they all seemed to hate the country and the rough life, 'after having been in America where they get high wages and have lots of money to spend'.[37] Unfortunately, Arthur's own morale was not holding up so well, due to several clashes with his superior, Dr Bradford, who visited Medua on 4 December:

'Dr Bradford has been out here for the night. As usual he wanted to upset everything and we had our usual scrap. He is an absolute failure as an administrator and has tried all along to spoil my show.'[38]

When an Armistice was finally arranged on 3 December, Arthur pretended to official observers that he was under the direct orders of General Martinovitch, and that the 'local Red Cross man' (Dr Bradford) had nothing to do with Arthur's activities.[39] Unfortunately the Turks refused to recognize the Armistice and the fighting continued. A Peace Conference was opened in London on 16 December, but with little hope of success. Now all kinds of people began to turn up at Antivari with money and equipment, including a medical student who came out independently, and a Miss Lucas, supposedly the sister of Lord Lucas, loaded with equipment, but

'None of them do any good as there is no organization to get them to the right places and the amount of money being wasted is enormous. Our six nurses seem to be enjoying themselves. There is nothing for them to do, but they may as well be helping to spend the money as anybody else. England would do well, before subscribing next time, to see first that there was a reasonable chance of the money not being altogether wasted. Our hospital here is wonderful; there is a looking-glass for every member of staff, and so many beds and mattresses that it is difficult to get into the place and everything else in proportion except drugs and antiseptics of which there are practically none.

I believe when Dr Bradford sent home for clocks the Red Cross struck and Sir F. Treves sent him an awful stinker. It was only my pig-headed obstruction which prevented Dr B. from sending home for 30 nurses. Perhaps it would have been better if he had and they would have found him out quicker.'[40]

In the first week in January, during the worst of the winter weather, there was an apparent end to the fighting, and it was hoped the Armistice would hold. Arthur's unit was ordered by the Red Cross to return to England. Arrangements were made for them to cross the Adriatic to the Italian port of Bari, and then go south by road to catch the Brindisi Express. Arthur was utterly frustrated by this move, as peace was not yet in being, although all parties were gathering in London for a peace conference; he was easily persuaded by the British Minister at Scutari, the Count de Salis, to sever all ties with the Red Cross and stay on. He explained to his mother that he would receive no more pay from London, but

'Being recalled in this manner is the climax to what has been the most disgraceful and muddled piece of organization all through. The people at home have been too bad for words and our boss out here has been worse. It would have been far better that we should not have come at all. I had no idea of the condition of things because I have been with the army practically all the time. It would probably be impossible to have found a person better able to make trouble wherever he has been than our Boss. He is about the last man in the world who should have been sent to Montenegro. Don't publish this letter.'[41]

The *Times* reporter sent the following to London:

'In view of the possibility of a continuation of hostilities at Tarabosh and the need of the Martinovitch Army for medical assistance, one doctor and several members of the British Red Cross Mission have decided to remain in Montenegro on their own account, while the Unit is returning to England.'[42]

In spite of the peace talks in London, fighting continued, in some areas as fiercely as ever. Early in February a three-day attack on Tarabosh by the Montenegrin Army provided Martinovitch's troops with their worst experience so far, resulting in thousands of casualties, and stretcher cases and walking wounded poured into Arthur's hospital at Antivari. Militarily, very little real progress was made, even with considerable assistance from Serbia. Poor organization and inadequate measures for the evacuation of the wounded increased the number of deaths and serious wounds, and the *Times* correspondent was critical of the Red Cross:

'It must not be forgotten that throughout the war Montenegro has been almost entirely dependent for medical assistance on foreign countries. The withdrawal of several of these missions, including the British during the Armistice, has left the country most inadequately provided with surgeons and skilled helpers. While, therefore, it is impossible not to criticize the manner in which the Montenegrin authorities have failed to profit by experience with regard to the transport of the wounded, such criticism cannot but be tempered by the unpleasant thought that England and other nations, which, by sending Red Cross missions to Montenegro, assured this country of help, have by the premature withdrawal of this help left her in the lurch at a most critical moment.'[43]

The Montenegrins licked their wounds for a month, before resuming the attack on Scutari. On 23 March the Great Powers intervened and allotted the town to Albania. This spurred King Nicholas's army to greater efforts, and they finally stormed Tarabosh. A Great Powers fleet arrived in the Adriatic to emphasize the position; peace in Europe was not (on this occasion) to be jeopardized by events in the Balkans. Still the Montenegrins fought on, finally capturing Scutari on 23 April. It was a pyrrhic victory. As Arthur was only too aware, the Montenegrin losses had been huge. And Scutari was only held for eleven days. Pressure from the Great Powers compelled King Nicholas to hand it over to them on 4 May, commenting:

> 'We have all to thank God that Scutari was in our hands, even for such a very short time. The prestige of our country and the honour of our arms have likewise been exalted even by this irreparable national loss.'[44]

The King presented Arthur and the remaining members of his unit with the Order of Prince Danilo, in gratitude for their services to Montenegro. Only now that the fighting was over was Arthur prepared to leave Antivari. He and his orderlies packed up and left for England, where, of course, no Red Cross official welcome awaited them. He went straight on from London to High Cross, disgusted at the way things had turned out.

The next month he set off for India to resume work with the Bengal-Nagpur Railway. He therefore missed the reception given by Queen Alexandra at Marlborough House on 8 July, 1913, at which she presented the BRCS Special War Badge, made in silver-gilt and enamel and with the word 'Montenegro' on the clasp, to those who had served in the Balkans. Arthur was presented with a badge *in absentia*, and it was sent to Marshalls to await his return. Six thousand pounds remained, unused, in the BRCS Balkan Fund; the money was expended during the 1914–1918 War.[45]

CHAPTER NINE

'A Uniform Does Everything Now'

Life at Garden Reach settled down once again into familiar routine. Arthur had arrived back in Calcutta to find the changes heralded by the Delhi Durbar of 1911 already beginning to take place; during that first visit to India by a reigning monarch, when the King and Queen were crowned Emperor and Empress of India, George V had announced the removal of the Raj's administrative headquarters from Calcutta to Delhi, a devastating blow to the 'City of Dreadful Night'. As usual, Arthur enjoyed his annual Cold Weather hunting trip at Christmas, 1913, in the jungle of the Central Provinces, and continued to train with the Railway Volunteers. Word reached him from Marshalls that, at last, the problem of Thorpe Hall seemed to have been resolved; following a succession of unsatisfactory tenants since the death of Arthur's father in 1893, and after a rather unsavoury High Court dispute in which Mrs Martin-Leake was victorious, to her great relief a buyer had been found. In July, 1913, General the Hon Julian Byng, commanding the British force in Egypt, bought Thorpe Hall at auction and moved there with his wife Evelyn in the autumn. General Byng, inevitably, was rarely in residence at Thorpe, but Arthur's family were gratified that such a socially acceptable couple were the new owners. They paid a rent to Arthur's mother for the use of some adjoining land (£100 per annum), and Evelyn Byng set about redesigning the gardens, her favourite activity.[1]

During the early months of 1914 the British news that most concerned Arthur was the Irish Question; as the summer wore on he also wrote home about the Suffragette 'outrages' that were being reported in the papers. But in Europe the Balkan Question would not go away. The assassination of the Austrian Archduke Franz Ferdinand and his wife in Sarajevo on 28 June caused only a minor ripple in the pages of the Indian newspapers. Arthur, like many others, did not think the event worthy of comment in his letters home. Instead, on 23 July, he asked his mother,

> 'What are you going to do about the women? There seems to be lots of talk about it but precious little doing to stop the anarchy.'[2]

As the conflict drew nearer and the armies of the Great Powers were placed on a war footing, a man like Arthur was undoubtedly getting himself into a state of readiness too. He had rushed to volunteer for South Africa and again for Montenegro, and when news of the outbreak of war broke in India on 5 August, twenty-four hours after it was declared in the capitals of Europe, he gave notice to the BNR, paid off his servants and made arrangements for his polo ponies and dogs to be cared for. He left his Victoria Cross, in its case, in a cabinet in his shared bungalow, intending to return, of course, when the war was over – 'by Christmas'. Then he took the first possible train to Bombay where he arrived on 9 August.

The earliest ship available for Europe was the P and O Steamship *Caledonia*, which was carrying a consignment of gold for England and numbers of soldiers bound for Aden, as well as hundreds of passengers hurrying home at the prospect of war. The ship's sailing was delayed for a few days due to rumours that a German cruiser was in the area,[3] but eventually got under way. Arthur's travelling companion was Captain Reginald L. Benson, a member of the Viceroy's staff, who also hoped to see action before the war ended. All officers' leave in the British Army in India was cancelled by the authorities, to prevent a wholesale defection to the seat of war. Arthur was free to leave at any time, but Captain Benson was able to slip out just before the ban came into force. They brought their military uniforms with them to make enlistment easier in Europe. The khaki worn by Arthur with the Railway Volunteers might prove to be very useful.

Arthur would have preferred to go straight to Marseilles, but the *Caledonia* was not scheduled to go there, so Malta was seen as the next best alternative. On 22 August he wrote to his mother,

'We arrive at Malta tomorrow. Then we shall take a ship for Marseilles or any French port. There is another Englishman on board with the same object in view, and we are going to wander along together till we find the Expeditionary Force. He comes from the Viceroy's staff and got special leave to join his regiment. I am not coming to England first because they might give me a home job.

'I don't suppose you are hearing much news at home as there seems to be very strict censoring going on. We cannot imagine in the least what England is like, but I expect you are much quieter now and are getting more or less used to the conditions of war. Our Frenchmen on board are most amusing and there was no holding them when they heard that their army was in Alsace. Race hatred goes a long way with the soldier and the Kaiser could not have over-estimated the feeling in France against him.

'I am sure you will agree with my efforts to join the army on the continent, and forgive me for not coming home first.

Remember, I have had experience of these people (Government officials) before, and now want to short-circuit them if possible. I have brought my uniform and think there will not be any great difficulties in getting across France. I also have money in gold. I expect to be attached to some hospital, or sent home as not required. Have no anxiety about me. Mine is quite a peaceful job and I am not likely to be exposed to any danger.'[4]

Benson and Arthur waited for two days until a boat was ready to sail for France. The harbour at Valetta was filled with the French Mediterranean Fleet, waiting for orders, and the air was filled with rumours of spies and sabotage. Captain Benson had a letter from the Viceroy asking that he be given every assistance, so he showed this to the British authorities. At first they were co-operative, but on the third day the Governor of Malta ordered them both to be detained and sent directly back to England. They pleaded for more time to find a ship, and were granted twenty-four hours. Arthur told his mother,

'Fortunately that evening this boat came in on her way to Marseilles, so we went on board and stayed all day and so escaped. This ship [the SS *Queen Eugenie*] is a tramp carrying a cargo of wheat for France. She is quite a good boat of her kind, very clean and well-kept. The skipper is a gentleman and takes much trouble to make us as comfortable as possible.

'Our stay in Malta was quite interesting. Half the French fleet were there and we went on the Admiral's ship to call. The Admiral gave us permission to go on any French war boat that was going to France, and of course that might have been useful if we had not found this ship. There was very little war news to be obtained but as far as it went, it appears that the Germans are not making any progress and that they are having rather a bad time. This must be an awful knock to the Kaiser and I hope now we shall soon see his complete downfall. Just on leaving we heard a rumour that our Expeditionary Force had been fighting hard with most satisfactory results. I wonder if this was so. . . .

'There ought not to be any great difficulty in getting across France as we have a letter from the French Consul at Malta saying that all help must be given. You won't get this letter for some time as the ship may be delayed at Marseilles.'[5]

After disembarking at Marseilles on 29 August, the intrepid travellers made their way to Paris, where they arrived next day. Arthur wrote home from the Hotel Bristol:

'We have just arrived after a quite uneventful journey from Marseilles. A uniform does everything now and we did not pay for tickets. *Entente* wherever we go. I don't think we shall have any trouble getting on from here, but it may be difficult when we get to the Army. I shall have to get hold of some high official in the Medical Department.'[6]

While Arthur spent the next few days in Paris, going to the British Embassy and any other potentially influential institutions, Captain Benson joined his regiment, the 9th (Queens Royal) Lancers. Five days later the Royal Army Medical Corps (which Arthur persisted in calling 'The Medical Department'), had taken him on (in spite of the 'permanent incapacity for military duty' certified in Calcutta in 1904) and attached him to 5 Field Ambulance with the Second Division. Each division in the 1914 Army consisted of three brigades, which together with artillery and support services numbered about 20,000 men. Three Field Ambulances were allocated to each division.

As the German invading forces had swept all before them, wheeling through Belgium towards Northern France in accordance with the now-famous 'Schlieffen Plan', recruitment in Britain had proceeded rapidly, an enthusiastic populace encouraging men to answer the call to arms. War Secretary Lord Kitchener's face – the face of the man who had tried to prevent Arthur being awarded the Victoria cross in South Africa (though Arthur probably never knew this, the relevant Public Record Office files remaining 'closed' until 1953) – pointed and stared in streets throughout Great Britain. Arriving at the Front straight from Paris Arthur had seen none of the posters.

He was aware from the newspapers, however, that the British Expeditionary Force had been hastily assembled under the command of Sir John French. General Douglas Haig's I Corps, consisting of the 1st and 2nd Divisions, along with II Corps and several infantry and cavalry brigades, had been heavily involved in the battle and retreat from Mons between 23 August and 5 September. The French 5th Army under Lanrezac and four British divisions had found themselves being trapped by thirty German divisions and were forced to fall back. Mons had been held by the British for a day, allowing the French to escape, and the BEF had managed to inflict serious losses on the surprised Germans, but had then been forced to withdraw. II Corps under General Smith-Dorrien turned at Le Cateau on 26 August and fought back, but the retreat continued. Great concern was felt in London, and Lord Kitchener crossed the Channel for discussions with Sir John French in Paris on 1 September, and the decision was taken to support our allies the French, but to continue the retreat towards Paris. The retreat had lasted thirteen days when it came to a halt on 5 September. British casualties

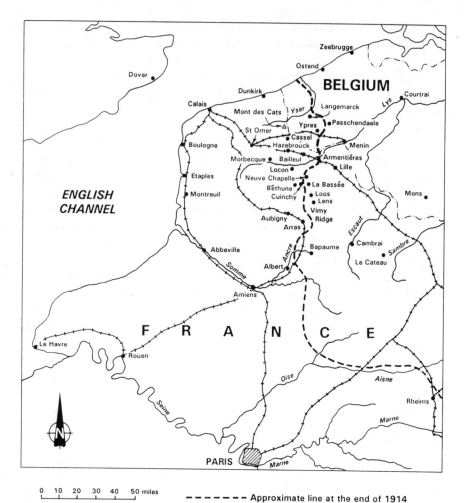

0 10 20 30 40 50 miles

‒ ‒ ‒ ‒ ‒ ‒ ‒ Approximate line at the end of 1914

THE WESTERN FRONT 1914

numbered 15,000 wounded, killed and taken prisoner, and quantities of equipment and perishable supplies had been lost.

Arthur joined 5 Field Ambulance on the day before the offensive known to posterity as the battle of the Marne began. It was immediately apparent that the organization of Britain's military medical services had undergone fundmental changes since he had last come into contact with them in South Africa. Now the Royal Army Medical Corps, founded as recently as 1898, had the benefit of support from various agencies, like the Queen Alexandra Imperial Military Nursing Service. There were training schemes for its personnel, and career prospects for doctors were much enhanced. At the beginning of the Great War an agreement was reached with the British Medical Association whereby doctors aged forty-five or less were accepted for general service, while those older than this would be allocated to home hospitals. At forty years of age Arthur's distrust may well have been misplaced, but he was taking no chances and preferred to join up in France. When he arrived with his India kit and the rank of Captain, the authorities were 'altogether nonplussed',[7] as the normal procedure was to commission civilian doctors as Lieutenants in the first instance. Accordingly the *London Gazette* on 31 December pronounced him Temporary Lieutenant, backdated to 3 September. In August, 1914, there were 3168 Medical Officers including Territorials, but as the only way for a doctor to practise at the Front was as a member of the RAMC this number increased rapidly. By the end of the war there were 13,152 Medical Officers in the Corps.[8]

Organization of medical units at the Front was soon firmly established in a pattern that persists today in many of its features. The primary requirements were to find efficient ways of evacuating the wounded and of treating the less seriously hurt so that they could be returned to duty as soon as possible. Diseases of war also had to be catered for, and the new disorders that began to emerge as the war went on, due, many of them, to the kind of warfare being waged, had to be allowed for in the RAMC's plans. Static trench warfare meant that a pattern could be set up, regulated, and quickly taught to newcomers.

The first medical point of contact for a wounded man was with his Regimental Medical Officer at the Regimental Aid Post, where a preliminary assessment would be made and the appropriate dressing applied. If able to walk, the man would be directed to one of the three Field Ambulances attached to his division; if too badly hurt, he could be moved by stretcher or any other available means. From the Field Ambulance, whose personnel would man the Main Dressing Station, a man would be evacuated by horse ambulance, motor ambulance, wagon, car, light railway, or even, on canals and rivers, by barge, to a Casualty Clearing Station. This unit would have equipment to enable operations to be carried out, perhaps an X-Ray apparatus, and usually a mobile laboratory. From the CCS there would follow a journey by Ambulance Train or Motor Ambulance Convoy to General or Base Hospital; thence to the United Kingdom by Hospital Ship.[9]

In the 2nd Division, Field Ambulances 4, 5 and 6 had been hastily designated and equipped as soon as war was declared. Number 5 assembled at Aldershot and sailed to Boulogne from Southampton on 18 August. Arthur joined it at Chaumes, south-west of Paris, on 6 September, when it had already seen some lively action. It was commanded by Lieutenant-

Colonel R. J. Copeland, a senior officer who, within a few days of Arthur's arrival, took over temporarily as the Division's Assistant Director of Medical Services (ADMS) when ADMS Charles Dalton was wounded by a shell; Colonel Dalton died a few days later. There could not be a clearer indication that in this war even senior men in non-combatant positions might find themselves in mortal danger, in spite of efforts by men like Arthur to reassure their families as to their safety.

Just as Arthur joined the unit he heard that the Martin-Leake family had very nearly had a casualty of their own. His brother Frank, now aged forty-five, who had been promoted Captain in the Navy in 1911 was, at the outbreak of war, in command of the Fourth Destroyer Flotilla, patrolling off the east coast of southern Scotland off St Abb's Head. His own vessel was the flotilla leader HMS *Pathfinder*, a light cruiser of almost 3000 tons and with a crew of 264. On 2 September a German submarine, *U21*, commanded by Lieutenant-Commander Hersing, entered the Firth of Forth and penetrated undetected as far as the Forth Bridge at Queensferry. The U-Boat cruised around, apparently unhindered, until, at 4.30 on the afternoon of 5 September, it encountered *Pathfinder* and fired a single torpedo. Frank's cruiser was hit square on and it seems that her magazine exploded, because *Pathfinder* went down within four minutes. The explosion was seen from the shore and destroyers and small craft hurried to the spot. Only fifty-eight crew members were rescued, including Frank. He was wounded, picked up unconscious and taken to Queensferry. Here was the so-called 'Hospital Ship' *Sheelah*, which in peacetime had been a pleasure yacht belonging to Admiral Lord Beatty and his wife. Now the lounge had been turned into an X-Ray room and the saloon into an operating theatre.

The newspapers[10] persisted in the view that the ship had hit a mine: it seemed incredible that a German submarine could have come so close, completely undetected. In any case, the Government did not wish to spread alarm, but by 11 September the newspapers were telling the true story. Crew members had persistently stated that they had seen a periscope sticking out of the water.[11] Frank also had known all along exactly what had hit *Pathfinder* and wrote home as soon as he was able:

> 'We were returning from a sweep out to sea to investigate shipping etc. I had just left the bridge and was in my after cabin standing by the table when the screws began to stop. I started a bolt to see what was up, but before I got away from the table, she gave a veritable stagger and tremble and everything movable came tumbling down. I got up the ladder, pushed the hatch cover up (it had come down), then got the boy (my valet) out, and had

a look round. Every sort of thing was in the air – shell room for'd. seemed to still be going up – the torpedo got us in our for'd. magazine and evidently sent this up, thereby killing everyone for'd. Her upper deck was flush with the water for'd. and it was only a question of how long she would float. Both our cutters were smashed up – the whaler was whole so all that could be done was to get this boat out and throw all floatable matter over – a badly hurt man was brought aft and put on the QD [Quarter Deck].

'While this was going on she began decidedly to do down by the bows and the 1st Lt gave the order for jumping overboard. He judged this very well. Personally I stayed too long and found myself on the after shelter deck with the ship rapidly assuming an upright position. I decided to stand on the searchlight stand and take my chance. This soon went under and self as well, came up again, ship still there. Had another dive and then got shot right clear – the situation then developed, an oar came along and then a bluejacket – then another – looked for ship, found her still standing on her nose (probably on the bottom). She then fell over and disappeared, leaving a mass of wreckage all round, but I regret a very few men amongst it, for at the time they were all asleep on the mess decks and the full explosion must have caught them, for no survivors came from forrard.

'I found one of the sailors with me had a broken leg; this prevented our propelling our oars to where more wood was, so I swam away to a more plentiful supply, and met a Meat Safe, I knocked the end out of this and was busy at the other end when I snuffed out for a time. On recovery I found myself being well-rubbed with rum in a bunk on *TB26* and she was getting alongside this yacht to deliver me to the tender care of these people who have done every possible thing imaginable for me. I somehow got a cut on the head – getting clear of the ship I expect. This evidently bled and accounts for loss of senses. Here they pumped salt and water into me until I objected. I now have a normal temperature and nearly healed head. I hope in a day or two to hear of a new ship.

'This outfit is run by Lady Beatty, the wife of the Admiral commanding 1st Battle Cruiser Squadron. I like her very much and appreciate her kindness. Sir Alfred Fripp is on board with another surgeon, McNair, and two topline nurses from Park Lane. I am the only patient here. Please write to her Ladyship and thank her, also to Fripp, he is a very good sort.'[12]

By the same post a letter reached Marshalls from Lady Beatty. *Pathfinder* had been the first ship of the war to be sunk by enemy submarine, and the staff of the *Sheelah* were delighted to be looking after her captain:

'It only took five or six minutes for her to go down and alas a great many of the dear sailors with her. Your son went down with his ship and came up and got hold of a bit of driftwood but as a poor bluejacket with a broken leg got hold of it too he left it to give him a better chance. He was found two hours later in an unconscious state and was brought here. The wound in his head thank goodness was not a very bad one. Since then he has been going on so well, he talks so much about his ship and we do feel so sorry for him. We are all so fond of him and you may be sure he will have every care and attention and two very good nurses never leave him day or night. We will let you know each day how he is.'[13]

Surgeon Alfred Fripp also wrote, calling Frank 'a fine fellow', and congratulating his mother for 'providing a noble batch of fighters for their country.'[14]

Arthur was greatly concerned about his brother, until he was assured that the wound was slight. Unfortunately Frank suffered serious underlying damage from the incident, but this only manifested itself after the war.

The situation for the personnel of 5 Field Ambulance was extremely busy just now, as much movement of material and equipment was taking place during those days in early September, while the British Expeditionary Force braced itself for the forthcoming advance to the Aisne. The unit's War Diary recorded moves to Le Mee, Boitrun and Verneuil, at the same time treating so many wounded Tommies that dressings ran out. The Battle of the Aisne was practically over when, on 16 September, Arthur was sent to the village of Soupir to help relieve a log-jam of wounded from the 4th Brigade. It had now been decided that pursuit of the German forces was no longer feasible and 'consolidation' was to take place. As the Germans seemed to have the advantage, both in terms of observation and of artillery power, by the end of September the British Army had ceased all offensive actions, and gathered its strength for a flanking move to the north, the so-called 'race to the sea'.

Trench warfare had arrived, accompanied by the bombardment of each others' positions, and 5 Field Ambulance had to deal with hundreds of the dreadful wounds that were to characterize this war. The results of shellfire, for example:

'It was found that the tremendous blast of air which followed the bursting of a shell produced severe injury to the lungs of the men

124

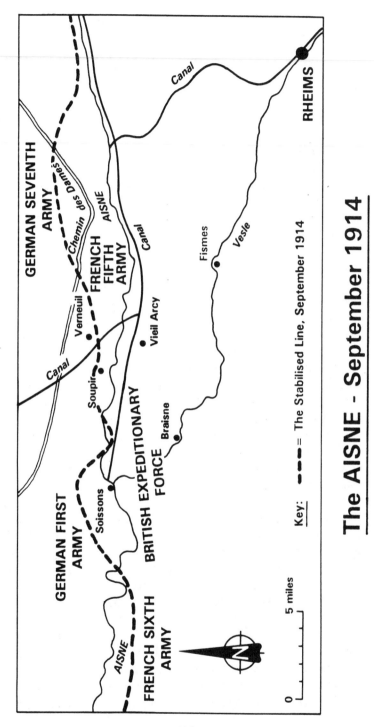

The AISNE - September 1914

Key: ▬ ▬ ▬ = The Stabilised Line, September 1914

GERMAN SEVENTH ARMY

GERMAN FIRST ARMY

FRENCH FIFTH ARMY

BRITISH EXPEDITIONARY FORCE

FRENCH SIXTH ARMY

RHEIMS

Chemin des Dames

AISNE

Canal

Verneuil

Vieil Arcy

Soupir

Soissons

Braisne

Fismes

Vesle

Canal

0   5 miles

standing near, and also that men in the neighbourhood suffered from concussion, which in many instances killed them outright. . . . Amongst the lesser effects of shell concussion observed were sudden blindness without injury to the eyes, deafness, and nervous prostration.'[15]

Due to long and often complicated lines of evacuation and the highly fertilized soil in which the trenches had been dug, wounds were likely to become infected, and tetanus, gangrene and gas gangrene were all too common. The problem of removing the wounded from the field greatly concerned the army medical authorities, right down to the commanders of Field Ambulances.

5 Field Ambulance's War Diary gave a full description on 19 September of the disposition of its strength:

'[Based one mile south of the Aisne at Vieil Arcy, L'Hôpital Farm]. The Regimental Aid Posts collect the wounded during the day and send them down at dusk to SOUPIR or VERNEUIL, as the roads are shelled heavily by day. At SOUPIR No 4 Field Ambulance is now established with all its wagons. At VERNEUIL Captain HISLOP is posted and helped by Bearer Sub-Division of No 6 Field Ambulance. Wounded are collected there. Ambulances are sent up at dusk and remove all cases to L'Hôpital where the remainder of Nos. 5 and 6 Field Ambulances have formed a Collecting Station for all casualties of II Division. Here they are dressed and fed after arrival and sent on in the afternoon by Ambulance or by Mechanical Transport to BRAISNE which is now acting as a Clearing Hospital. One Medical Officer and 4 men accompany each convoy.

'The "wards" consist of 2 large open barns capable of holding 50 cases each. These have been enclosed by walls of straw and are airy and satisfactory. The other wards are large sheds arranged around a courtyard the centre of which is a large hollow filled with manure and stable refuse to a height of about 3 feet and in such an advanced state of fermentation that it was judged wiser not to attempt to move it. The smell from this is at times very unpleasant. The sheds used for patients had at one time been used for stabling oxen but were in a comparatively clean state and when swept out and covered with a thick layer of clean straw made quite decent wards. There were several rooms in the residential part of the farm but these were too small to be any use for the sick. They were therefore used as offices, operating rooms, dressing rooms etc. The stairs were very narrow so that the rooms upstairs could not be utilized for sick and were used by Medical Officers. A large greenhouse was turned into an Officers' Ward for 9 cases. The RAMC personnel were accommodated in the lofts of the farm.

'The water supply is abundant but not good. A large proportion of the wounded have been found septic, as on several occasions it has been found impossible to bring the wounded away for 2 or 3 days. The men's clothes are in a filthy condition as they have been worn day and night since 5th August and are caked with mud. Men have slept in mud, slush, etc. The proportion of shell wounds is as high as 95% and are very severe. In the case of night attacks wounds are necessarily dressed by touch as no lights are allowed. In the case of German prisoners all the wounds are in a lamentable condition, as most of them have been over 4 days undressed and could not be brought in sooner from the field. These septic cases are treated as much as possible in a separate building in the village.'[16]

This was a quite different kind of military doctoring from that required during the war in South Africa. Many Medical Officers must have experienced difficulty in coming to terms with the insanitary conditions in which they had to work; Arthur's recent exploits with the Montenegrin Army had perhaps prepared him for this kind of war more than most, but he found the constant shortages of accommodation, dressings and drugs in these early months as irritating as ever. On 20 September even blankets and stretchers were in short supply, and a week later the Ambulance only had eighteen doses of anti-tetanus serum to meet the needs of the Division's three Field Ambulances. Diarrhoea was prevalent among both staff and patients; towards the Front the Regimental Dressing Stations were similarly afflicted and calling for help, but there was nothing the Ambulance could do. Clothing supplies were erratic; though desperately short of size nine boots, when a consignment did arrive they were 'only fit for boys' and had to be re-ordered.[17]

Before the war was two months old cases of self-inflicted wounds were occurring. One Private C. S. Walker was sent down to the Base with a wound that could not be accounted for, and where 'the clothing over the place was not pierced or injured'. A few days later four cases were discovered 'in which there was more than a suspicion that they were done purposely with the intention of avoiding their duty. One case was shot through the forearm and three through the foot.' The Divisional General ordered that cases of this sort should be inquired into and if necessary tried by Field

Court Martial. They should not be transferred to the Base Hospital until the case was fully investigated.[18]

Added to all these problems, it was the task of the Commanding Officer to account for all stores used and to keep records for the benefit of the owner of L'Hôpital Farm of just what amounts of hay, straw and firewood were used. Compensation could then be claimed by the farmer, M Chauvaux, who was especially demanding; the process was later to be very well described in R. H. Mottram's *The Spanish Farm*.

At the end of September a joint decision by the British and French High Command led to the removal of the British Expeditionary Force to the north, i.e. on the left of the line. Lines of communication with Great Britain would therefore be shortened and the BEF could be reinforced more quickly. The evacuation of the Aisne took place in secrecy so that the Germans could not respond with a move of their own. 5 Field Ambulance War Diary recorded on 15 October that the unit had

'Travelled all yesterday and last night without halting for refreshment or relieving nature. Passed through Amiens and were told a halt will be made at Calais for 35 minutes. At Calais men prepared breakfast and used latrines etc. Train moved off after twenty minutes leaving several officers and men and all breakfast material behind. Train stopped after a mile and the majority of absentees rejoined. Several still missing when train moved off. Detrained at Cassel at 1.50. Marched out at 3.20. Had tea 4 p.m., and marched to Morbecque, 8 miles. Arrive in dark, 6.30 p.m. No billeting officer present. Mayor gave us the school. No other troops present. Brigade marched in during the night. Sent Bicycle Orderly in to Hazebrouck to report arrival – no sign of H.Q. of Brigade or Division. [16 October] – Foggy and chilly. Reveilled at 5.30 a.m. Dark. Found Brigade HQ in MORBECQUE Square. Report. Had bike mended and bought bran for sick horses. [17 Ocober] – Marched to GODEWAERSVELDE. Billets in farm filthy and unfit for occupation. Applied for fresh billet but too dark to move.'[19]

There were constant reminders of the sad and unpleasant impact of war. On 19 October Arthur's Commanding Officer, Colonel Copeland, received notice that some British and Germans were badly buried on the north side of an ancient chapel at the trappist Monastery, Mont des Cats. A burial party of stretcher bearers was sent out with Arthur in charge, and found the bodies of three officers – Captain J. K. Gatacre of Probyn's Horse (11th Lancers, son of General Gatacre), Lieutenant F. E. Levita of the 4th

Hussars, and Lieutenant W. M. MacNeil of the 16th Lancers, who had all been killed on 12/13 October. Several German bodies were found too, and, though they had only been dead for seven days, the bodies were too badly decomposed to be exhumed, and it was only possible to pile earth over them to a depth of three feet.[20] [The three British officers now have graves in the Military Cemetery at Meteren, a few miles from the Mont des Cats.]

And so the somewhat erratic progress of the Second Division went on, Arthur and his colleagues making the best of frequently appalling living conditions and inadequate transport. From 21 to 24 October the Division was involved in the Battle of Langemarck, north-east of Ypres, and the Field Ambulance was moved, via billets in the brewery at Poperinge, to a school at Vlamertinge; from there a tented party was sent to the Market Square (the 'Grote Markt') in Ypres to provide a Dressing Station for the wounded coming in from the front line. The Ambulance's 'Bearer Division' went out into the Salient, assembling at Saint Jean with three forage wagons and two water carts. Commanded by Captain A. H. Heslop, four other officers including Arthur were with this party. The so-called 'First Battle of Ypres' was about to begin.

The battle officially lasted from 19 October to 22 November, 1914. 'Ypres' was the name by which it was known, both to the official historians of the war and to the participating soldiers, because the decision had been taken that Ypres would not be allowed to fall, no matter what sacrifice was required of men, guns and equipment. The spires of the old, walled, medieval town were perfectly visible from anywhere in the Salient, knocked about though they were during the prolonged bombardment. But to the men on the ground, other towns and villages had names that became equally well-known, either as deadly places where one tried not to linger, like Gheluvelt or Ploegsteert, or as welcome areas of rest and recuperation, like Poperinghe along the road leading west away from Ypres. Arthur spent almost three weeks out in the Salient with an Advanced Dressing Station, finishing up at a location near Zonnebeke, a sector that was already well-known as a 'hot spot', and here he displayed for the second time the bravery that won him Britain's highest military decoration.

CHAPTER TEN

'A Very Gallant Fellow'

In Ypres 5 Field Ambulance took over the cloisters of St Martin's Cathedral to provide accommodation for the reception of the wounded. On 21 October the cloisters were found to be:

> 'a very large building in process of building which has already been partly equipped as a hospital. Large stone-paved halls are capable of holding 50 to 60 cases – the basement is occupied by French troops. The first floor is provided with mattresses, pillows, sheets etc., with a kitchen at one end, and blankets of sorts. The upper floor is fitted with 56 beds, mattresses etc. The total accommodation is above 250, including passages. But no latrine accommodation of any kind. Trenches have been dug in the courtyard, which is a most unsatisfactory state – used as french kitchen and latrines indiscriminately. Oil lamps have been provided. The wounded arrived throughout the night; resources very strained. The municipal authorities have been requested to make some latrines for our use. They have agreed to erect pan closets etc. In the meantime we are looking out for more suitable accommodation. All 180 cases treated have been evacuated at night by ambulance train and ambulance motors. 5 died.'[1]

Soon the French took over the cloisters, and 5 Field Ambulance moved to the Communal Schools at the junction of St Jean and St Nicholas Streets. Here the wooden floors of the Girls' School were fitted out with 150 mattresses. Orders had been received that all wounds cases must be injected with 'anti-tetanic serum', but there was none to be had. Because the normal dose of the serum was too large for the usual syringes, Colonel Copeland had to scour Ypres to obtain some, but in any case he had to wait for the arrival of more serum requisitioned from the base. The Girls' School had no lighting or running water, another indication of the grave difficulties faced by Field Ambulances in these early months. In the Boys' School, next door, there was accommodation for the RAMC personnel in the upper storey, but most of the building was occupied by Belgian refugees from the countryside out in the Salient. At Copeland's request, the refugees were removed on 25 October, leaving behind them overflowing latrines and mattresses so stained that they were unfit for further use.

Arthur, meanwhile, out at Saint Jean, was experiencing trench warfare at its worst. On 26 October he wrote home when the battle for Langemarck was over and he had a few quieter days:

'I have not been able to write for some time as we have been moving about a great deal. I have had a good bit of work to do – you will know from the papers where we are. There is a lot of fighting going on – as far as one can make out things are going very well. . . . Of course, it is only a matter of time and these German pigs will be completely squashed.

'This country is very like our parts of England in many ways, but the people don't seem to be up to much. They are a dirty, untidy lot and, though the land seems rich, the farms are bad. We are living in a farm now and it is a filthy dirty place, like all the others about these parts. They go in largely for dairy produce and we get plenty of excellent butter. There are also lots of chickens and rabbits. Now I have got a camera you should have some photos if the weather will improve a bit. I could have had some fine partridge-shooting on the Aisne, only I could not get hold of a gun. Please ask Isabel to send me a toothbrush and some carbolic tooth powder. I should also like some warm gloves.'[2]

Letters from Marshalls offered fruit and walnuts from the gardens, but Arthur assured his sisters that there was plenty of fresh produce in the abandoned farms and gardens around Ypres. The family at home were quite excited at the news that Belgian refugees had arrived at nearby Wadesmill. In such ways the war was coming closer to English homes than had any war for centuries. The ever-growing casualty lists in the papers served to emphasize the point. For the Martin-Leake family, one son, Frank, had already almost lost his life but was now recovering well at home following the torpedoing of the *Pathfinder*; Steenie and Dick had also volunteered for the Territorial Force Reserve as musketry instructors, each with the rank of captain. Arthur thought they were 'very energetic', and hoped

'they will make some good soldiers to send out here. Our infantry is so vastly superior to the Germans. The New Army [Kitchener's thousands of recruits] might be quite good, if they can get good

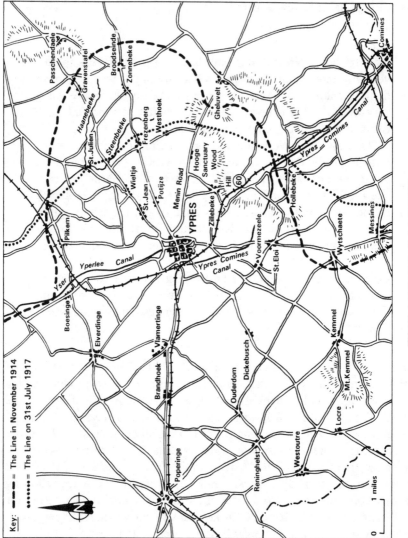

THE YPRES SALIENT

Key:
▬ ▬ ▬ = The Line in November 1914
•••••• = The Line on 31st July 1917

0   1 miles

officers for it. We hear that some of the Indian troops are actually
fighting now, but shall not believe it till we see them'[3]

The rumour was correct. Indian troops were serving in the area and did so
for the first year of the war, but the cold, wet winter made them susceptible
to illness and in November, 1915, they were transferred to Mesopotamia
with its warmer climate. Some Indian cavalry units remained.[4]

Arthur asked his sister Bella to send him a tin of curry powder with which
to enhance the omnipresent bully beef, and wanted Willie to send him an
electric torch, small enough to carry in his pocket, and an extra battery and
bulb. Willie, now forty-nine years old, was making great efforts to get out to
the front, a foolhardy enterprise, in Arthur's opinion:

'I hope Willie is not coming out; he should stick to some job at
home; this is too hard a life for anybody getting on in years.'[5]

Arthur himself, nine years younger than Willie, was not finding soldiering
exactly easy:

'I find that this sort of life is rather trying when one's years are
increasing and the habits of India don't help one to fit into it.'[6]

His letters home contained nothing about his own actions at Zonnebeke. 5
Field Ambulance's War Diary describes hard and heavy fighting every day,
and on 32 October Ypres itself was shelled and the Communal Schools had
to be temporarily evacuated. The three chaplains with the unit, Presbyterian,
Church of England and Roman Catholic, were kept very busy. There were
several more cases of self-inflicted wounds to deal with, and a flood of sick
soldiers suffering from rheumatism (treated with aspirin and returned to
duty within three days), and diarrhoea (treated with cold milk and fasting).
By 1 November the Field Ambulance was moved out of Ypres to a position
along the road to Vlamertinge, and the stretcher bearer party near the front
was split, Arthur's section being sent to the large village of Zonnebeke a few
miles east of Saint Jean. Their Advanced Dressing Station was in a large
house known as the 'White House', at a junction of two lanes about 500
yards from the trench system. Lightly wounded cases either walked here or
were brought by their regimental stretcher bearers, their wounds being
dressed if necessary before they were sent on down the line. Severer cases
were kept at the 'White House' until nightfall and sent back by horse
ambulance to the Dressing Staton on the busy Ypres–Vlamertinge road,
where the main part of 5 Field Ambulance was now situated. This was a
distance of more than five miles, so the horse ambulances could only

complete one journey each night. Occasionally wagons might be borrowed from other units, but there was no evacuation by railway because the Ypres Railway Station had been shelled. In the midst of it all Arthur told his mother:

> 'You will know from the papers that the fighting has been pretty heavy during the last few days. We seem to be doing quite well. At any rate the enemy has not made any progress and he has been trying very hard. The casualties have been very heavy here and we are full of work.'[7]

The next day there was more of the same:

> 'Here we are, still hammering away. The Germans have been trying very hard for the last four or five days to smash the line and get through, but they don't seem to have made any progress. They seem to take a lot of smashing and have endless numbers to bring up. Lots of French are arriving and something decisive should happen soon. The country round here is in an awful mess and nearly every farm and village is battered and burnt. A very fine church and château are both destroyed. What a jolly good thing that this war is not taking place in England. There have been a lot of casualties lately and our people have been fighting splendidly, holding their own against very violent German attacks. The Germans must have lost enormously as they have done the attacking and they don't seem to care at all about losses.
>
> 'What is going on in your part of the world? Are the Herts people coming forward as they should? Every man will be wanted for this show and of course the world will be intolerable unless the German hog is thoroughly put under. They say the Kaiser is in front here – everybody hopes he is.'[8]

Arthur was correct in reporting the presence of the Kaiser nearby; he had installed himself at Courtrai, no doubt ready to claim Messines or Wytschaete or whatever else his guns might capture.

On 6 November Arthur described his billet at Zonnebeke:

> 'At present I am living in quite a good house with every comfort and plenty of coal in the cellar. The only disadvantage is that it has been smashed up a good deal by shells, and we have to be content without any glass in the windows. We have shelter-pits to go to in the daytime when they begin to shell. The nights are

always quiet and, when the wounded have been sent off, we have great peace and comfort. We had roast pig for dinner today. The beast was reported officially to have died from shell wounds!! It is extraordinary how often edible creatures meet this end. I should think you will see some news about this part before long and I hope it will be that the German has trotted off.'[9]

Still the bombardment by both sides went on, only darkness bringing respite from the deafening noise of screaming shells and shattering explosions. Arthur was very conscious of the importance of artillery in this war:

'The German infantry is no good, and fights cannot be won by artillery alone. There was one amusing incident here the other morning. The Highland Light Infantry were attacked at dawn one foggy morning and they suddenly found the Germans standing in front of their trenches demanding them to surrender. The HLI proceeded to polish off the lot. Every German was, I believe, accounted for, either killed or taken prisoner. Our infantry are magnificent. If this war was carried out without machinery we should have played with the German as we liked. It is his infernal big guns which save him. You must have seen in the papers that Kaiser Bill had settled to be in Ypres at the end of last month. As he can't get there he is knocking the place to pieces. It is now a terrible wreck, after the weeks' shelling which it has had. This is nothing but wanton mischief and must be done out of pure malice and spite. The German population must be thinking now that William is a bit of a blown-out pig.'[10]

On 7 November Colonel Copeland went out to Zonnebeke to inspect the 'White House' Dressing Station. He found everything in order, but made no mention in the unit War Diary of any noteworthy actions on the part of any of its personnel. On 12 November the 'White House' was hit by a shell. Private D. Wolfe, who was serving with Arthur, recalled seeing a hole in the house 'the size of a bus':

'but Captain Leake wasn't perturbed at all, very quiet; said: "Well, we'll be moving to another situation tomorrow."'[11]

In fact the shell burst had also damaged four ambulance wagons and killed two horses; four other horses had stampeded and two were permanently lost, one had drowned in a shellhole and another had been made lame. The War Diary recorded an 'indent' for three sets of harness, two sets to replace those lost in the 'stampede', and the other to replace the set cut off the drowning horse in at attempt to extricate it from the morass.[12]

For a detailed description of Arthur's actions at Zonnebeke his family had to wait for the official account to be published the following February. They had no idea from him that he had done anything more than his ordinary job as a doctor in a Field Ambulance. He was now more concerned with the way in which the RAMC was organizing medical services. A letter from Sir Victor Horsley, Arthur's friend and mentor from University College days, bemoaning the unwillingness of the Army medical authorities to engage experienced civilian surgeons, was published in *The Times* on 2 November:

'The care of our wounded needs immediate supplementation . . . by notably increasing the staffs and equipment of the Base hospitals in France by sending out a number of hospital surgeons of experience. There are a number of Territorial Medical Officers like myself who found ourselves practically unemployed by the War Department as soon as we had completed the preparation of the Base hospitals. . . . I addressed a Memorandum to the Director-General venturing to suggest that the appointment of consultants as in the Boer War would not be so useful as the addition of a number of us to the Expeditionary Force as supernumerary surgeons of hospital experience who could be sent to serve Base hospitals wherever the pressure was greatest. This suggestion, however, has not so far been accepted, and I cannot help still feeling that our wounded are not receiving all the surgical help their splendid services deserve.'[13]

Arthur commented on it in a letter home:

'I know nothing about the work at the Base, but the great difficulty they seem to have had has been caused by the constant change of base. Our arrangements up here leave plenty of room for improvement and the organization is very out-of-date in many ways. Of course the RAMC are very prejudiced and hate the civilians, and have probably tried to keep out the big surgeons from home.'[14]

In the event Horsley was accepted for active service and was sent as consulting surgeon to the Mesopotamian Expeditionary Force, where he died of heatstroke on 16 July, 1916.[15] He is buried in Amara Military Cemetery, Iraq.

5 Field Ambulance seemed to be almost constantly on the move as well.

Arthur's party was ordered to return to Ypres, and Arthur told the family at Marshalls that thousands of French troops were in the area and it was very hard to find accommodation. But by 18 November,

'We are just now living in the bar room of a little pub. The business has ceased but the people are still here and living as best they can. There are a fair number of civilians in the houses around and we have been wondering whether they are spies or not. We may move at any time. Nearly all this Division has gone back for a rest and we shall not be at all sorry to follow.

'Some of us resided for a time in the most magnificent château, richly furnished and with every luxury. These places are, however, not as a rule as comfortable as they sound because they always get shelled sooner or later. At other times we live in barns, stables, lofts, sometimes in the open. I have been rather lucky and have nearly always had a roof of some sort over my head. The troops are always billeted if possible, but, situated as we are now, the majority are in the open. This is not really bad because Tommy very soon digs himself into the ground and puts a roof on.

'The Herts Territorials are here and I have been interviewing some today. They only came up yesterday and already a large number have been trying to go sick. This always happens with a new lot as the fainthearts invariably try to get back. I gave a severe lecture to some and told them that Herts expected great things of them. It is disgusting to read in the papers that the able-bodied men at home will not join. England ought to see Belgium; the people would then know what an invasion by the German Barbarian means. It was the women in Africa, also in Montenegro, who had such a tremendous effect in making the men turn out to fight and they should do so at home. The female driving influence would probably be more powerful than legislation if it would really start. A Montenegrin soldier never dared to go home, however much he wanted to, and we couldn't even get the sick ones to face home in many cases.'[16]

For the moment 5 Field Ambulance's close proximity to the war was at an end. The First Battle of Ypres was practically over and the 2nd Division was ordered out of the line to a position south-west of Ypres. Packing up in haste, Arthur and his colleagues were told to be ready to move at any time. On 19 November the Ambulance marched to Bailleul and was billeted in two farms to the north-west of the town, a comparatively safe area.

Nevertheless, at High Cross Mrs Martin-Leake was in a constant state of anxiety about her sons and about the ultimate result of the war. Arthur tried his best to reassure her:

'You must not be in the least anxious about the result – it can but go one way and probably will not take a great time longer. The German is already beaten and it is only a question now of smashing him up completely. We are full of cheer here and always get the maximum amount of amusement out of the show. The French are doing splendidly and, though they can't fight like our people, they make up by numbers. They are a very cheery lot and it is a fine army.'[17]

On 22 November Arthur left the Front for seven days' leave at home, and put his mother's mind at rest, at least for the time being. When he returned to Bailleul on 30 November he found that Colonel Copeland had gone down to take charge of a Base hospital at Boulogne and Captain H. Carter was now commanding the Ambulance. There was little interesting work in this behind-the-lines area to keep Arthur occupied, so one Sunday he wandered along to Church Parade, but was not impressed – 'Rotten sermon, the Padre would be better at home'.[18] While there he met Captain Benson, his companion on the journey from India, bemoaning the fact that there had been little for the cavalry to do so far. Then came a black-edged letter which took Arthur back to his schooldays at Westminster:

'I enclose a letter from my old schoolmaster. He is more polite than when I last had anything to do with him. Of course I admit that I never left a stone unturned to irritate him.'[19]

Mr Tanner's letter read:

'Dear Leake,
It was a curious coincidence that my son [Captain Ralph Eyre Tanner, The King's (Liverpool Regiment), died 23.9.1914] should have been under your care. I have been told that you treated him with great skill. For this I thank you very warmly. I only wish that he could have remained under your hands and not had the two days of the railway journey which must have been very bad for him. Apparently it was owing to this that the wound in the leg got poisoned and tetanus supervened in the hospital at Versailles. It is all very heartbreaking but we have to try to win through somehow. I like to think that Ralph was treated by a

138

Grantite. I hope you will be able to come and see me when you come back.'[20]

Arthur endorsed the letter with the words 'This was before anti-tetanus serum was brought up'.

As the first Christmas approached and the war showed no signs of reaching its expected end, all along the Front an endless stream of parcels and letters began to arrive for the troops and the Marshalls household added its bit by sending cake, pudding and chocolate. The pudding was kept to be eaten on Christmas Day, and on 23 December the unit moved to Locon. Arthur sent the news to his mother:

'We marched all night and arrived here this morning. We were very lucky in the weather as there was no rain, but it was very cold. The Indians are here and have been doing a good deal of fighting. I have not seen many of them yet. It is funny to see the black man here and he looks most out of place in the mud. I suppose we shall be in this neighbourhood for some time, though probably not in our present billets.

'England has at last had a little of the shelling [at Scarborough on 14 December] and it will probably do her a great deal of good. Recruiting should go well now. It will also do Germany's cause a lot of harm, if they had any friends left in the world to sympathize with them.

'We have had a great change in our Padre staff. Two have left. One has already been replaced and another new one is to come. The new one is a real live Bishop, the Bishop of Khartoum [Right Reverend L. H. Gwynne]; he seems to be a very nice man and a great sportsman. We were much perturbed about what his title should be, but on his arrival we found that "My Lord" would be much out of place. He shows great keenness and wants to see all that he can.

'Willie is nearby [at Bailleul] but I haven't managed to see him yet.'[21]

On Christmas Day, plum puddings were issued to the men and every man received a card from the King and Queen, but there were too few for the officers so more had to be applied for. Arthur sent his 'Princess Mary's Gift Box', containing tobacco and matches, home for Steenie and Dick, because he felt they were doing such good work for the country. The pipe he kept for himself.[22] The famous 'Christmas Truce' had been experienced in the Locon sector of the line, a few miles north of Béthune, when an Indian

Regiment had exchanged cigarettes and rum with Bavarians in the opposing trenches – Germans who said they had no ill-will towards the British.[23] The authorities were greatly displeased and gave orders that such an unofficial armistice must never happen again. Arthur hoped that 'by next Christmas there will be no chance to have a party of this sort'.[24] On the first day of the New Year the Ambulance moved to Zelobes, near Béthune, where it remained, static for all intents and purposes, for most of the year.

Now much of 5 Field Ambulance's time was taken up with treating 'trench foot' – not called that just yet, but common throughout the armies of both sides. Arthur had not come across it before, even in Montenegro in 1912:

'We are having a good many cases of bad feet now – they are caused by standing in water and mud in the trenches and, though it has been pretty cold, there has been no frost for some time, and that does not seem to be necessary to cause the trouble. It occurs in those who are subject to chilblains and is in fact an exaggeration of that condition. Some of the cases are very bad and will be of no further use as soldiers.

'This is a monotonous time. A few men are occasionally wounded by snipers. It is no good worrying about the war; it will come to an end in time. Lots more lives have got to be lost yet, but the war has to be finished, so this must be taken as a matter of course.

'There is a large brewery in this village. The manager is still here and she makes very good beer once a week. On the remaining days it is used as a wash house for the Tommies. This does not seem to spoil the flavour of the beer at all. 400 have been washed there today – 50 women, natives of the place, are employed to iron the clothing to kill all vermin and do repairs. It is an excellent thing and should do much to keep the troops fit. I believe they have started many other such places. Willie is washing his men in a Lunatic Asylum. The Bishop has just been here to conduct a service – a splendid chap and gives an excellent service for the men.'[25]

Early in January word came from the BNR in Calcutta that employees involved in the war would receive half-pay for the duration, as well as their Army pay. Arthur felt quite gratified that he would therefore not be out of pocket at all. When colleagues in India wrote to him bemoaning the dullness of life at Garden Reach he commented, 'They don't know when they are

25. 'The lady in question was Winifred Carroll' (p.211). With Dick on her first visit to Marshalls, October, 1930.

26. '… or simply relaxing in picturesque surroundings' (p.213). Winifred, Central Provinces, India, December, 1930.

27. 'A particular favourite of them both was a terrier, Billy William' (p.213).

28. Arthur's saloon on the Bengal-Nagpur Railway, December, 1930.

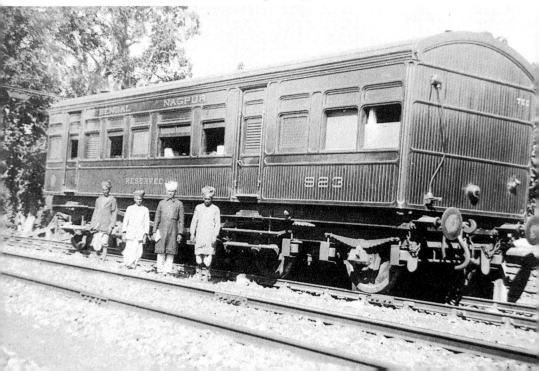

29. '… and soon bought himself a Gypsy Moth' (p.20). Dum Dum aerodrome, Calcutta, December, 1930.

30. Marshalls from the air, late 1930s, photographed by Arthur.

31. Arthur at Marshalls, 1950, aged 76 years.

32. Arthur's grave at High Cross.

GEORGIANA MARTIN-LEAKE
1863 — 1945
RICHARD MARTIN-LEAKE
1867 — 1949
ARTHUR MARTIN-LEAKE
VICTORIA CROSS AND BAR
R. A. M. C.
1874 — 1953
DIED AT MARSHALLS, HIGH CROSS
ERECTED IN PROUD AND LOVING
MEMORY BY THEIR COUSINS
HUGH & JOHN MARTIN-LEAKE
PARI ANIMO
1956

well-off out there'.[26] Life was quiet for Arthur too, and he urged his mother not to worry:

> 'We are living here in perfect peace and might almost be in a peaceful country. It is most awfully monotonous and one feels as if one is doing time. You need not have a moment's anxiety about me as we are just as safe as you are at Marshalls.'[27]

Once again, he hated inactivity:

> 'The Indians came and relieved our people, and the Indian Field Ambulance took over our dressing stations. There are really more Field Ambulances than are required for this kind of fighting and the majority of us are doing very little now.'[28]

He was bored, and to help pass the time he concocted a code to be used in his letters, to foil the censor. Letters of the alphabet were given numbers, so that he could indicate his location. He began to comment freely upon foreign news, having time on his hands in which to read thoroughly every newspaper that came his way. He had designs on the health of the Kaiser:

> 'The Kaiser wants something stronger than cascara and I should very much like to have the dosing of him. I am very fit and only suffering from the want of a little work to do.'[29]

In February Willie, now almost fifty, returned home to Marshalls, ill. The whole family felt that his talents had been wasted in France and Arthur wrote angrily:

> 'His position is not in the trenches, and if our d – d stupid, pig-headed idiots refuse to see when they have got a soldier of experience and ability, they don't deserve to get him at all. It is perfectly ridiculous the way material is wasted because the authorities won't take the trouble to use it in the right way. The number of men with knowledge of military matters cannot be too great now, and it is perfectly wilful to go and misapply an old soldier in this way. There is no doubt that the right plan for Willie is in Kitchener's Army where he can teach soldiering. Any of these half-baked soldiers can do the trench work and they are no use anywhere else. I think his pluck and endurance have been most wonderful. Nobody can form any idea of the kind of existence which the infantry have out here unless they have

actually been on the spot. I have seen enough to know what a hard time it is even for the strong young fellows. To meet complete amateurs holding high rank and knowing as much about soldiering as you or I, and then to find Willie doing the work of a Captain is simply ridiculous. There is no doubt that now he is at home he should make a great effort to get a more fitting job.'[30]

Arthur put in a request to be moved to a regiment:

'I asked our chief Tin-Pot for it and shall be glad of a change. A Field Ambulance is all right when things are more active, but it has been very dull now for some time back. Thanks much for the offer of a jigsaw, but I don't think it is worth sending out, especially as we have not much room here and no table to do it on. . . . I am glad to hear the blockade on Germany is to be tightened. The Navy is very splendid and is certainly knocking the hot wind out of the inflated sausage. The health of the Army is outstandingly good, most of the sickness round here is due to this sort of influenzey [sic] cold which is about. What a tremendous effect the typhoid inoculation has had on the war – the cranks who are preaching against it should be strung up without any exception. It is a pity the Government won't make it compulsory and do away with all this nonsense.'[31]

As he prepared to go on leave on 20 February, Arthur heard that Willie was still ill and was suffering from neuritis in a nursing home staffed entirely by female nurses. Arthur blamed the length of the illness on Willie's doctor who had failed to diagnose it – 'it puts my profession to shame', but saved his really barbed remarks for the nurses:

'Willie's experience of the nursing home does not seem to have been pleasant. I hope I never get into the clutches of these interfering females. Expect they are all suffragettes and run their shows accordingly. This is the sort of end one would wish Kaiser Bill with.'[32]

Before he left for England, Arthur had been told by his Commanding Officer that his name was about to appear in the *London Gazette*, but he said nothing about it until he reached Marshalls on 21 February. There he found his family and the village people agog with the news, that he had been awarded a 'Clasp' to his Victoria Cross. The word 'Bar' was soon in common use.

The terminology was naturally uncertain even in the highest of places, for such an award had never been made before. The citation read:

> 'For most conspicuous bravery and devotion to duty throughout the campaign, especially during the period 29th October to 8th November 1914, near Zonnebeke, in rescuing, whilst exposed to constant fire, a large number of the wounded who were lying close to the enemy's trenches.'[33]

The previous day he had been 'Mentioned in Despatches'.[34]

This was only the second RAMC Victoria Cross of the war. The first had been awarded posthumously to Captain H. S. Ranken on 16 November, 1914. He died on 25 September and is buried in the town cemetery at Braisne in the valley of the Aisne.

The award of a Bar to a Victoria Cross may have been entirely without precedent, but Major-General C. C. Monro, the Officer Commanding the 2nd Division, had had no hesitation in supporting it. His recommendation to BEF Headquarters at St Omer, dated 26 November, 1914, read as follows:

> 'This officer has shown such conspicuous gallantry that I recommend his case be favourably considered, and that he be granted a bar to the Victoria Cross that he already holds.
>
> At Zonnebeke, when he was with the Bearer Division of the 5th Field Ambulance, in a most exposed position, he went out continually over the ground in between the English and German positions in search for wounded, and although always fired at, and often having to crawl on hands and knees, he was able to get away large numbers of wounded men who would otherwise have been left to the inclemency of the weather and the continued shelling of the enemy. These operations often took him many hours to accomplish. There can be no doubt that by his devotion many lives have been saved that would otherwise undoubtedly have been lost.
>
> 'His behaviour on three occasions when the dressing station was heavily shelled on the 5th November, 9th November and 12th November, was such as to inspire confidence both with the wounded and the Staff. In such a case it is not possible to quote any one specific act performed because his gallant conduct was continual – and the fact that he repeatedly successfully accomplished his dangerous mission makes his case, in my opinion, all the more worthy of reward.'[35]

The unit War Diary, it may be noted, mentions only one incident when the Dressing Station was shelled on 12 November.

On 28 November General Douglas Haig, commanding 1 Corps, agreed:

'Captain Leake, RAMC, has repeatedly done most gallant acts, and I concur in recommending that a bar for the V.C (which he now holds) be granted.'[36]

The dates of the action to be included in the citation required clarification before the award could be published. The Warrant that established the conditions under which the Victoria Cross might be awarded had been amended several times,[37] but it laid down that the date, or dates, for the action must be engraved on the Cross along with the recipient's name. So the Military Secretary at the War Office, Sir Frederick Robb, sent a telegram to General HQ in France on 5 February, 1915:

'Please wire date of gallantry of Martin-Leake when with 5th Field Ambulance at ZONNEBEKE. STOP. We have recorded the dates 5th to 12th November in this case. STOP. Is this correct?'[38]

Back came the reply within forty-eight hours:

'Martin-Leake performed acts of gallantry every day between October 29th and November 8th.'[39]

29 October as the starting-date of the action was presumably chosen because on that day the Battle of Gheluvelt, in which Arthur's Division was involved, was officially deemed to have begun.[40] That the date did not accord with Major-General Monroe's version of events is obvious, and 5 Field Ambulance's War Diary throws no further light on the matter.

The award of a bar was provided for in the Fourth Clause of the original Royal Warrant, dating from 5 February, 1856. This laid down that 'no person is entitled to a bar unless, after he has received the Cross, he shall again perform an act of bravery which, if he had not received such a Cross, would have entitled him to it.'[41] A bar had, on several occasions, been refused to men who thought they should have one, because they had not actually been *awarded* their first Cross, although a recomendation was in being. This could not have applied in Arthur's case as he had received his Cross some thirteen years previously. Nor could it apply in Captain Noel Chavasse's case in 1917; he had actually received his first Cross a year earlier.

Following the announcement of Arthur's bar in the *London Gazette*, there was a great deal of excited correspondence in the papers. Many people were convinced that bars had been awarded before, and were determined to prove it (an indication of the interest evoked by the Victoria Cross ever since its inception, an interest that continues unabated today). The *Daily Telegraph* declared that Arthur was

> 'believed to be the only man besides Lieutenant-General Sir C. J. S. Gough, K.C.B., who has been awarded the clasp to the V.C., although the Cross has many times been awarded an officer or soldier for more than one act of bravery. Sir Charles Gough's Cross had three bars, thus showing that on no fewer than four occasions did he win the award.'[42]

This was entirely erroneous. The *Hertfordshire Mercury* hastened to put things right:

> 'The late Sir Charles John Stanley Gough, one of the two famous brothers who won the Cross in the Indian Mutiny, was credited with possessing three bars. It is true that he was decorated for no fewer than four conspicuous and separate acts of bravery, one of which was saving the life of his brother, Lieutenant Hugh Gough, who also won the VC, but he was not gazetted until October 21 1859, when these various acts were enumerated.'[43]

A Miss Ethel Day wrote to the *Daily Mail* stating that her father, Captain G. F. Day, had won the bar in the Crimean war, but this was quickly refuted by others, who pointed out that two or more dates engraved on a Victoria cross were quite common, but did not signify that a clasp or bar had been awarded.[44] Another correspondent recounted how he had read, on a tombstone in the cemetery at Lansdown, Bath, that Major-General Jerome received the Cross three times, the inscription reading:

> 'Severely wounded in the Indian Mutiny campaign, in which he was awarded the VC on March 17, on April 3, and May 28 1858'.[45]

Thus a basic misconception about how the Cross could be awarded, and exactly what constituted a clasp or bar, was compounded – as the *Daily Mail* commented:

> 'Is no official record in existence to which one could refer? At present it is easier for inquirers to discover the names of past secretaries of insignificant football clubs than those of winners of the VC.'[46]

Fortunately the views of the man who had the final word in the matter of the award of the bar to Arthur, King George V, are known. It happened that he inspected the Fleet, and had a conversation with Arthur's brother Frank about it, on board HMS *King George V*. Frank told his mother:

'Since Tuesday the King has been here paying us a visit. All Admirals and Captains have had a meal with him. I lunched today with him on board the *King George V*. I was pointed out to the King as being the double VC's brother. He remarked that "Your brother is a very gallant fellow" and that "he has puzzled me by doing so many things. I could not give him a VC every week so gave him a clasp." The King was very emphatic on Arty's clasp being the first given, and said the papers contained a lot of nonsense about it.'[47]

To his Aunt Rose, Frank explained it again:

'The King said he was lost as to a reward for Arty, but eventually decided on a Bar to his VC, and said it was the only one ever given in spite of what the papers said.'[48]

Another newspaper controversy concerned Arthur's rank. He was gazetted for the bar under the rank of Lieutenant, but Major-General Monroe and General Haig both referred to him in the confidential correspondence already cited as 'Captain'. In the *London Gazette* of 4 March it was announced that he was promoted to Temporary Captain.[49] *Town Topics* on 6 March contained the following explanation:

'Martin Leake [sic] VC is a captain, although all temporary appointments of civil surgeons to the RAMC for the war were made under special conditions of pay and with the rank of lieutenant. Martin Leake has worn the uniform and badges of a captain throughout this war with the consent of the authorities. His name appears as a captain in the Quarterly Home Army List in the list of V.C.s.'[50]

Others joined in. A letter to the *Morning Post* opined that the promotion was

'evidently the result of some strange inadvertence, as this brave man, after serving through the Boer War, where he gained his first VC, owing to the injuries then received was invalided out of the Army with the rank of Surgeon-Captain. He was therefore entitled to rank as captain, as everyone knows, on being again accepted for service in the present campaign. Hence promotion for further heroic conduct was meant to raise him from the rank he held, as of right, to the higher grade of major, RAMC.

'The public, which is in no mood to tolerate petty official mistakes, must see to it that the War Office at once remedies this inadvertence and corrects the official notice in the *Gazette*. Otherwise a grave injustice will have been inflicted on our double VC, who, between the first and second campaigns mentioned, served, it will be recalled, with the Red Cross in Montenegro in the First Balkan War.'[51]

So it was believed that Arthur's promotion had been made as a reward for his valour. The suggestion that he should properly have been promoted major was not followed, and he was only accorded that rank some eight months later.

As in 1902, and perhaps with increased enthusiasm, Marshalls was showered with congratulatory letters. One of the first was a telegram from Baden-Powell, and another came from the South African Constabulary Association at Pretoria. There were also numerous letters from members of the family, near and distant. In reply to one from his Uncle William, Arthur wrote:

'Will you please accept my very best thanks for the very kind congratulations from yourself and your family. Your letter has given me great joy and satisfaction, because I am very pleased to think that any little thing that I may have done should give my family pleasure.'[52]

The press waxed effusive. *The Lancet* declared that 'the whole medical profession unites in honouring him,'[53] and *The Tatler* proclaimed that 'his deeds have set the whole Empire a-ringing with his name. . . . Mighty Nimrod, most modest of men, first-rate doctor, a man to read of and about whom is a privilege.'[54] The *Hertfordshire Mercury*, after describing stirring deeds performed by its battalions in the Bedfordshire Regiment, announced that

'Now a still greater fame has been brought to the county by the unprecedented heroism of one of its sons. All England is ringing with the story.'[55]

From India came an account of the hero by one who knew him in his life there:

> 'When news came that he was in the thick of the war his friends were in no way surprised. They took it as a matter of course that wherever the fighting was hottest and the danger was greatest he would be sure to be found. He is a man of many friends, but none of them could claim to have ever heard from his lips any stories of the personal part played by him in the campaigns in which he has won such high distinction. He is even more modest than the average VC, which is saying a good deal. In India he is known as a first-class doctor and a good all-round sportsman, and all the world over as one of the bravest men in the British Army today.'[56]

When he returned to the Front on 2 March after his leave, Arthur found telegrams and letters from the Bengal-Nagpur Railway, the Hertfordshire Yeomanry, University College Hospital, the British Red Cross, and countless others. Not being a great letter-writer (except to his mother), he found the task of answering them all somewhat daunting:

> 'On arrival found a large pile of letters, which will take weeks to answer at the rate I go. It is a most infernal nuisance and this, together with an order to dine with the General, has brought home the lesson of the situation. I enclose you a few cock-a-doodle-doos which are the only ones of any interest. I enclose a cutting from an Indian paper – it is the usual kind of rot.'[57]

It was with a sense of relief that he turned his attention again to matters of war.

CHAPTER ELEVEN

'The Germans Must Be Squashed'

During the early spring of 1915 Arthur was commenting vigorously on the war news: 'What a fine thing it will be when we take the Dardanelles – This should just about finish off the Turk,'[1] and on developments at home. His whole family seemed to be involved in the war, even his sister Georgiana ('Sittie') was now working at a convalescent hospital in Ware and, like her brother, was chafing at all the interference she was having to suffer from higher authorities.[2] Frank now had command of a new ship, HMS *Achilles*, and Willie, in spite of his rheumatic tendencies, was now based at Hounslow as a Staff Captain in the Adjutant General's Department. In March family optimism was shaken by news of the death in action of a distant cousin and near neighbour, Captain A. B. R. R. Gosselin of the Grenadier Guards, whose family lived at Bengeo Hall, a few miles from High Cross. He lies in Cuinchy Military Cemetery, very close to where Arthur was then serving.

They all worried about the poor health of their mother. Now eighty years old, she was becoming weak and 'nervy', was constantly anxious about Arthur and Frank, and spent much of her time resting. An invalid carriage had been procured, and Dick, Steenie and Bella took her for gentle outings along the garden paths when the weather allowed; on warmer days she sat under the old mulberry tree on the lawn, writing letters to her son and many relatives and friends. She tried to keep up with village affairs, often receiving the vicar, Mr Overton, for afternoon tea, and pasting up her books of cuttings and items of interest; one of these books was kept for each of her sons. She was somewhat remote from the everyday life of the village, and a story persists to this day that during the Great War, when the public was being exhorted not to waste food, Mrs Martin-Leake sent one of her household servants to offer 'the poor' some *once-used* tea-leaves from the Marshalls kitchen. The family certainly took seriously the necessity to produce as much food at home as possible, and a letter from Frank on board *Achilles* indicates how successful the walled kitchen garden was:

'Thank you for the vegetables. The artichokes have seen the
Faroe Islands and those left are now close to the end. Conse-

quently the passage of the next cabbage will be shortened by 2 days in transit. Everything was fresh and very good. Sparrowgrass [asparagus] has possibly less flavour in the post and sea cooking, although I have a good cook'.[3]

Arthur was to remain with 5 Field Ambulance until November. The boredom from which he often suffered was only occasionally relieved by questions from the Base which had to be answered, like why the number of bayonets arriving with wounded men was always less than the number of rifles.[4] The Army authorities had decided to clamp down on unauthorized cameras at the front, a great disappointment to Arthur as photography was one of his favourite hobbies, in the absence of game to shoot. He told the family:

> 'I am sending some photos. Several are of the Bishop of Khartoum and one of him in a trench. This is a communications trench called Hertford Street: it was made by the Herts Territorials. An Army Order has come out saying that cameras are all to be sent home at once. There have been many orders saying that no photographs are to be taken, but this time certificates have to be given by Commanding Officers, stating that there are no cameras in their units. The trouble all arises from people sending photos to the papers, and it is hard on the harmless amateur. I am packing my camera up and it will arrive in a few days.'[5]

But this was not the end of Arthur's photographic career. A few days later, with complete disregard for the censor, he sent yet more photographs, this time showing a Dressing Station called 'Number One Harley Street' on a narrow road containing at least four Dressing Stations near Cuinchy:

> 'The trenches all have names here, mostly called after London streets. I sent you a photo of Marble Arch the other day. An attack was expected today because it was Bismarck Day but it did not come off. We have just got 6 new Sunbeam Ambulances just arrived. They are splendid cars, but just now there is very little work for them. I am sending home a box of souvenirs (tops of shells). A man going on leave is taking them as far as London and will book them on.'[6]

He was not without a camera for long. In May he asked for one to be sent, but suggested that a description of the contents should not be written on the outside of the parcel. Within a week a package arrived, containing 'the unmentionable article'.[6] He continued to take photographs of anything interesting thereafter.

The newspapers were full of discussion about how excessive drinking was affecting the war effort, particularly in munitions factories. King George V took the matter up and on 6 April ordered that from now on no alcohol would be consumed by the Royal Household.[7] Few of the King's subjects were moved to do the same; Arthur commented:

'You seem to be having a great dispute over the drink question – something should be done to make these disgraceful rotters work. . . . But I am very sorry to hear you are thinking of giving up your port wine. It will be a great mistake. I shall certainly not give up my rum ration and if you give up your port I shall double it. It might be a good time now to stock our cellar. Perhaps some of the Royal wines will be going cheap.'[8]

His forty-first birthday on 4 April was celebrated with a birthday cake baked by Sittie, but he had little time to relax, as the Field Ambulance at the time was inundated by Territorial Medical Officers who were being assigned to the unit for instruction. They spent a day at each of the four Dressing Stations and watched the work and looked at shells bursting in the distance, many of them seeing artillery activity for the first time. Some days the front was quiet and the Medical Officers expressed great disappointment at not seeing any 'war'. Other days were frighteningly noisy and the new doctors found it less amusing than expected.[9]

Not far away, Neuve Chapelle and the Aubers Ridge were the scene of fierce fighting but the Field Ambulance was far enough behind the line, near Béthune, to know very little about it. Arthur had time to contemplate growing some mustard and cress and got Bella to send some seeds, but, as one of the Field Ambulance's frequent moves seemed imminent, he gave the seeds away to a Frenchman.[10] In the north, as the Second Battle of Ypres got under way, word arrived of the Germans' first gas attack, on 22 April, on French and Canadian troops near St Julien. The Canadians had held on and Arthur remarked:

'We are a long way away from the fighting and know very little about it, but how splendid of the Canadians. They must have done some very fine fighting. It is difficult to believe the Germans got through by their stinks. They have made some ground at Ypres but it is of no consequence and must have cost them heavily. I am sending my warm clothing home; please send me some thin vests. We have been having some lovely weather, almost hot, and it has brought on the trees like anything. The woods around here are beautiful and full of nightingales which sing like anything.'[11]

But he was bored; once again, there was not enough work for the Field Ambulance, situated behind the lines. He reflected that there seemed to be 'no shortage of doctors in this country, and probably some could be spared for home work if required'.[12] The unit War Diary recorded with disgust:

'It is noticeable that the new officers coming from the Base are unable to ride. From this point of view they are useless in a Field Unit. The last three come under this head.'[13]

There was hardly ever a chance for Arthur to do any surgery, and a request for a transfer seemed a distinct possiblity.

'I am thinking rather seriously of getting a transfer to some large hospital to try and get some work. This sort of life is uninteresting after about eight months of it. . . . Of course the Germans are the worst savages the world has ever known and they must be squashed, though it is a very tough job. The Prince of Wales has been here, and took a very keen interest in the German prisoners. He never missed an opportunity to see a batch when they were brought in. Today [21 May] we have come right back [to Locon] and are now miles behind the fighting [in the Battle of Festubert, 15–25 May]. This Division has done splendidly but the losses have been heavy and they will have to get up to strength again. A good bit of progress was made and a fairly large number of prisoners taken. The weather became very bad on the second day and made things very difficult. A large force of Canadians are fighting now [1st Canadian Division] and we hear that they did very well yesterday. They are a splendid lot and quite mad to get at the Germans. They are quite convinced that some of their people were crucified the other day at Ypres and they mean to have their own back. The Dardanelles are still going well, so the war may still be over by the end of the summer. We were jolly glad to get back for a bit. I have not had my clothes off since Sunday last and had lodgers – have now had a bath and put on some of the things you sent the other day.'[14]

His commentary on the latest news in his letters home helped to compensate for the enervating ennui of Field Ambulance life. Lacking what he regarded as real action in his own life, he read the newspapers furiously and put forward his views on everything from obvious propaganda to the new Cabinet and the possibility of conscription in Britain:

'You must have seen by the papers that a whole lot of Germans wanted to surrender and got shelled by their own people. This I believe is quite true. I suppose you are still very busy Cabinet-making. We must have Conscription and it would have a real good effect on Germany – the Germans think we are only playing at this show yet. We hear that the Italians are going to send support to Servia and push forward from there. Our Territorials are doing very well and fighting like Regulars. This is of course splendid and points to the work our new armies will do when they appear on the scene. Some of the old troops who have been fighting since the beginning want resting now. The country should force the Government into having Conscription at once – our system is most unfair and inefficient and just the thing to make the war drag on indefinitely.'[15]

After leaving Locon on 30 May, the Ambulance moved to Noeux-les-Mines, south of Béthune. Here a Dressing Station was opened in a school that had previously been used by the French – 'the latrines were in a disgusting condition, cess-pit choked and faeces heaped up on the seats.'[16] Arthur's misgivings about foreign standards of hygiene seemed to be fully justified. He wrote home describing the new area:

'We are now in the centre of the mining district and living in a mining town. It is very dirty and frightfully dusty. I have just met an old University College Hospital man. He went into the Navy and then retired to Private Practice. He tried to get back into the Navy but the authorities, with their great talents for putting people into jobs for which they have least experience, drove him into the Army. I have not seen him since 1898.

'Rather an amusing incident here this morning. I was asked to see a Guards officer because he was suffering from supposed "itch". He had previously been treated for obscure digestive troubles which caused over-heating of the blood and consequent irritability of the skin. On my arrival it had just been discovered that he was lousy – great consternation and a panic on a small scale. He must have been lousy for quite a long time as all his bedding and everything were crowded. I nearly called him a B.F. Perhaps a good thing I did not because he is head of a large banking firm and belongs to a well-known Herts family, with many representatives in our neighbourhood.'[17]

Reinforcements arriving from England were impressive, Arthur thought:

'I saw one or two Scotch regiments of Kichener's Army yesterday, and was much struck by their firm appearance. We should have the best of this show in the long run of course, though there is some check just now (at Givenchy). I have written to the King to put my spare cash with the War Loan, so the country will be all right now.'[18]

Arthur's family were just about coming to terms with his two Victoria Crosses, although unsure about how to address letters to him. His sister Sittie, somewhat self-consciously, tried 'Captain A. Martin-Leake, VCs', but was told by him not to do this: 'It is not correct,' and he was more than happy with just 'VC' – although his modesty would have avoided even that if it were possible.[19] He also had to instruct Sittie that he should be designated 'Captain RAMC', and that the addition of 'FRCS' was unnecessary. Meanwhile his original Cross had arrived from India and had been sent on to the Military Secretary in Whitehall by Willie on 31 March.

The design for the Bar had caused some ripples at the War Office. Messrs Hancocks & Co, on the corner of Bruton Street and New Bond Street in London, had been the manufacturers of the Victoria Cross since its institution in 1856. The firm produced some sketches of their design of the so-called 'Clasp' which were submitted to the War Office in April. The first sketch showed a laurel wreath, in the same gun-metal, linking the Bar with the 'suspender' from which the Cross hung. This meant that a large part of the dark red ribbon would be covered. Indeed the sketches, which survive in the Public Record Office, suggest that the Cross itself might be overshadowed by the wreath, and the Bar would look almost insignificant. Lieutenant-Colonel B. R. James, head of the section of the War Office dealing with the matter, seems to have agreed, commenting to the Military Secretary, Major-General Sir Frederick Robb:

'The circular wreath seems neither beautiful nor necessary. Will you please decide?'

Robb instructed Hancocks to make the Bar:

'exactly like the bar from which the ribbon is suspended, the dates of the acts of bravery being engraved on the back.'[20]

During the summer the War Office was looking for an investiture date when Arthur's Bar could be presented by the King in person. But in early July he was allowed a period of leave to have a minor health problem dealt with. Frank told the King all about it when they met on board HMS *Achilles*:

'When I told the King Artie had come home last Sunday he said, "I must get hold of him and give him the Clasp". I told him he was going to undergo an operation and when he said what for I said, "Piles". However, as Wigram (Equerry) asked me for his address, Artie must stand by for a summons.'[21]

Arthur stayed overnight at the Grosvenor Hotel and entered University College Hospital on 5 July. He told his mother on 8 July that 'the operation was a huge success. I am feeling quite fit this morning.'[22] Willie came to see him, and he soon returned to Marshalls for two weeks' convalescence. His surgeon had gone on a fortnight's holiday and would not allow Arthur to return to the front until he saw him again. The expected invitation duly arrived by telegram:

'Your attendance is required at Windsor Castle on Saturday next the 24th inst. Service Dress. Proceed by 12.5 train from Paddington. You are invited to lunch at the Castle, or if unable to lunch there is a train leaving Windsor at 1.20. Kindly telegraph acknowledgement of summons stating whether able to remain to luncheon. Lord Chamberlain.'[23]

Two more Victoria Crosses and twenty-two other awards were presented at the same time, including the Companionship of the Order of St Michael and St George to the Hertfordshire Member of Parliament Lieutenant-Colonel Henry Page, serving with the Hertfordshire Regiment. Arthur described the occasion, in meagre detail, to his Uncle William:

'Thank you very much for your very kind letter of congratulations. The King said a lot of nice things and gave us an excellent lunch, but nothing stronger than cider cup to drink. It was a very wet day and Windsor was not looking its best. I return to France on Saturday and then perhaps the weather will improve; it always seems to rain when I come to England.'[24]

Arthur's mother, in writing to her sister-in-law Louisa, gave a few more details of the ceremony:

'I am very proud of Arthur and of all of them. At Windsor Castle the King had a very good talk with Artie. The ceremony went off well, but it was not so magnificent as King Edward's was. King Edward was most exact and particular about all the outward signs of a good personal appearance. Artie remarked the difference, but he was dressed up to his standard of King Edward's requirements, and he looked very well. The clasp is simple and adds greatly to the simple beauty of the VC.'[25]

On 30 June, a few days before the presentation of the Bar, the British Medical Association met and awarded Arthur its Gold Medal for 'Distinguished Merit', but he was not able to collect it in person until after the war.[26]

He returned to 5 Field Ambulance on 1 August, again meeting a friend from his medical student days: 'War is a great place for meeting all sorts of people.'[27] Another good friend had gone, however; Bishop Gwynne had been appointed Deputy Chaplain-General, with the rank of Major-General, and had moved to BEF HQ at St Omer.[28] Sad news had arrived in High Cross for the vicar, Mr Overton, whose son Tom was killed in Gallipoli on 30 July while serving with the Lincolnshires. He was buried in Redoubt Military Cemetery, Helles. Arthur was sorry but philosophical about it:

'I saw Tom's death in yesterday's *Times* – as there are not other casualties reported I suppose he had the misfortune to meet a shell. Am very sorry for the Overtons, but these things have to be. I am certain there is another winter's soldiering in view for we amateurs.'[29]

During the late summer the Ambulance involved itself in cricket matches and sporting contests. Concerts were staged once a week, which pleased the soldiers very much, according to Arthur: 'Tommies are very fond of singing mournful songs'.[30] There were some severe gas attacks in the area in late September, and the number of sufferers was large.

'During 24 hours 8 a.m. 25 September to 8 a.m. 26 September we treated 705 cases. The large number of walking cases that trooped in swamped the Dressing Station. The men were covered in mud and had no equipment in the majority of cases. We could not sort the serious from the slight. The only thing was to clear the place to make room for others, and very slight cases must have slipped away [to the Base].'[31]

Arthur was becoming conscious, through the newspapers, of another theatre of war – the Balkans. He told his mother that he would not be in the least surprised if something began to happen there soon.[32] In October he noted that

> 'The Balkan tangle is huge, I hope we shall send a large force down there, so that we can really smash them. It won't do to let the Germans through. . . . We have lost our big RAMC man: he has been sent off to the Balkans. A great loss to us as he was a very good man and has run this Division very well since the early days of the Aisne. He was always very keen on giving everybody as much leave as possible and treated me very well in this respect as you know.'[33]

On 22 November, no doubt as a result of his acquaintanceship with the 'big RAMC man' [Surgeon-General W. G. Macpherson], Arthur was recalled to England by direct order of the War Office. On 27 November he was promoted Temporary Major,[34] and by 1 December was on his way to Paris. A Mission was being sent to the Balkans, and once again Arthur was heading in that direction too.

CHAPTER TWELVE

'A Bally Awful Muddle'

Perhaps the most impenetrable and contentious issue in international affairs during the century before the Great War was 'The Balkan Question'. Problems in the area between the Black Sea and the Adriatic had led commentators throughout the nineteenth century and right across Europe to introduce this phrase into common parlance, regardless of language. By 1915 everyone knew what it meant – the vacuum caused by the decline of the Austro-Hungarian and Turkish Empires being hotly contested by the forces of nationalism that were growing ever stronger in the region. A crisis over the annexation of Bosnia and Herzegovina by Austria-Hungary in 1908 had solved nothing and had led to prolonged enmity between Austria-Hungary and Serbia. One result of this antagonism was the assassination of the Archduke Franz Ferdinand in June, 1914, providing the spark from which the Great War had been kindled.

The invasion of Serbia by Austria that followed the assassination was repulsed within days, but Austria launched another onslaught in September, 1914. She was again thrown back when Serbia rallied after receiving fresh supplies of munitions from France. Arthur-Leake commented:

'What a splendid victory the Serbs have had. They may be past masters at atrocities, but they are splendid soldiers as well.'[1]

It was in the Allied interest to keep Serbia afloat because she lay between the Central Powers and their ally Turkey, and her neighbour Greece's pro-German neutrality helped the situation not at all. However, the Greek Prime Minister Venizelos was prepared, on his own responsibility, to allow allied troops to land at Salonika, the principal port through which cargo and munitions could reach beleaguered Serbia.

British medical aid had been sent during the first winter of the war, when an epidemic of typhus fever threatened to bring Serbia to her knees. The Serbian military medical organization could not possibly deal with the 70,000 Austrian prisoners now in Serbian hands; typhoid and smallpox also raged, exacerbated by severe shortages of drugs, linen and disinfectants. Various medical missions travelled independently to Serbia and Serbian Relief

Committees were established in Britain, France and America. The husband-and-wife team of Dr James Berry and his wife F. May Dickinson Berry, working under the auspices of the British Red Cross, arrived in Serbia early in 1915.[2] It was considered prudent to take complete British units rather than simply send piecemeal help, because Serbian methods were so different and co-operation was severely hampered by language problems. Dr Berry commented on the deep-seated compulsions that urged the Serbs to battle on for their national homeland:

'National independence is to the Serbs the same tacitly accepted and exalted idea that it was to the Italians in the time of Garibaldi. They hate Austria more than Turkey, because Turkey only scourged their bodies, while Austria has stifled their souls. The only foreigner a Serb fears is the Bulgar, and the moral effect of the entry of Bulgaria into the war [on 15 October, 1915] was obvious and profound. Over all other races, the Serbs are willing to boast their superiority. [For a Serb] it is improper to condole with a mother who has lost her son in war. She is to be congratulated on the honour rather than commiserated on the loss.'[3]

The first unit financed and sent officially by the British Red Cross arrived at Vrntsi in February, 1915, and the Scottish Woman's Hospitals and Serbian Relief Fund units followed, doing sterling work and developing round them an aura of feminine heroism epitomized by doctors like Elsie Inglis and Alice Hutchison. Supported by numerous dedicated and enthusiastic nurses and VADs, they experienced the same hardships as their patients, and were described in the British press as 'these noble women'.

Arthur Martin-Leake, with his well-established distrust of women, read in *The Times* of their exploits during that first year of war with particular interest because of his own experiences in Montenegro in 1912. He had met Serbs and Albanians before, and had forged ongoing friendships with several Montenegrins. Serbia was now being subjected to fierce attacks from Austria-Hungary and to powerful threats from Turkey and Bulgaria, and it was obvious to anyone that without substantial Allied assistance Serbia's future would be in jeopardy. If she fell, Germany would be allowed to connect directly with Turkish forces from Constantinople. The attempt to wrest control of Gallipoli from the Turks, begun with such optimism in April, 1915, was, by the summer, foundering under the combined power of German-reinforced Turkish defensive measures, heat, flies and disease. But Turkey could also be challanged through Salonika and the first British and French troops landed there on 5 October. For three years they were virtual prisoners in the port and its hinterland, unable to make contact with the enemy. A British Naval Mission at Belgrade could not prevent the Serbian capital being overrun by the Austrians, and when Bulgaria declared war on the 14th there was little hope for the Serbian forces.

Arthur read with dismay the accounts in *The Times* as the Serbian forces were increasingly driven into their own mountainous region, trapped between the invading forces and the Adriatic. Fortunately Italy had entered the war on the side of the Allies in May, and her ships, together with supplies provided by Britain and France, were Serbia's best hope of salvation. By the end of October the British Government had decided to send out a 'Mission' to the Serbian Army, on the assumption that part of it might have to fall back through Montenegro and would need to be supplied via the Adriatic.[4] This 'task force', subsequently to be called the 'British Adriatic Mission', commanded by Brigadier-General F. P. S. Taylor of the Army Service Corps, was the unit to which Arthur was summoned by War Office telegram on 22 November. The first party reached Scutari on 24 November, and men of the Royal Engineers were employed in repairing roads. Apart from a small group from Number 143 Field Ambulance, this was the only part of the British Adriatic Mission ever to set foot on Balkan soil.

One wonders why Arthur was plucked from his work behind the trenches of Northern France and sent to the obscurity of the Balkans. The single reason given in later accounts of his war career, namely that his experience in Montenegro three years previously had prepared him, uniquely, for participating in the relief of the Serbian Army, is a valid explanation, but is not the whole story. The General appointed to the command of the Mediterranean Expeditionary Force, in succession to General Sir Ian Hamilton, was Sir Charles Carmichael Monro, a Boer War veteran who had formerly been commanding the Second Division on the Western Front.[5] This was the same General who had recommended Arthur for the Bar to his Victoria Cross. Monro, whose home was in the Craiglockhart district of Edinburgh, had won for himself a reputation for sound judgement and a noteworty realism. Arthur thought quite highly of him.

His first task was to examine ways of relieving Serbia, and there is no doubt that a doctor who was a serving Victoria Cross holder would raise the medical profile of his Command. As Arthur had already noted, the First Army's 'big RAMC man', Surgeon-General W. G. Macpherson, had also been sent to the Balkans as Director of Medical Services at Salonika, and Arthur knew him well. Arthur's years in India would surely be useful in Salonika if he ever got there, where numbers of Indian troops were being deployed. In the event he was unable to exercise his medical skills or employ his experience except in very minor ways, and once again he spent most of his time with the Mission chafing irritably against official restrictions and what he saw as ineffable incompetence. He now understood exactly how Steenie and Dick felt, stuck in England on the sidelines of the war, their talents, in their opinion, wasted.

Victoria Cross holders were certainly being used in propagandist or morale-boosting roles such as recruiting campaigns or encouraging people to invest in War Loans. It may well have been thought in Whitehall that the inclusion of the only 'double V.C.' as a member of the Adriatic Mission would enhance its role and would help to refute suggestions that the British Government had been slow and half-hearted in sending help to Serbia. At the end of October the French Commander-in-Chief, General Joffre, visited London, and the public acclaim accorded to him demonstrated clearly where the sympathies of the British people lay. *The Times* noted:

'The people of this country are as eager as France to save Serbia from ruin. They have been deeply touched by the heroic resist-ance of the entire Serbian race, and are conscious that one of their proudest objects in drawing the sword was to save the smaller nations of Europe from brutal destruction. . . . Serbia will not be left to perish. Extensive preparations are understood to be in progress.'[6]

In Parliament the next day Prime Minister Asquith declared that:

'Serbia may be assured that her independence is regarded by us as one of the essential objects of the Allied Powers.'[7]

But the preparations were, in reality, far from extensive. Arthur wrote home from Paris on the first leg of the train journey to the Adriatic:

'We are making a slow journey. We are going by Rome so it will be new country for me. There are two Montenegrins in our party, and a chap who has lived most of his life in Italy, so the language question is settled.'[8]

Three days later he told his mother:

'We have orders that we are not to go but stay here. All luggage was booked through to Brindisi by another train, so at present we have nothing. Fortunately I had washing and shaving materials with me, so I can carry on. We will probably remain in

Rome for ten days or a fortnight. There seem to be great difficulties in the way, in fact the whole thing is rather in the air at present. We went to the Opera last night and saw all sorts of old things in the afternoon. There is no sign of war at all and the town is very gay and smart. It is rather curious being in a town which is brilliantly lighted at night, after London and Ware.'9

As the days went by his patience began to evaporate. Still no orders came, and the Serbs were complaining that they had been let down by the Allies; Arthur had every sympathy with them:

'We spend our time wandering about seeing the sights of Rome and having quite an interesting time. The various people on this show are scattered about at different hotels in the town and I have not met many of them yet. As far as I can make out the thing is still rather vague and it may be a good long time before anything happens. Why they sent me out in such a hurry I don't know. We got our kit yesterday from Brindisi – a tremendous bill to pay for it. However, we are lucky to get it back whole. . . .

'We went to the Vatican today and saw a little of it. The old Roman things are not so hugely interesting, I find, chiefly because I was a naughty boy at school and did not learn anything about them. They must be very interesting to the good boy who did his lessons well. The people here are very gay and seem to live for the most part in the streets, and on their fiesta days it is difficult to walk along because of the crowds. The place is packed with men of military age, and if they would take the loafers who spend their time selling picture cards etc. they would get a small army. At least this is the impression one gets.

'With regard to our show, I don't know anything about it and have almost forgotten that one is here for any other object than amusement. I can, however, tell you that it is being much cut down and seems to be daily getting smaller. It is quite on the cards that I shall be returned home before long.'10

The British Government's resolve does seem to have been weakening only weeks after the Mission set off for Italy. General Monro was having to direct all of his attention towards the evacuation of the Gallipoli Peninsula, so it was hardly surprising that the Mission's activities were given a much lower priority. But terrible descriptions of Serbian suffering were appearing in the Press as a retreat to the coast began in earnest; thousands of soldiers, and similar numbers of refugees, were trudging painfully through the Montenegrin and Albanian mountains, harassed by the inhabitants of the latter who took their revenge for alleged Serbian oppression in the previous two or three years. Typhus, pneumonia and dysentery raged, the mud threatened, as the soldiers dragged their remaining guns and other equipment with them, and the peasant refugees struggled with their pathetic bundles. Inevitably thousands died, and from the retreat went out a vociferous criticism of the Allies for sending no help. Some British women, the stubborn doctors and nurses whose Scottish Women's Hospitals had been forced to close, were also with the retreating army, and they were in the impossible situation of attempting to explain the lack of Allied response.[11] Astonishingly, the Serbs brought with them more than twenty thousand Austrian prisoners, who had been a burden on resources for many months. Their mortality rate more than equalled that of their disheartened captors.

A contemporary observer thought the Allies emerged from the situation deserving of high praise:

'Perhaps when the history of the war comes to be written, one of the most remarkable feats of the allied navies will be found to be the transportation of Serbia's soldiers to Corfu in less than five weeks without an accident.'[12]

But, as the days went by, Arthur was singularly unimpressed and repeatedly complained of the Mission's inactivity:

'Nobody knows what we are going to do, or if we are going to do anything. As far as one can see this looks like some political business now. They keep saying in the House [of Commons] that the Serbians are to be (or are being) fed and clothed by the English and Italians, so we are kept here to look as if something is being done and to enable our beautiful Government people to give their usual evasive answers. The Italians, for their own reasons, don't want us over there and have put all difficulties in the way. At present it looks very much as if it is going to end in smoke, or at any rate become merely a question of shipping supplies over for the people over there to distribute. It is not advisable to say too much in a letter so I will close on the subject.'[13]

Now the French had also organized a Mission, under the command of General de Mondesir, whose objective was to 'reorganize' the Serbs to fight another day. The efforts of the British Mission, by contrast, were being targetted at simply alleviating the sickness and starvation being endured.

The two Missions knew nothing of each other's existence, until their members met each other 'in the field'. Two days before Christmas Arthur and his colleagues left Rome for Brindisi, but still 'nobody knows what is happening next':

> 'Our big people are in Rome and a few people are somewhere over the other side in Albania. We hear a little foodstuff is being sent across now and then. I expect to stop here indefinitely. There is nothing good to be said about Brindisi (I prefer Rome). The Italians are an absolutely useless lot. They are obstructing any chance of assisting the Serbians either by the French or the English. Their Navy seems to be very contemptible and bolts every time it sees anything.'[14]

On 15 December Italian warships had set out from Brindisi, carrying supplies of food and medicines drawn from stockpiles that the French had organized in the port. The 'few people' in Albania were actually in Durazzo, where a trickle and then a torrent of soldiers, prisoners and refugees began to arrive from the mountains to the east. Supply lines of sorts were slowly being established by the British, French and Italians, although frequent shelling of the supply ships and of the Adriatic ports by the Austrian Navy were a constant hindrance to progress. In Durazzo itself the command was now under Rear-Admiral Troubridge, late of the abortive Naval Mission at Belgrade. Austrian pilots even managed to bomb the town, killing several Serbian officers, and it was all but impossible for the large number of Serbs to be evacuated from the port. The beaten army had to trail wearily through the coastal marshland for a further sixty miles, south to Valona; from there it was hoped they could be taken off by French ships and transported to the island of Corfu. The island was chosen because it seemed to offer the necessary facilities for receiving the troops, and it was sufficiently near to Salonika to enable the Serbs, when re-equipped and fit again, to take part in further military operations there. On 11 January the French established control over Corfu by putting ashore a squadron which was to prepare for the arrival of the Serbian Army.

Because there was so much sickness, it was decided to send medical reinforcements out from England and a detachment from Number 143 Field Ambulance was despatched to Durazzo. The new men travelled through Brindisi and passed on the latest rumours from England. Arthur commented:

> 'I understand there are some more doctors and men coming out shortly. Why more doctors it is not easy to understand. There are many mosquitoes and much malaria here. We hear many

accounts of the Kaiser's cancer and the latest rumour, brought by a man who has just come out of England, is that he is dead. I hope this is not true, as a long illness will be good for him.'[15]

He was concerned with the situation at Durazzo and feared that the whole Mission might soon have to be written off:

'I believe there is only one possible move which the show [the Mission] can make now, probably even it is hopeless and medical staff will not be able to bolster it up for much longer. You may see me before long.'[16]

The move he referred to was to Corfu with the wretched remnants of the Serbian Army, and on 28 January he and his colleagues were taken to the island by a French naval vessel. He was appalled at what they found there. The British Adriatic Mission seemed to have foundered completely:

'I have moved on to an island further south. A large consignment of doctors has arrived and with every possible stretch of the imagination there is only work for 2 or 3. We are in the ultimate stage of chaos here, and are absolutely wallowing in ineptitude. Experience gained with this 'Bally Awful Muddle' has filled me with much sympathy for Steenie and Dick. One knew nothing about this side of the Army in France. The French have taken over this island and we are trying to establish ourselves also. The whole Question seems a complicated one and there is more in it than feeding the Serbians.'[17]

He managed to take a few photographs of dispirited Serbs, but almost before he knew it he found himself back in Rome. The waste of time did nothing for his temper:

'Returned to Rome this morning from Corfu. We were in the island for 5 days. The Serbians are arriving there now at the rate of 4-5,000 per diem, so the whole army will soon be around. The French are in possession of the island and are putting themselves in sole charge of the Serbian Army. We went, as far as I can understand, to try to get a finger into the pie. The situation is most involved. The medical arrangements are most inadequate and not much is being done for the sick Serbs. They all look pretty bad and the French doctor in charge says that about half are sick. They die at the rate of 100 per diem.'[18]

With his next letter home Arthur enclosed a cutting from *The Times* of 2 February. Censorship about what help was reaching the Serbs had been firmly exercised by the French authorities, and so far there had been only vague reports in the press. Now the rules had been somewhat relaxed, but the *Times* correspondent, based in Rome, gave a totally erroneous account of the situations in Arthur's opinion. The report stated that

'the retreat of the Serbian troops to the coast has only been rendered possible by the co-operation of the British, the French, and the Italians. Food has been supplied by the British and French jointly. The Italians have provided most of the shipping and escorts necessary to transport it across the Adriatic. Its distribution has been arranged for by the members of the British Adriatic Mission under General F. P. S. Taylor, C.M.G. . . .

'The very difficult situation created by the co-operation of three separate authorities and the complicated division of labour have been dealt with satisfactorily, and if there has been some delay the results attained and expected speak most highly for the good will of all concerned.

'The work providing supplies was in the hands of the British Mission, but could never have been accomplished without the ready and generous co-operation of the Italians. The Italian Army made jetties, unloaded ships, transferred food to the coasting steamers, provided mule transport, and in short supplied all the means for getting the food from the base depots to the Serbians. The Italians have also done a great deal of valuable work making and improving roads in their sphere.'[19]

Arthur's reaction to this version of events was scathing in its criticism, both of the Press and of the BAM:

'When I met the *Times* reporter here yesterday I told him it was one big lie from beginning to end; his only excuse was that it had been given to him ready-made by the Mission. Told him his paper was disgraced for ever by putting in such stuff. You can see plainly from this account what is being done to bolster up this miserable show. The whole thing has been the most outrageous muddle from beginning to end and a perfect scandal. Men, material and money have been squandered right and left. The work accomplished could have been done by William Whiteley & Co [a local Hertfordshire firm of furniture removers] with two men and a boy. Our staff are now trying to bluff the world by sending these lying accounts to the papers. I hear, now, that the work is all over in Albania; they are advising that the different departments should be kept out here to prepare some country (unknown at present) for the advance of the Serbian Army (as yet unorganized or even collected together). The main principle of the Missions has been, all along, to keep going on the largest possible scale with the largest possible staff so as to make a very big display.

'There are not too many jobs going in these days which offer the comforts and luxury of the best Hotel in Rome, and when such a job is obtained it must be kept at all costs. I believe if this Mission could become the subject of an inquiry it would show up as one of the greatest scandals of the war. The staff alone is wonderful; there are about 700 officers and men all told. To run this, there is in Rome one General with 3 Staff Officers and 5 motor cars, a Postal Department with an officer and many men, a Records Office with one officer and many men, and, they say, tons of material. Inland water transport – 12 officers and many men. Army Service Corps – 3 Colonels, many other officers and men. Engineering Department – 1 Colonel and many officers and men, together with 1 officer and a complete air-line equipment [sic]. Medical organization large enough for half a division.

'The only excuse is that the Mission in the first instance was to have been a big show. It was intended that it should have lines of communication far into Serbia so as to keep the Serbs fighting in the field. It was obvious before it started from home that the opportunity had been missed and it was too late. When we got here it was quite obvious that the most the Mission would do would be to feed the Serbians at the ports of Albania, or at most send a certain amount of food a short way inland. Instead of the staff being reduced to meet the new requirements, it has been kept up as far as possible to the original size. Even now attempts are being made to keep it to its full strength.'[20]

And still the Serbs were landing at Corfu; by 11 February 75,000 were on the island. A number had also been taken to Bizerta, the French naval port in Tunisia. Some elements of the British Mission remained, and a few personnel were sent on with the Serbs to Salonika in the early summer. But Arthur's service with the Mission was over. On 19 February he wrote with heavy sarcasm:

'As a matter of fact the Mission is only being allowed to exist at all by the kindness of the French, because its wails and lamentations on the shores of Corfu were so piteous when it was thought it would have to go home.'[21]

Ten days later he went to Naples for a few days' 'holiday', and on 6 March returned to England. On the same day coincidentally, General Taylor left Rome for Corfu to make arrangements for a new British Mission to the Serbian Army, command being exercised by Taylor's Chief of Staff, Lieutenant-Colonel W. C. Garsia. The French General Mondesir was to be in overall command, and every effort was made to reorganize the tattered Serbian Army once again. By May, 1916, 125,000 Serbs had been transferred to Salonika where they did indeed fight another day, albeit within the restrictions of what had become known as the Allies' 'largest internment camp'. The last remnants of the British Adriatic Mission left the Balkans on 18 July.[22]

At home in High Cross Arthur enjoyed two weeks' leave before returning to France. It transpired that there had been great excitement in the village because the vicar, the Rev F. A. Overton, was being moved, after twenty-three years, to a new parish at East Barnet. Arthur rather unkindly commented that 'it will be a good thing to get Mrs Overton out of the place'.[23] He had always found Mrs Overton to be a gossip and a busybody, but then he thought that about most women. His mother had certainly enjoyed the friendship of the vicar's wife, and would miss her frequent visits, particularly as old age and ill health took their toll. Both Arthur and his brother Frank often wrote to their eighty-year-old mother, advising her to take things slowly and rest more. She enjoyed sitting under the old mulberry tree in the Marshalls garden, or being pushed around the country lanes in her reclining wicker invalid carriage. At New Year, 1916, she wrote to Arthur's brother Willie:

'Thank you very much from us all for your good wishes. It is so very delightful to think you wish me many more New Years, for I give trouble to you all. Still, I love to be with you and you are all so very good to me. . . . The Kaiser is in the fashion, a boil on his neck – lots in our village. All are well here. Taxes are very high, I pay off my bills as they come, in case money may vanish, but I get used to it all and am happy over it.'[24]

Georgiana was living at home and was no doubt a great comfort to her mother. Bella's work in the convalescent hospital kept her away for many hours each day, and her own health deteriorated as a result of her work; she suffered from boils (like the Kaiser), and from nervous exhaustion, both of which necessitated several weeks' residence in a nursing home. Dick and Steenie were both in the Territorial Force reserve, serving at Watford and Woolwich respectively, but by 1916 Steenie had more or less retired. Dick had purchased a motor cycle and roared up the Marshalls drive every weekend. Willie was, by the middle of 1915, receiving 'Retired Pay', but still active as a Staff Captain in the Department of the Adjutant-General to the Forces. Promoted in 1917, he spent the remainder of the war in the Department and lived in Kensington.

The Zeppelin menace, which had begun in January, 1915, was the main threat to the tranquillity of Marshalls, and on several occasions there were alarms when the silent airships passed overhead. Bombs had been dropped on Hertford in October, 1915, and quite frequently jittery observers caused false alerts. Mrs Martin-Leake was always fearful and exhausted by these, although Steenie and Dick used to leave the house in great excitement to patrol the lanes and fields 'just in case'. In April a genuine raid passed close by, and Arthur's mother described it to Willie:

'We did not know till the morning. Steenie and Sittie heard something but were too sleepy to realize. We suppose tonight will bring them again. I long to hear you had no waiting about from the Zepp. A balloon has just gone over here; it did not seem quite in order. Steenie tells me it had been down at Wadesmill; it was short of gas and turned out three men.'[25]

Willie, who had been on his way back to Kensington, had indeed had something of an adventure:

'Just a line to tell you how I got caught last night. Clapton 10.20 p.m., train stopped – all lights out – air-raid guns soon began – H. E. [High Explosive] bursts quite good – very cold – no means of getting on with the journey – all trains stopped. All Clear at 12.20 a.m. No move on the part of the train until 1.20 a.m. Stopped at Hackney Downs and Bethnal Green and several times in between. Arrived Liverpool Street 1.45 a.m., no tube, underground or taxi. Went to Liverpool Street Hotel, got last empty bedroom, Number 376. No lift – opened door of bedroom, turned on light, found two beds with a man in each. Went down to Manager. Very sorry, meant 276. Got new key, told porter to call me at 7 a.m., got to bed at 2.45 a.m. Called at 6 a.m. Damn the Huns. No definite news of damage. On Saturday night, they appear to have dropped a bomb on the Officers' quarters at

Chelsea Hospital. Last night St Pancras Station Hotel, Fleet Street and Woolwich seem to have some beastliness dropped on them. To Hell with the Kaiser.'[26]

When Arthur arrived at Marshalls he found anti-aircraft guns in a neighbouring field, and his family full of talk about the apparent dangers from the air. But the garden was flourishing, seeds were being planted in the vegetable patches and the house was being kept in a good state of repair by Dick and Steenie. He noticed that the household cats had multiplied greatly, and there was a profusion of tame guinea pigs. Life seemed really very peaceful, but, after the fiasco in the Adriatic, he was quite glad to return to France. He received orders to report himself to Casualty Clearing Station Number 30 and left England on 22 March, 1916.

CHAPTER THIRTEEN

'I Am No Soldier . . .'

'This is quite a new part of the country for me. It seems a much more interesting district than any I have been in so far. A CCS [Casualty Clearing Station] is of course quite a new experience and I don't understand much about the working of it yet. This one has only been here a week and is not yet established in its permanent quarters, consequently we are in rather a muddle. The permanent place is a French hutted hospital and the French have only just left it. The huts are very good and everything is substantial and well done, except the choice for the site and the sanitary arrangements. The site is bad because it is a wet and low-lying bit of ground. The sanitary arrangements are characteristic of this country but our people are already on to them. A CCS is the next step from a Field Ambulance. They are situated back from the fighting area and on railways so that trains can come up and empty them frequently. All serious cases are operated on and kept if necessary till they can be moved.'[1]

Arthur's first letter home from his new posting helped to reassure his mother that he was not in any danger. 30 CCS had just arrived in the village of Aubigny, a few miles north-west of Arras, where part of the supporting infrastructure for the forthcoming Battle of the Somme was being put in place. By this stage of the war the system of medical treatment and evacuation of casualties had become both sophisticated and reliable, and Arthur had described the role of the Casualty Clearing Station very accurately. Although CCSs were originally intended to be mobile, i.e. moveable in eight or nine three-ton lorries, the nature of trench warfare had led to them becoming static units. As the months went by they were supplied with improved equipment, and skilled surgeons were often drafted in from civilian life, so that detailed surgery could be done there and fewer cases had to be sent back to the Base Hospitals. The personnel of the CCS consisted typically of eight medical officers (one of whom would be a dentist) and seventy-seven other ranks, with three chaplains and a number of nursing sisters – five originally in 1915, later increasing to seven. A distance of at least 12,000 to 14,000 yards from the front line was deemed safe for a CCS.[2]

A Motor Ambulance Convoy, or sometimes a light railway, or even a barge, would bring the injured and sick from the Advanced Dressing Stations near the fighting to the extensive tented or hutted hospitals waiting to receive them. Three or four CCSs would often be grouped together, each with perhaps 800 beds. The aim of the medical staff at a CCS was firstly to ensure that any man who could be rendered fit should be returned at once to the Front. A prime reason for setting up these hospitals at all was that they were aimed at reducing the numbers of men who might have to be evacuated from a battle area; evacuation was costly, both in terms of manpower and of vehicles and fuel.

If a man did have to be removed from the CCS because he would receive more appropriate treatment elsewhere, he would be sent 'down the line' to one of the large Base hospitals at places like Etaples or Boulogne. From there he might be given a 'Blighty ticket' to a military hospital in the United Kingdom. Of course, a CCS would find many of its beds filled, especially in the immediate aftermath of an attack, with men whose condition was so bad that they could not be moved. Serious casualties often died at the CCS to which they had first been taken, so it is not surprising that the position of each CCS was soon marked by a military cemetery in an adjacent field. Today the regular lines of graves denote to the visitor that here men died in their beds, and usually there would have been time for a proper funeral, even if the funeral service was, of necessity, shortened.

The Commanding Officer of the CCS was usually a Lieutenant-Colonel, and Arthur, with the rank of Major, was second-in-command of Number 30. While his spirits may have slumped at the sight of the nursing sisters, he would certainly have brightened up when he saw the full operating facilities available. And, generally speaking, Mrs Martin-Leake could rest easy in the knowledge that her son was safe, although occasionally the Red Cross flag flying over the CCS was not enough to protect it from aerial attack.

The first few weeks at Aubigny were very quiet, with little more than everyday illnesses to be dealt with. The French and British High Commands were moving up men and munitions in enormous quantities, in preparation for 'The Big Push' on the Somme, the area between the Rivers Ancre and Somme forming the starting-point for the British part of the attack. Rumours abounded, and Arthur wrote home on 29 June:

'Everything seems to point to the Bosch having serious times and it looks as if one time is not far ahead.'[3]

The preliminary bombardment of the German positions was noisy enough; when the attack itself began on 1 July with the detonation of nineteen enormous mines beneath German strongpoints it is certain that the staff of 30 CCS were shaken by the distant thunder. But still they waited, too far from the action to have any realistic expectation that casualties might be transported as far as Aubigny. While thousands of British soldiers were being killed or were lying wounded in the open under the hot July sun, Arthur and his colleagues had nothing to do. Indeed, they believed, falsely, that the battle was going well for the Allies. On 3 July Arthur wrote to his mother that 'the news is good'; though a few wounded trickled in from the northern end of the line, he continued to believe until 18 July that the Germans had been practically routed.

Then came an urgent summons for medical personnel to be transferred to hospitals in the Albert region, where Casualty Clearing Stations were labouring under the huge wave of wounded that threatened to overwhelm them. Arthur's surgical skills were in great demand for the six weeks he was there, but out of concern for his mother he filled his letters home with comments not about the war but about the countryside:

'It is quite nice country in these parts and the crops are very fine. No leave is likely, so I don't expect to see your strawberry crop this season. I hope the crops are bad in Germany to help finish this show.'[4]

By the middle of August he was again writing optimistically:

'The crops here are good. The French are wonderful agricultur-ists and it is surprising the way they keep the land going during wartime. The Somme is a great river for fish and angling is most popular, British on one side and French on the other. As far as I have seen the Frenchman understands more about his fish than the Englishman. The Germans are being pushed back. I went to see our newly-acquired territory the other day, it is interesting to see, and the German fortifications are wonderful. Steenie and Dick should be pleased with the Army they have helped to train. We seem to be still gaining ground slowly, but the most important thing is we are killing plenty of Germans.'[5]

In September he was allowed three weeks' leave. He found that in the south of England a big attraction was to go and see the site of the crashed Schutte-Lanz airship SL11, which had been shot down over Cuffley, some ten miles south of High Cross, by the Royal Flying Corps on 3 September; the pilot credited with the 'kill', Lieutenant W. Leefe Robinson, was awarded the Victoria Cross within forty-eight hours of the action.[6] Arthur and his brothers were very taken with the wreckage which burned for three days, and by the stories being told by locals of how they saw the airship caught in the beams of the searchlights.

It appears that Arthur was particularly impressed by the exploit of Lieutenant Leefe Robinson; for the first time he openly showed an interest in flying, a fascination that was only to be satisfied much later in his life. For now, he was prepared to give up his wartime medical role and join the Royal Flying Corps. Some months later he wrote to Major-General Sir Maurice Holt, a former colleague:

> 'I am now at a CCS and learning this war surgery. It is all new to me and I am fortunate to be under a really good surgical specialist. I left the RAMC last September and joined the RFC, but the ADMS expressed a wish that I should come back as he was very short of Medical Officers, so of course I had to. It was a great disappointment as I have always had a great wish to fly.'[7]

He did not tell his family of this brief flirtation. Instead he returned on 10 October to Number 30 CCS at Aubigny. The Battle of the Somme was grinding to a close with Allied casualties of 750,000, exceeding those of the Germans, and public unease was so great that, at home, Asquith's government fell by the end of the year. But Arthur still found himself with too much time on his hands. A day or two were taken up in moving to a different billet in order to escape a manure heap under his window, and he discussed the question of food rationing that was being aired in the papers. He approved of it.[8] His reaction to German prisoners-of-war who turned up for treatment was predictable:

> 'I have two Huns in my ward at present. Took the appendix out of one yesterday and should like to do some more to him if there was any possible excuse. He was very fat and they are being fed too well in the camps, considering the way our people are being treated in Germany. The other speaks English a bit, and says he doesn't want to Straff England and is very glad to be over this side.'[9]

A meeting at this time between Arthur and an RAMC orderly is recorded in the Diary of Private G. H. Swindell of 77 Field Ambulance, who was sent to 30 CCS for three weeks' duty at the end of 1916. The description is revealing of the awe in which experienced soldiers and Victoria Cross holders were held by the ranks, although Private Swindell was mistaken in thinking that Arthur was a Regular:

'Some of us were sitting in a ward and in came an Officer, he was rather a gentle looking individual, but we knew he was a regular by the South African ribbons. He spoke to several of the patients and on going out called me over, asked me all about the Ambulance. I must have been talking with him for half an hour. I was very much surprised when he got up to leave me, for him to pat me on the back and say, "Well, young man, you will all have a lot more to do before this ghastly business is over. I wish you the best of luck and play hard and work hard, like you have, and that is all you can do, but above all remember the Corps you belong to, and let no man deride it." He shook me by the hand and off I went. [I was told the next day] he was Major Leake, double VC, the only man in Britain who had ever won the V.C. and a Bar'[10]

But *Arthur* could 'deride the Corps', and did so freely as the war continued and he expressed what he regarded as justifiable criticism of his superiors. He only disparaged them to his family, however; Arthur was no fool, and fully realized the importance of loyalty and commitment if the men were to give of their best. As an officer, and drawing on his experience in South Africa and India, he accepted that one of his most significant duties was to instil these qualities into the men who served under him. He was right about 'this ghastly business'; it had a long way to go yet, and morale must be maintained. Many years later a fellow doctor described Arthur's conduct under fire at 30 CCS. While others scrambled for safety into a shallow trench dug for the purpose, Arthur sat reading in a deckchair, as if nothing at all were happening around him.[11]

On 18 December President Woodrow Wilson repeated his efforts to end the war by negotiation; he sent a formal Note to the belligerent powers, a note which contained the unfortunate sentence, 'The objects which the belligerents on both sides have in mind are virtually the same'. Arthur was aghast at the idea that the aims of the British war effort might be the same as Germany's, especially as the Americans were not even in the war yet:

'You are no doubt full of surprise over old Wilson's Note, like the rest of the world. It fairly puts the cap on it when he says we are all fighting for the same thing. These Yanks really are the extreme limit, and when their turn comes they are not likely to get much sympathy or help. Everybody here has unbounded confidence in Lloyd George and he will fix them up alright.'[12]

So here was the third Christmas of the war, with no more likelihood of an early end to the fighting than in 1914 or 1915. Arthur was in charge of the hospital during the festivities when the Commanding Officer went home on leave. He was now coming across men of many different nationalities:

'We have an extraordinary number of patients in hospital now – Japs, Russians, Americans, and we have had one Swede. The reason for this is because the Canadians are here and they have a lot of these foreigners with them. . . . I am hoping the weather will be soft when I next have leave, so that cultivation can be carried on [at Marshalls]. If there is plenty of manure in readiness I can start off on preparing the potato patches. You will want every bit of ground possible put under cultivation for the potato crops.'[13]

Rumours flew about that the Americans would soon enter the war. Many 'Yanks' were already at the front privately or with the Red Cross, and Arthur came across one of them in the middle of January:

'A very amusing thing has happened here. A Yank doctor started last summer with some wonderful apparatus and proposed to be able to take photography by wireless. He showed some wonderful pictures of the brain and other organs damaged by bullets. The story goes that he also killed a cow at a long distance and showed a Zeppelin passing over on a very dark night. The authorities took it up, especially some of the big medical people, and gave him much money and opportunities to carry out his research. This went on for a long time, before they found out that he was one big fraud. He has now got 18 months. The whole thing is being kept very dark.'[14]

The weather that month became very severe, and when he arrived home for two weeks' leave it was impossible to do any gardening at all. In any case Arthur was more concerned with his mother's health; she seemed to be deteriorating with every day that passed, particularly as the weather was so cold. Ponds and streams around High Cross froze, and he was reminded of earlier peacetime days when they all used to go skating with the Giles-Pullers. By mid-March, though, back at Aubigny, both the weather and the progress of the war seemed to be improving:

'We had tremendous excitement here yesterday. A Bosch flying-machine was brought down close by. All turned out, as well as the civilian population, and the show reminded me very much of the visits to see the Zepp. last September, only it was on a smaller scale, fitting the bird. The Bosch was whole, unfortunately, and they say he was glad to surrender. We have heard the news that old Count Zepp. has died. Hope he is frizzling now like the Bosches he sent over England. At any rate it is nice to think he lived to see the complete rout of his machines.'[15]

He was now offered the chance to command his own Field Ambulance, and while in the medical sense this was something of a backward step in that the chance of surgery would be very slight, yet he thought it would be more interesting to be a little nearer the action once again:

'I have been here a year now and shall be sorry to leave the work and comfort. It is, however, an old man's job and I shall be better pleased doing something more active.'[16]

As he approached his forty-third birthday he did not regard himself as in any way 'past it'. Nevertheless he was nervous about his new role in command of 46 Field Ambulance, serving with the 15th (Scottish) Division:

'Don't be surprised if you see me following other amateur soldiers in getting the Order of the Boot before long. I am no soldier and shall probably soon make a mess of my new show.[17]

The Ambulance was situated in the suburbs on the western side of Arras, where the Third Army was deployed in preparation for the forthcoming pushes to the east. The Germans had, since February, been carrying out a massive withdrawal (Operation 'Alberich') between the Aisne and the Ancre, in order to shorten their line and consolidate on a newly fortified position that became known as the Hindenburg Line. In the Arras region, however, particularly in the Vimy Ridge area to the north, the German front line remained very close to that of the allies, and the Anglo-French plan in the spring of 1917 was to dislodge the enemy from its strongholds. The plan was largely the proposal put forward by the fiery Third Army Commander, General Sir Edmund Allenby in February, 1917.

The British First Army under General Sir Henry Horne included four Canadian divisions, which were commanded by Lieutenant-General the Hon Sir Julian H. G. Byng, and to them fell the task of the assault on Vimy Ridge, two previous attempts by the French having failed, with enormous

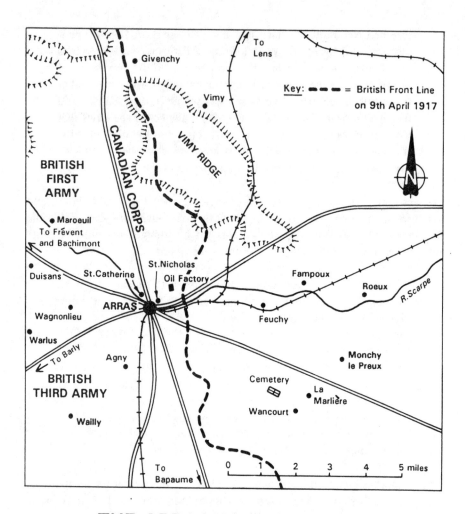

THE ARRAS SECTOR - 1917

numbers of casualties. Under Vimy a complex network of tunnels was constructed, and under Arras a system of medieval caves and tunnels – the 'Boves' – was adapted to be used in the battle. The Citadel of Arras, part of the seventeenth century fortifications carried out by Vauban, was to appear frequently in Arthur's record of 46 Field Ambulance's work, but he referred to his section of it, protruding out from the main city wall to the north west, as 'The Bastion'.

At one o'clock in the afternoon of 19 March he was installed as Commanding Officer of the Ambulance. He began the task of completing the unit's War Diary, which he wrote every day for the next fifteen months:

'Took over command of 46th. Field Ambulance at 1 pm yester-day. This morning went to see ADMS at DUISANS but found he was out. Inspected the horse lines at that place. Found the Highland Division [51st] horses and mules in good condition, but some of the riding horses are not very grand. Captain Day tells me they had a very rough time on the Somme and poor food. I understand they are improving now under the better conditions and feeding. Inspected the medical arrangements of the Ambulance and the building. Visited the Bastion and looked into the work going on there.'[18]

Obviously his main task was to establish lines of communication, transport of the wounded, and accommodation for the numerous casualties that were sure to be brought in once the battle commenced. On his second day he received his orders from the ADMS and scoured the once-beautiful town of Arras for locations with potential as Aid Posts:

'Took over some cellars in Rue des Martenaux as a Dressing Station for the Brigade in that area. Sent a working party to have it cleaned out. Visited the Left Relay Post which is under preparation. Started making another exit in the Bastion to the south side in case the exit at present in use should become impossible. The wall is about 10 feet thick and it will take some time. Two sections of 47th F.A. got shelled coming into the town last night and unfortunately suffered casualties. Captain Robin-son was killed and Captain Blake was wounded.
[22 March] 'Some alterations have been made in the bastion to the gas defence arrangements, as some of the openings were not completely protected. Horse blankets have been put up at the entrance. New exit hole is progressing. Another water tank has been put in and this will make a supply of over 600 gallons. The cellars in Rue des Martenaux are now in use. . . . Work continues on left Relay Post and we have taken over two old dugouts close to it, for more accommodation for [stretcher] bearers. Enemy shelling becomes more active and there have been a good many casualties admitted from different parts of the town.'[19]

The attack was due to begin on 9 April, so the intervening days were fully occupied in making preparations. It was planned that a Horse Ambulance should take the wounded back to the village of Wagnonlieu, and Arthur walked or rode over the route several times, but was ultimately pessimistic about its usefulness; it was a third class road full of potholes and almost impassable in wet weather. So another cellar was taken over in Arras, in the Rue de Rosatis, so that if men could not be evacuated they could at least be reasonably well housed. But within twenty-four hours this cellar was needed for something else, so the Ambulance had to move everything out again. Arthur tried to get hold of some space in the cellars beneath Arras Prison but was unsuccessful at first; ultimately the Ambulance was given these cellars and ordered to use them for the treatment of German prisoners. A path and a ramp had to be constructed to enable walking wounded to leave the Bastion, and one of Arthur's least pleasant tasks was to inspect the town's sewers to see if they could be utilized. He visited the Ecole Normale, situated near the Prison on the north-west side of the town, and had two cellars there cleaned out ready for use. He planned, once the attack had begun, to post a small party there to escort casualties to the Main Dressing Station in the Bastion.

In the middle of it all he found time to write home:

> 'We are in a very old town which you often see mentioned in the communiqués. It has been very much knocked about and most of the old buildings of interest have been destroyed. There are still a few inhabitants here. They stop because of the opportunity they have of making money. The French shopkeeper is a regular Jew and nothing will move him when he is making huge profits.'[20]

Good news had arrived from Marshalls on 31 March: Frank, still commanding HMS *Achilles,* an armoured cruiser of 13,550 tons, had been on the 'Northern Patrol' with the armed boarding steamer *Dundee.* On 16 March, 1917, they had engaged the German cruiser *Leopard* and sunk her with all hands. In June Frank was decorated with the Distinguished Service Order for this feat[21] and Arthur was delighted:

> 'I call it absolutely magnificent and send him my very best congratulations. The satisfaction of having got a really satisfactory 'coup' in must be intense, especially in his case. I should certainly get drunk tonight, only the circumstances are such that one cannot.'[22]

The *Achilles'* ensign was eventually placed in the church at High Cross, where it may still be seen; a brass plaque commemorates six men from the *Dundee* who lost their lives in the incident.

April was ushered in by severe weather, cold winds and snowfalls adding to the misery of the troops preparing for the attack. Arthur was promoted to Temporary Lieutenant-Colonel on 3 April, and the next day he and his staff moved to their 'battle stations' around the town; notice boards were put up both in the streets and in the trenches, directing walking wounded to the nearest Aid Posts. German shells were causing constant damage and streets were being blocked with rubble every day, but Arthur had to try to ensure they were kept clear, as stretchers would be held up otherwise. On the 7th he took his command position in the Bastion, annoyed because the Field Ambulance's motor cars were taken away and added to the general pool, leaving the Ambulance to rely entirely on the Motor Ambulance Convoy. He resented the loss of flexibility entailed by this development. He made strong representations to the ADMS about it but received no concessions. His annoyance was increased by the fact that eleven clerks were now attached to the 15th Division and nine padres; they took up valuable room and had to be accommodated in the Ecole Normale.

In Arras, zero hour, which was 5.30 am on Monday 9 April, was awaited, perhaps with more apprehension than eagerness in the minds of men who remembered the Somme; 46 Field Ambulance was as prepared as it could be, and had only a short time to wait before casualties began streaming back. Up on Vimy Ridge General Byng had declared, 'On Zero Day, the Canadian Corps will capture Vimy Ridge',[23] and certainly by 12 April the ridge was theirs. Further south, the Battle of Arras lasted for almost six weeks, and only officially came to an end on 17 May.

On the day the attack began hundreds of German prisoners began to arrive and had to be interned in the Prison. Arthur was pleased with the way the injured arriving at the Bastion were being quickly dealt with and evacuated where possible. In spite of his earlier doubts the Motor Ambulance Convoy system was working well:

'The MAC have taken the cases away quite as fast as we could put them through and they now have plenty of motor buses running. The horse ambulances are taking the lighter cases for the first 36 hours over part of the road to Wagnonlieu, and then sitting cases were sent by motor ambulance direct to Warlus. Several cases which started by horse wagon had to be taken to CCS, because they could not get further. The bearers have been working very hard and are getting done up. They are doing relay bearing between 45 FA at FEUCHY and the Oil Factory. There has been a heavy fall of snow and the weather is very cold. The ground is in a dreadful state of mud and bearing work is very heavy. I tried to get some help for the bearers but without success. Captain Proud captured a German dugout and took 30 prisoners; they were glad to surrender and did not show any signs of resistance. The German wounded have been attended by 2 of their own doctors who were captured. This has enabled me to withdraw the MO from the Prison to work in the Bastion.'[24]

An idea of the work done by 46 Field Ambulance may be obtained by the evacuation figures; on 10 April fifty-seven officers and 2692 Other Ranks passed through and were moved on; on 11 April ten officers and 1299 Other Ranks, and on 12 April twenty-three officers and 2421 Other Ranks. In the War Diary Arthur made some medical comments about this tide of wounded men:

'A great many cases came in walking which had to be put on stretchers as soon as possible owing to the seriousness of their wounds. A very large proportion of the cases were quite slight and did not require re-dressing. Perhaps the most noticeable feature was the number of cases requiring re-dressing on account of the tightness of the bandages. Wounds of every part of the body were seen and about the only class of case we did not get was fractures of the long bones of the lower limbs. Many chest wounds and a certain number of abdominal cases walked down. Taking the cases as a whole they exhibited the most wonderful example of pluck and physical endurance that it would be possible to see anywhere. Many slight cases got through that should not have done so, but the difficulty of keeping them was too great as there was no place to send them. Some cases were handed over to the Military Police when they [the MPs] came round. We could have handed over more if the Police had been in constant attendance.'[25]

Numbers of men, it would seem, welcomed the slightest chance of getting away from the fighting. But Arthur was delighted with the progress being made, and wrote to his mother:

'I hope you like the news in the papers. The weather had been awful and of course the country is a sight of mud, and movement is most difficult. . . . It is most satisfactory to hear that we have taken Vimy. I was in those parts [Aubigny] a whole year.'[26]

After a lull lasting a few days, pressure on the Ambulance began again, and five extra Medical Officers were sent out. On 26 April a further Advanced Aid Post was established at La Marlière to the south-east of Arras:

'This has made an excellent Dressing Station and the motor and horse ambulances have been able to go up on the WANCOURT road as far as the cemetery [Tigris Lane or Hibers Trench] so evacuation has been easy. The collecting has been difficult on account of machine-gun fire and snipers. Shell fire has also been very heavy.'[27]

On 28 April it was deemed that the 15th Division had had enough, and it was sent back to a rest area. The Field Ambulance was to continue to run the Corps Dressing Station in the Arras Bastion, but not many men were coming through and one Medical Officer could manage the work. During April Arthur's Field Ambulance had treated 230 officers and 13,491 Other Ranks, and six of its non-commissioned officers were awarded the Military Medal.[28]

On 7 May the Ambulance was moved to 18 Corps at Barly, a few miles west of Arras, and at midday Arthur handed over the Bastion to Captain Castello of the 2/3 London Field Ambulance. At Barly, where the main job was to collect and treat the sick of 46th Infantry Brigade, the Ambulance found themselves in a good hutted camp with plenty of accommodation and good stabling. The men were drilled and inspected, and equipment and transport was repaired or replaced. Of course, no sooner had they established themselves (and Arthur was even thinking of planting a vegetable garden), then they were moved again; as he said to his mother 'Two or three more of these moves will take us to the sea.'[29] But this time the move was only to Bachimont west of Frévent where Divisional Headquarters was situated, and Arthur was billetted in the château:

'There is accommodation in the Château for six officers and 45 men. The equipment is mostly Red Cross material. It is well fitted up but most of the crockery has been broken. At present there is only material for 3 officers. The linen on the beds is in a dirty state and will all require washing before it can be used. The water supply is difficult as there is only one pump in the adjoining farm and a very deep well in the village which we can use. The water carts will have a long distance to go, and the washing question for the personnel will be difficult. The only water supply for the horses is the deep well; it takes 5 minutes to get up a bucket of water. A water working party will have to be at work all day to fill the trough.'[30]

They soon replaced buckets with beer barrels, but it still took several hours to water the horses. The problems of a Field Ambulance were not confined to matters of medicine. But Arthur was quite enchanted with the Bachimont district:

> 'This is quite the best part of France that I have been in, very hilly and large woods – beautiful to look at this time of year. The woods are said to contain badgers, foxes and wild pig. The wild pig question is being investigated and yesterday we found a family and very nearly caught some squeakers but they got away in the thick undergrowth. They look very much like the baby Indian pig and show the same striped markings. Just at the bottom of the field here in front of the Château there is a wood full of fine beech trees, and a company of Canadian foresters are working at felling them. They have a sawmill working. These Canadians are real backwoodsmen and it is a treat to see them felling and cutting up timber.'[31]

There was little medical work for Arthur to do, and he was irritated, as one might expect, by the 'brass hats' who would keep visiting the unit, but as he said, 'this is part of the Army and has to be put up with'.[32] From 1-12 June he went home on leave, and spent most of his time gardening at Marshalls. Two issues that were earnestly discussed by the family were a strike in the munitions industry and the Daylight Saving Movement. The long drawn-out industrial dispute convinced Arthur that as usual the workers would win everything and make no concessions, and the situation gave him no cause for optimism about industrial peace after the war. Daylight Saving had been in force since the previous summer, generating considerable economies in fuel consumption in industry, and was now being applied to the Army in France, where Arthur managed to ignore it, finding that it made no difference to the time at which he woke up. At home, arguments made against it included the fact that the Germans and Austrians already followed the practice of putting the clocks forward, and this seemed to many an excellent reason why Britons should not.[33]

When he returned from leave Arthur discovered that an American doctor had been sent to 46 Field Ambulance to learn something of the work. This was J. A. Campbell Colston, whose Diary of his time with the unit comments on the Commanding Officer's reputation for 'utter fearlessness'.[34] Arthur thought Colston seemed 'quite a nice chap', and was pleased to note that the Americans, now that they had entered the war, did not intend to be 'slack' about it.[35] Meanwhile, plans were being made for another great 'Push' by the Allies, this time in Flanders, an attack that had as its objective the taking of the Passchendaele ridge north-east of Ypres. At Bachimont Château the Field Ambulance began to pack up, to move with its Division to Belgium.

An NCO and two men were left in charge of the furniture in the Château until arrangements could be made for the Red Cross to collect its property. Arthur was very impressed with the entraining procedure that was carried out at Frévent:

> 'All arrangements were very complete and rapidly carried out by a party of 9th Gordons. We had nothing to do except look on, and it was a very gratifying sight to see this regiment work in such a wonderful way.'[36]

In the early hours of 18 June he was back in Flanders for the first time since January, 1915.

CHAPTER FOURTEEN

'War Is a Fearful Waste'

As the men of 46 Field Ambulance trudged along the Poperinghe-Ypres road towards their camp in the village of Brandhoek they could not help but be aware that an enormous concentration of men and materials was being built up in this area behind the shell-shattered town of Ypres. It was no secret that the British High Command had determined to follow through the recent success in the Arras region with a huge attack on the enemy in Flanders, with the stated aim of clearing the Channel ports and perhaps introducing 'open' as opposed to 'trench' warfare for the first time since the early weeks of the war. Field-Marshal Sir Douglas Haig, the British Commander-in-Chief, had wanted to carry out such a plan in 1916, but the French argued forcefully for the attack on the Somme and Haig was dissuaded from action in Flanders that year. Because of the Somme and Arras actions, the opening of this 'Third Battle of Ypres' had been considerably delayed, but now it was summer and surely good weather could be expected to contribute to success. Unfortunately the late summer of 1917 turned out to be one of the wettest for fifty years and Third Ypres was to flounder and drown in a sea of mud.

While Arthur's Ambulance was still at Bachimont, an early success had occurred in Flanders, when on 7 June nineteen mines were exploded simultaneously at ten past three in the morning on the Messines-Wytschaete Ridge. General Plumer's forces of the Second Army overran the ridge and all objectives were taken. For the next seven weeks preparations for the great attack on the Passchendaele Bridge were made: zero hour was eventually fixed for the early hours of 31 July.

On arrival at the camp, it was obvious to all that large numbers of casualties were expected. There were acres of hutted camps housing Casualty Clearing Stations; there was a light narrow-gauge railway between the northern suburbs of Ypres and the Brandhoek camps, running alongside the tree-lined *pavé* road between Poperinghe and Ypres. Ominously, within the central crossroads area of the village itself three cemeteries had been prepared. The area had been known to British soldiers since the autumn of 1914; many thousands of them had arrived by train just as Arthur had, alighting at Poperinghe or Hazebrouck, then tramping for miles in constant earshot of the heavy guns out beyond Ypres. That first day at Brandhoek Arthur wrote in the War Diary:

'We have taken over this camp from 97 F.A. It is a walking wounded station and has accommodation for 1000 cases. All are under canvas with the exception of one hut used for a dressing room. Have had some difficulty in finding stabling for the horses and the mules have to remain in the open. We have orders that we are to work with 2/1 Wessex F.A. in their Dressing Stations as this Division [15] takes over part of the line held by the 55th Division [West Lancashire Territorials].'[1]

It was the Ambulance's main function to man a Main Dressing Station for the 46th Brigade in the cellars under the prison at Ypres, so Arthur soon saw for himself just how much damage had been done to the ancient medieval cloth town since he had helped run an Aid Post in the crypt of St Martin's Cathedral in 1914. In addition, Aid Posts had to be established as near to the front line as possible. The front line at the beginning of Third Ypres lay some two miles east of Ypres along the Menin Road. Arthur described his first tour of inspection, travelling by motor ambulance, the American Doctor Colston tagging along with him:

'[19 June] I went to Ypres to see the Dressing Station in the Prison and then the Advanced Dressing Station on the Ypres-Menin Road. We supply 1 officer and 20 men for the prison (half the staff), and at present 1 sergeant and 5 men for the ADS, also 1 NCO and 4 men for a relay pool in the trenches. All these left camp at 5 p.m. today under Captain PROUD who will be in charge at the Prison. The Left Collecting Post will be at POTIZJE, this is at present being worked by the 2/1 Wessex.

'[20 June] Inspected the Prison, found more work required, sending working-party there daily. We are trying to get pit props, elephants [corrugated iron], nails etc. from the Royal Engineers. The 46th Field Ambulance will supply half the stuff for the Post at Potizje. We evacuate from the ADS on the Menin Road, and from the Potizje Post every other day.

'[23 June] The Menin Road Dressing Station has been damaged by a shell and the water from a cesspit adjoining is now getting into the cellar through cracks in the wall. We have started pumping the sewage out of the cesspit and hope to stop it running into the cellar. This neighbourhood is being heavily shelled with 5.9s.'[2]

Dr Colston recorded his impressions of doing tours of inspection in Arthur's company:

'This sector was very active in preparation for the offensive which started around 1st August, and which is now known as the Passchendaele Battle. The enemy was well aware of these preparations so that shellfire designed to harass traffic towards the front lines was often heavy at such vulnerable points as the Menin Gate, Suicide Corner, Hellfire Corner, Shrapnel Corner etc.

'Colonel Leake was always most solicitous and considerate towards me and I am sure that he realized that I had never previously heard any noise louder than a twelve-gauge shotgun. When I accompanied him we would usually leave in the early morning and arrange to spend an hour or two in the shelter of the Prison. The hour just before dawn was usually chosen by the enemy artillery to subject the front lines and supporting positions to heavy fire for the purpose of breaking up any impending attack and during this time our own infantry was always on stand to with fixed bayonets. As soon as daylight came, artillery usually slackened and it was this time that the Colonel usually chose to take me to inspect the forward aid posts.

'Our reception at Battalion or Company Headquarters was friendly, of course, but one could clearly read in the faces of the tired infantry officers the thought "just two more MO's on a Cook's Tour of the front line when things are quiet", but when they saw the Colonel's crimson ribbon the transition was immediately apparent.'[3]

To his mother Arthur toned down the alarming parts of what was happening:

'There is plenty going on in these parts and we are kept fairly busy. The Boche spends his time trying to destroy everything and our people are always constructing. War is a fearful waste of everything, and the sooner the Boche is wiped off the earth the better. . . . This country is most fertile and the farms and gardens are looking wonderful. There is a good deal of hop cultivation and it does not look as if the Belgian is going to give up his beer. How is your hay crop getting on?'[4]

His mother informed him that his sister Bella was ill again with boils, which was generally attributed to overwork and poor blood condition. Arthur instructed her to 'take herself in hand and have some treatment – she has probably been doing too much and not taking care of her insides. Shall be anxious to hear how she gets on.'[5] As always, he commented on the news, and had some acerbic comments to make following the recent report (June 1917) of the Mesopotamian Committee which had censured the commanders in the campaign, including Lord Hardinge, Viceroy of India:

'The findings are very interesting, and most people who have been to India will be pleased that that "little god", the Indian Government official, should be well strapped. They have shown up very badly, also some of those hopeless "old dodderers" in the Indian Medical Department. The Mesopotamian Expedition in the early days, when India ran it, seems to have been just as bad as it possibly could have been.'[6]

Most of his time was inevitably taken up with the huge redistribution of the Allied armies that was taking place prior to 31 July. Arthur took part in the discussions with the Divisional Director of Medical Services, Colonel Pollock, about optimum ways of dealing with the wounded. The War Diary recorded on 25 June:

'Went round the front line this morning and visited the posts, roads etc. to form a scheme for collecting and evacuating the wounded. Evacuation to St Jean and then by Light Railway is under consideration. It is important to have routes for evacuation outside the town if possible, and if this arrangement can be worked with the Division on the left [55th] we shall have the means of evacuating cases to the north and south of the town and need not go through Ypres if it is heavily shelled. ST JEAN Aid Post is finished – it consists of 2 elephants and will take 24 stretcher cases. There is very little accommodation in the Advance Aid Post at POTIZJE, not more than 10 cases could be sheltered here. And 30 cases in the MENIN ROAD ADP. This consists of 2 large elephants and a medium ridged one. They are above ground in a stable, but fairly well built up with sandbags; stretchers cannot be got in but it will be a useful post for bearers and perhaps walking wounded.'[7]

All the Ambulance's outposts might come under fire at any time and had to be constantly repaired. As night fell on 25 June bombs were dropped from an aeroplane right over the camp at Brandhoek, resulting in one death and four men seriously wounded. The Ambulance had to be moved with all its equipment and tents to a new position on the other side of the Poperinghe-

Ypres road, because it had been decided to build a siding for the light railway on the site; latrines were dug and field kitchens constructed, but within hours they had to move again because it was now planned to position a Casualty Clearing Station there. The Menin Road Aid Post also had to be moved on 28 June because of unwelcome attentions from the enemy, and on the same day the Main Dressing Station at the Prison in Ypres was heavily shelled.

The CCS, Number 32, arrived on 3 July. It was commanded by Lieutenant-Colonel Sutcliffe, and was to specialize in the treatment of abdominal wounds. Its equipment included a full-scale Operating Theatre and 'Röntgen Ray' [X-Ray] apparatus. It was soon under attack.

'[4 July] During the night the camp and crossroads were shelled with 5.9s and something smaller. One 5.9 dropped in the centre of the CCS site and damaged the tents. They were empty at the time. Some local casualties were brought in from the road. One Ambulance motor-cyclist was knocked out by a shell on the Menin Road; he was much shaken up but not wounded. The cycle was seriously damaged and could not be brought away at the time.

'[6 July] The second motor cycle was badly damaged at the Prison yesterday. I have had to borrow a cycle from 47 F.A. as both of ours have been knocked out by shellfire. I am sending what remains of one in to the [repair] shops; the other on the Menin Road could not be found and was evidently picked up by some passing car. We cannot get any trace of it. One of our cars was damaged in the Potizje road today, fortunately not badly and neither patients nor driver hurt, so it got back all right. . . . A road is being made for the cars which will evacuate our wounded from here. We have difficulty getting stone for it.'[8]

Such entries had to be made because the Commanding Officer of the Ambulance would have to account for loss or damage to equipment. However, in the battle to come so great was the confusion and chaos that such misfortunes were easily glossed over.

As July wore on the preparations continued; there were lectures for non-commissioned officers as well as for Commanding Officers, so that all were familiar with the likely conditions to be faced, and Arthur got his men to dig a new well for the new position of the Ambulance and was pleased when they struck 'a fair supply of water'. As always in the heat of battle, (and high summer temperatures could be anticipated for this one), shortage of water added greatly to the sufferings of the wounded. This particular summer in

Flanders had so far been drier than usual, and local farmers had even gone to such lengths as chaining and padlocking their wells.[9]

In the middle of the month the enemy sent large numbers of gas shells over Ypres, and Arthur discussed this extra hazard in detail:

'[13 July] During the night large numbers of men were caught with the gas, they are still being evacuated. Over 600 have been sent down already. It seems to be a new form of gas shell and this accounts for so many men having been caught. It does not appear to have a marked smell and as there were many other shells coming over at the same time nothing unusual seems to have been recognized until the effects began to appear. The most important feature about this poison is its delayed action; the effects do not begin to show themselves for some hours and increase in severity for 24 hours or more. One of our Medical Officers (Captain Day) who has been evacuated said that "he had no trouble at all for 5 hours after he passed through Ypres". Our men at the Prison did not begin to feel the effects until after 6 a.m., and they had been working loading cars at the Prison Gate most of the night. In places where the poison is more concentrated the menace affected more quickly. Blankets are a complete protection. In the Prison cellars where the openings are well-blanketed there were no cases.

The cases complain of pain and smarting in the eyes, sneezing, running of eyes and nose, headache, and sooner or later retching and vomiting. Most of the cases when they arrived here had extreme conjunctivitis, swelling of the eyelids to such an extent that they were separated with difficulty and when opened a copious flow of tears took place; the tears were in many cases under such pressure that they squirted out. The lips and face presented a bloated appearance and there was a thin watery discharge from the nose. Vomiting of a yellowish fluid in the majority of cases and the conjunctiva highly infected all over.'[10]

On 14 July the Field Ambulance dealt with 645 cases, some of which exhibited different symptoms such as blistering on face, hands, back and buttocks. The delayed action of the gas was further demonstrated when many cases also developed swelling of the neck in the area of the thyroid gland and inflamation of the skin of the scrotum and penis, leading Arthur to wonder whether the gas, once inhaled, was now being secreted through the sweat glands. Phosgene gas as well as the lachrymatory kind could now be detected, and a few men died. A gas expert from the American Army was sent to investigate and the gas was identified as mustard gas. (Incidentally, Arthur did not mind the occasional American, but was of the opinion that "we don't want to be swamped with them".'[11] He was correct in his belief that this gas was new. Even nurses and orderlies were made ill through contact with gas victims.[12] The Casualty Clearing Stations were in danger of being overwhelmed, and orders came back that all except the most serious cases must be kept in Field Ambulances and returned to duty as soon as possible. Nothing must be allowed to jeopardize the success of the forthcoming attack, the preliminary bombardment for which began on 16 July. The noise from then on was tremendous, with retaliation in kind whining and whistling overhead from the direction of the German lines.

On 24 July a trench raid took place along the Potizje road and Arthur had to send stretcher bearers to the Aid Post there in case of casualties. The raid was a great success, he wrote, because 800 German prisoners were taken.[13] Now a 'dump' of one hundred stretchers was being formed at the Potizje Aid Post, and a fifty-gallon water tank and sixty petrol tins filled with water were also left there as zero hour approached. On 28 July Potizje Château was handed over to 46 Field Ambulance to use during the battle, and cases under treatment at the Ambulance at Brandhoek were being cleared in readiness. On 30 July the stretcher-bearers designated for duty along the Menin Road were sent to Ypres Prison, from where they would move towards the jumping-off trenches just before Zero hour.

But Arthur still found time to write home, discussing in detail the recent Cabinet changes which had led to the reinstatement of Winston Churchill, dismissed from his post as First Lord of the Admiralty in May, 1915, following the Dardanelles fiasco. Since then Churchill had held the largely 'ornamental' post of Chancellor of the Duchy of Lancaster;[14] now he was to be Minister of Munitions in Lloyd George's government, and Arthur disapproved, echoing the views of many Britons when he told his mother:

> 'It looks as if we shall beat the Germans in time, but nobody can ever hope to squash Churchill. Lloyd George seems to make great speeches but talking won't kill the Boches and it is impossible to forget that he has just put Churchill back in a job.
>
> I am afraid there is nothing to write about. Our work is always the same and intimately connected with future events so of course cannot be written about. Our Yank [Dr Colston] is turning out to be quite a good chap and very keen on his job, which is more than can be said of some of our latest additions. Sometimes we wonder whether the medical examinations held in parts of Great Britain are only held for the fees they bring in.'[15]

15th Divisional preparations for 31 July were carried out in tandem with those of the 55th (West Lancashire Territorial) Division, whose sector adjoined the left flank of that of the 15th. The 55th's Main Dressing Station was at Red Farm, close to Brandhoek crossroads, and it had Aid Posts and collecting posts very close to that of 46 Field Ambulance at Potizje. Inevitably, therefore, in the heat of the battle, casualties from each Division mingled and were carried back by bearers and motor ambulances of either. Both Divisions could use the services of the Ambulance Trains running from Saint Jean and the Canal Bank dugouts to Brandhoek on the light railway. Provision had been made for each train to consist of four trucks, each of which could accommodate eight lying and six sitting cases.

At Brandhoek the Red Farm Dressing Station for the 55th Division and Arthur's Ambulance on the other side of the road for the 15th Division would unload cases and allocate them to the appropriate Casualty Clearing Station. Head wounds and lachrymatory gas cases were to go to one of three CCSs at Mendinghem (Proven), abdominal cases to 32 CCS at Brandhoek and 'Not yet Diagnosed' patients to Dozinghem and Bandaghem at Haringhe; the humorous nomenclature of these three sites had been provided by the ordinary Tommy, but found its way into Divisional Orders.[16]

At zero hour, 3.50 am on 31 July, the whistles blew and the attack began, the men moving forward to their designated objectives under the protection of a creeping barrage. There were successes at first, but considerable casualties were inflicted by the retreating German artillery and the enemy machine-gun nests that held up portions of the advancing lines for hours. The first cases for treatment began to arrive from the Potizje Aid Post less than two hours after zero hour, and Arthur made up the War Diary on the same day:

'[31 July] The first cases arrived at 5.10 this morning. Other cars were sent up at once. The first car from the Menin Road arrived two hours later. Clearing [of casualties] has been satisfactory except on the Potizje side, especially during the afternoon up to about 8 p.m. The difficulty was caused by the amount of traffic on the Potizje road. The cars took a very long time to get up and down this portion of the route. The accumulation of cases at one time reached about 40 but I don't think it passed this figure. The posts were cleared by 10 pm completely. A good many stretcher cases were carried to the Prison by Germans and cleared from there by car. A good many walking cases found their way to the Prison and char-a-bancs were sent for them. Here work has gone smoothly and there has never been any great accumulation. We have had 4 Medical Officers working. No dressings have been changed unless there was some special reason, and cases sent on to CCS with as little delay as possible.'[17]

During the first twenty-four hours the Ambulance had seventy-four officers and 1990 other ranks through its hands, as well as eighty-nine prisoners. To his anxious family waiting for news at Marshalls Arthur wrote on the second day:

'You will know by now that things were pretty busy over a large part of the line yesterday. Whether we have done much it is hard to make out, but one gathers that things were fairly good and a good many Boches have been sent through. The weather began to give out during the evening and soon reached a steady and settled downpour and is still (7 pm) doing it. It does not take much rain to make this country very bad as it is a sticky clayey sort of stuff. All seems to have stopped now and I suppose the Push is held up for the time being. It is very bad luck on the troops after so much preparation. However, things will improve before long. We were very busy up to this morning, since when our work has more or less finished. I believe the casualities have, on the whole, been slight, and certainly more were expected in these parts.'[18]

On 2 August, cases were still arriving but in fewer numbers. One of them was noted particularly by Dr Colston:

'An Ambulance came up late tonight and in it was Captain Chavasse, VC, RAMC, of the King's Liverpool Battalions of the 55th Division. His face was unrecognizable, all blackened from a shellburst very near and he seemed to be unconscious. As he had an abdominal wound besides I did not take him out of the Ambulance which was sent on direct to 32 CCS where he will probably die.'[19]

Captain N. G. Chavasse, Medical Officer of the Liverpool Scottish (1/10 King's [Liverpool Regiment]), was indeed fatally wounded and died on 4 August. He is buried in the New Military Cemetery at Brandhoek, one of the three cemeteries specially opened for the third Battle of Ypres. Arthur had seen him, but only later did the meeting assume any significance for him: on 14 September it was announced that a second Bar to a Victoria Cross had been awarded, this time posthumously, to Chavasse.[20] He and Arthur were the first two, and both won their Bars while carrying out their duties as Army doctors. From Zonnebeke where Arthur had won his, to

Wieltje where Chavasse was killed in the winning of his, was only a distance of a few miles, hardly signifying at all in the scale of the world war in which they both distinguished themselves. In 1956 Dr Colston described them both as *'chevaliers sans peur et sans reproche'*.[21]

The total casualties for Third Ypres were enormous, but in the early days of the battle Arthur was not to know the scale of the tragedy. When the 1st and 2nd Canadian Divisions made their final rush and secured the high ground at Passchendaele on 2 November, the total Allied casualties were 430,000 killed, wounded or missing. Over 40,000 of these were never found and have their names on the Memorial to the Missing at Tyne Cot.

On 4 August 46 Field Ambulance was moved back to Winnezele for fourteen days' rest with the 15th Division. Arthur described the district to his mother:

'This is quite a good part and not in any way spoiled by war, though of course there are troops everywhere. We are near a place called Cassel. It is a little town on top of a hill about 500 feet. On a clear day the view from the top is wonderful – Calais, Dunkerque, Ostend, and even further into Holland can be seen. The other side as far as Lille. It is the most fascinating place to go on a clear day with glasses and I often visit it.'[22]

Then they returned to Brandhoek for a few days. Arthur's view was that 'the fighting was satisfactory as far as it went, but stopped too soon owing to the wet'[23] but the enemy was nevertheless turning the camp area into a veritable 'hot spot':

'[21.8] About 11 a.m. today shelling began in this neighbourhood. Two shells fell in our area close to the building. There were lots of patients about at the time but nobody was hurt; this is to be accounted for by the wet and soft ground where the shells pitched. Shells have dropped in the three CCSs, and Number 44 has had a nurse and orderly killed. The shelling has continued on and off all day, mostly near the Railway. CCSs evacuated in the evening.

[22.8] Most of our tents have had holes made in them, also the mess marquee. We have been moved further from the railway line.'[24]

News from Marshalls, that his sister Bella, whose health was giving great cause for concern, was at last going into a nursing home pleased Arthur:

'She should certainly undergo treatment and be put right. Rest and a proper course of treatment and feeding should give her every prospect of a cure. She should stay in the home until she is cured, no matter if it takes a long time. I have lots of money lying idle and it would be a good thing to find a use for it, so you have only got to let me know. Hoping you are quite fit and not trying to do too much work. During wartime the high standard of things at Marshalls should be allowed to slacken a bit.'[25]

Very soon the Ambulance left the Salient for good. On 2 September officers and men entrained for Aubigny and then marched to Habarcq near Arras. Two days later they were back in the familiar territory of Arras itself. They were supporting the line-holding operation in front of the town, and expected to have only the usual illnesses to deal with, and perhaps an occasional wounding or gas case. The town's 'Deaf and Dumb School' was taken over as the Corps Main Dressing Station, a large building much damaged by shellfire, but repair work was immediately started. The Field Ambulance's motors were deployed at the Rivage (quayside) to meet motor launches bringing sick and wounded from Fampoux; men would have first been transported on pontoons along the canal leading to the River Scarpe, and Arthur devised a system of hot water bottles in an attempt to keep them warm. Another motor ambulance met the trains on the Light Railway from Feuchy, south of the Scarpe.

On 19 September Arthur had an interesting chance meeting with General Julian Byng, who had commanded the Third Army since June. They talked about Thorpe Hall, Byng's home since 1913, but Byng told Arthur he had only spent nine days there since he bought it.[26]

A short leave spent at Marshalls came Arthur's way in October, but his return to his post near Arras seemed to bring nothing but personal discomfort and boredom:

'Bad weather, rain and cold. I have a stove in my tent but just at present it is not a great success because the smoke goes every-where but up the chimney. I shall get over the difficulty with more piping. I have also put in floorboards. We have been doing some rather successful rat-catching just lately. This town swarms with rats and they are a great nuisance.'[27]

Two more American doctors arrived at the Ambulance, but there was hardly enough work to occupy them. Average daily admissions were four wounded and thirty sick, the illnesses including trenchfoot, measles, colds and influenza. Another Dressing Station was being got ready in some stables in the town, with a large area being partitioned off for the purpose by the Army Service Corps. A system of 'central hot-air' heating had been devised, much of the heat being provided by incinerated rubbish.

Arthur's concern with keeping warm was not misplaced as winter approached, and on Christmas Day two inches of snow fell. As usual the soldiers managed to enjoy themselves:

'The Unit had Christmas Dinner and concert afterwards; all enjoyed themselves and it was considered a success. Much stuff was sent up the line to the forward posts and they also had a good time. Snow is still falling and we have several cases of frostbite. They mostly show dusky patches involving loss of skin or even toes. There is some trenchfoot too.'[28]

He was relieved that the impact of the rationing scheme about to be introduced would not be too great at home:

'It is as well that the family has reached an age when it doesn't get great joy and happiness from an over-distended condition of the stomach, and this condition is not essential for getting successfully through Christmas Day. Here, Tommy Atkins was determined to have as big a blow-out as could be arranged under the circumstances. There does not appear to be any shortage, as the French people are using everything they have in the food line to make money. The men had pork, plum pudding and lots of other things. We purchased locally a goose and turkey so did ourselves quite well. . . . Have just met a Yank from Paris. He says they are immensely busy and have already got a lot of men, planes and war material out here. Our pessimists are very fond of saying that they won't be able to do much on account of the difficulty in getting things over, but this is all rot and they will probably be fighting in the Spring.'[29]

In January the appointment of a new Director General of Medical Services was announced. This was Colonel T. H. J. C. Goodwin, who replaced Sir Alfred Keogh.[30] Arthur was becoming even more critical of the senior echelons of the RAMC, where there seemed to be a preponderance of Irishmen, but regarded the new DGMS (who had no apparent Irish connections) as a step in the right direction:

'The new DGMS will doubtless cause a great stir and much jealousy amongst the upper ranks. I should imagine it is a splended thing, but they will still want to comb out a lot of the useless senior people yet.'[31]

Within weeks his quarrel with his RAMC superiors took a more serious turn, but for now he tried to allay his mother's fears about the war, especially about the likelihood of a German victory now that an armistice had been agreed with Russia:

'There is no cause at all to be windy; the Boche may have a good many more men from the Russian side, but they won't be able to do much and it only means more of them to be killed, which is a good thing for the world when peace comes.'[32]

He spent much of his time giving lectures on first aid to his orderlies and stretcher bearers, demonstrating splints and bandages and administering anti-tetanus vaccinations. Boxing matches were held, the men played football nearly every day, and gas mask drills were frequent. A means of steam-heating the clothing worn by victims of gas attacks was devised, consisting of a large boiler over which the clothing was hung. It then had to be steamed for three hours and was deemed to be decontaminated. The 'Hay Box' cooking method was also tried, and Arthur pronounced it very successful for stews and rice. A spell of leave at home brought him back through Boulogne, where he was surprised at the apparent plenty:

'The shops in Boulogne were interesting, especially the butchers, of which I counted four in one street, and all packed full of meat. Such a change from England. Other provision shops were in the same condition and there were great masses of butter to be seen. One would imagine that France could easily export butter and eggs to England. . . . A circular has been sent round about cultivating land and growing potatoes. I am hoping they will give us some land and let us start at once. We have plenty of horse and man power being wasted during these times.'[33]

His impatience with inactivity was showing itself again. A plot of land was allocated to the Field Ambulance, (although the local French authorities caused difficulties about it), and work was soon under way. 'Dud' bombs were unearthed and apparently disposed of with gay abandon. Large tracts of land were being cultivated by the Army:

'but it does not look very promising as the ground has been out of cultivation for so long that it will take an immense amount of clearing and this should have been begun last Autumn. However, agricultural experts have been appointed in the true Army fashion so all must go right. . . . I wish I had known as much about digging when home on leave last. Your parsnip bed was not treated in the correct way and I would do it better now after the instruction I have been having.'[34]

Now began the enemy's final attempt to break out from his trenchlines and go on the offensive, before the American forces could be got ready to fight. Against all Allied expectations the Germans managed to mount a tremendous bombardment south of Arras, beginning on 21 March, and within a week had pushed the Allied line back forty miles. Arthur tried to reassure his mother:

'You must be somewhat anxious at home about the turn of events, but when you think that this is the greatest attempt the Boche is capable of you will not be discouraged because he has had some results. He is near the end now and all may change rapidly as it did at the Marne.'[35]

Arras and the supporting area where 46 Field Ambulance was situated was not directly involved because this part of the line held firm, but large numbers of shells were sent over and before long, on 23 March, the Ambulance had to move, this time to Haute-Avesnes along the road to Aubigny. The XVII Corps Rest Station at Warlus had to close down due to its proximity to the action, and Haute-Avesnes now became the new Rest Station. To all intents and purposes the Field Ambulance had become a small CCS, with tented and hutted wards capable of holding hundreds of cases. By 9 April it had 445 in-patients. Diseases were more common than injury, diphtheria and scabies being the most intractable. Arthur's morale was lifted by the news in April that he was being promoted to Temporary Lieutenant-Colonel,[36] but the last months of his career with the RAMC were marred by his bitter criticism of both his immediate superiors and the central Directorate. The exact reason for his anger is unclear; he was careful not to even hint at it when he wrote up his unit's War Diary, and his letters home were necessarily circumspect in view of the censor. He had obviously been able to explain the problem to his family when he was on leave in February, and thereafter he was able to refer to it in general terms, safe in the knowledge that they understood his meaning. At times, however, he allowed himself to complain vehemently about the men at the top:

'My immediate boss is going to another job as he has got promotion (to a Corps). Don't know who is coming in his place and don't like the idea of the change much. There are many quite impossible people in this branch of the Army. There is a rumour that a Field Ambulance may be taken away from each Division, so it is quite on the cards that one of us will lose a job.'[37]

When the replacement was appointed, rumours flew round the Unit:

'I hear the most alarming accounts of our new boss and only trust that he won't turn out quite as bad as the reports make out. He is, however, an Irishman so I am fully prepared for the worst. Experience teaches me that the only point in an Irishman's favour is that he is sometimes amusing. He seems to be quite untrustworthy in every respect.'[38]

When the new man arrived, Arthur seems to have immediately quarrelled with him:

'I expect my tenure in this job will be rather shaky. Our new appointment has mystified everybody as he is well known throughout the Army and certainly is quite the most unsuitable subject for the post. Unfortunately I have just had to sign a new contract so shall have to stick it for six months anyhow.'[39]

Arthur's forty-fourth birthday on 4 April dampened his spirits even more, and to cap it all he heard that his brother Dick might be sent out to France:

'I have great hopes that my next birthday won't be spent at war. Now the age limit is 50 I am well in it. Don't know what they mean to do with old people. Age is a great disadvantage to warfare and the hospitals are just choked with old men as it is now. No soldier is much good after 40, at least not for the front line. . . . I have an idea that Dick is over-age. [Dick was fifty-one]. He certainly is physically, owing to prolonged residence in the tropics and a tendency to rheumatism. If he is even called upon for an examination he should explain this as it would be no use his coming out here. Old people are worse than useless for active operations here, and it will be a great mistake if they are taken from useful work at home. Frank is quite right – "The nation is quite sound in spite of the political people." They form a scum on the top which makes the depths look foul. The British soldier is the finest fellow in the world and never better than when the odds are against him. The Frenchman is as good and on the whole better led. There is no cause for alarm as the Boche will not do much against the combination. Our men seem to be fighting magnificently and now Foch is Chief of the whole show, all will go right.'[40]

The Divisional ADMS went back to England for a time at the end of March and Arthur declared that, as he was an Irishman, his absence meant the war was nearer to being won.[41] The Unit moved to Lozinghem for a few days, and then to Maroeuil before settling into more permanent quarters at St Catherine, on the northern outskirts of Arras. Arthur was still very uneasy about the ADMS:

'I am expecting a change to come sometime. A low-class Irishman is intolerable and can drive anybody out. . . . I had orders to attend on the higher medical authorities [DMS at Heuchin] yesterday and now have to wait and see. But they nearly all come from Ireland, and think and act in the same way.'[42]

On 23 May he composed a diatribe against Irish doctors and sent it home:

'The Irishman has made a corner in Army doctoring and nothing can improve the service until these big officials, practically all Irishmen, die of old age or return voluntarily. There is a strong union amongst these people because each of them knows he cannot stand alone and needs all support to cover his gross ignorance and shady methods. It will take longer than this war can possibly last to get rid of these pests, but the country should see that it is not caught in this way again.'[43]

Two days later Arthur was again 'Mentioned in Despatches' (in Haig's Despatch of 7 April).[44] Then the Divisional ADMS was replaced but, said Arthur, "this won't be sufficient to break up the Irish gang." The new man had been a senior Medical Officer in the South African Constabulary, so Arthur felt this was a change for the better. Early in June a list of RAMC senior appointments was published, but too late to win Arthur's approval:

'The RAMC list means nothing except that the Irishman is a little bit frightened and thinks he had better put in a few Englishmen for a change.'[45]

A diary written by Captain G. D. Fairley RAMC comments on 46 Field Ambulance and its Commanding Offier at this time. Captain Fairley had been transferred from his position as Medical Officer to the 7/8 King's Own Scottish Borderers, and one of Arthur's first remarks to him was, predictably, that he thought Fairley had been badly treated by the RAMC. Fairley described him as "of small to medium height, neatly built, of middle age, very pleasant."[46]

On 13 June Arthur was ordered to take command of number 42 Casualty Clearing Station. It was situated at Aubigny, an area he knew well:

'The change is the result of my fight with the Irishman. It is looked upon as a more classy job, but I don't think so and would not have taken it unless I had been driven out of my Ambulance. Curiously enough it is the CCS next door to the one [Number 30] that I used to belong to, so I know most of the people in it. My old CCS has now been moved but this one is still in the same place and has been here for over 2 years. [Two Irish doctors were with the establishment.] You may think my experience on the subject of the Irish is not sufficient to enable me to pass an opinion, but being in the RAMC is nearly the same as being in Ireland and one gets a vast insight into the animal. I have escaped from one only to find myself with two'.[47]

Nor did he like the job itself, finding himself severely hampered by all the paperwork that was now required:

'I am trying to learn my new job, and at present don't think much of it. The Army has nearly throttled itself with all its returns and other forms of red tape, and a few more years of war will find it quite impotent as a fighting machine. . . . I would rather be back with my old unit.'[48]

The influenza that was to sweep the world during the next two winters had arrived on the Western Front that summer and rumour had it that the enemy was badly affected:

'No news except the Boche has got influenza in his army and this may be the reason why he doesn't attack. We have had a big run of it but now it is quite on the decrease and is probably dying out. Hope you won't get it at Marshalls, though it is for the most part quite a mild thing – it is a nuisance.'[49]

Women and the RAMC came in for some more strictures in August:

'There are 17 nurses here but thank goodness they are managed by the Matron and I have little to do with them. A large number of wounded have been through, and we have got on pretty well except when the Brass Hats pay us visits and inspect everything. Our officials (RAMC) are the absolute limit and I wish the Boche would catch the lot. Work would then get on all right.'[50]

42 CCS was moved a few miles north to Mingoval when air-raids became a threat; numbers of American troops were drafted in to help in the move, a considerable undertaking for a CCS that had been in the same position for two and a half years. Arthur was most impressed with their work but not with their short working day:

'Everybody is taken with the Yanks out here; they are excessively keen and determined to beat the Boche no matter how long it takes. There is very little doubt about them finishing the war well if we can only keep old Lansdowne [Editor of the *Daily Herald*] and his disgraceful lot from starting a peace movement. The Yanks work well when they are at it, but their working hours are not many. 8 hour day, half day Saturday and Sunday off. They will find that they will have to alter this. The reason seems to be that they want the time for their military training, inspections etc. Anyhow they know what they are about and are fighting so well down south that their scheme must be pretty good.'[51]

On 28 August he noted that the CCS was open but was still only partly complete.[52] This was his last wartime letter. His six-month contract, signed with the RAMC the previous March, expired on 3 September. Arthur did not wish to renew it. As soon as he could, he packed up his belongings for the last time and headed for home.

CHAPTER FIFTEEN

'A Simple Man'

Marshalls, and indeed the whole county of Hertfordshire, was a welcome haven of rural peace and quietness for Arthur on his return from France. The harvest was being gathered, in his mother's kitchen garden as well as in the fields surrounding High Cross. His whole family was convinced that the end of the war could not be long delayed, and for some weeks he was content to tend the flowerbeds, collect apples in the paddock and tomatoes in the greenhouse, his brother Steenie's pride and joy. Steenie chafed at inactivity now that he was no longer doing army work, and put his engineering skills to good use making crutches for disabled soldiers; his mother described the results of his handiwork as "quite nice-looking".[1] He was also a senior local magistrate, sitting on the Ware bench. He frequently went hunting and shooting with Major Arthur Percival from Ware, a good friend of the family who was ultimately to become, in 1950, Colonel of Willie's old regiment, the Cheshires.

Willie came home at frequent intervals, and promised to make this permanent by retiring from his post as Deputy Assistant Adjutant General; he finally left the military world that had been his lifelong career in the summer of 1920, at the age of fifty-five. Mrs Martin-Leake's health gradually declined from now on, though this was only to be expected at the grand old age of eighty-five. Because of this Arthur resisted for some time the letters that arrived almost weekly from friends and colleagues in India urging him to return to the Railway. He made up his mind to remain in England, at least until peace was restored in Europe.

The news of the collapse of the Central Powers was read with relish at the Marshalls breakfast-table. Stories of internal wranglings in the Berlin Reichstag between groups supporting and opposing an armistice gave great satisfaction, as did descriptions of the enemy's rapid loss of all the gains that had been made by Ludendorff in the Spring offensive. The deeds of General Byng's Third Army in the Cambrai area made the Martin-Leakes particularly proud of their connection with him through his home, Thorpe Hall. The collapse of Austria-Hungary on 3 November and the growing tide of revolution in Germany made the Armistice of 11 November, 1918, inevitable. An early signal announcing the ceasefire was seen by Arthur's brother

Frank, now Chief of Staff to Admiral Lewis Bayley, stationed at Queenstown on the east coast of Ireland. Frank wrote home:

> 'This is to send my best congratulations to you on the end of the war. It is hard to realize, and comment on paper is a poor susbstitute for what one feels about it. Things now will move very rapidly, and may we be spared an excessive dose of democracy. I feel Lloyd George should be instantly shot. British commonsense shall pull us through.'[2]

As the weeks turned into months, the family became accustomed once again to peacetime conditions. Gradually the papers stopped publishing war news and casualty lists, though many column inches were devoted to the peace negotiations taking place in Paris. Eventually Arthur's war medals arrived, as did those of his brothers; his were added to those of South Africa and Montenegro, and consisted of the 1914 (Mons) Star bearing the dates '5th August – 22nd November 1914'which indicated active service with BEF, the British War Medal and the Allied Victory Medal with oak leaves for 'Mentioned in Despatches'.[3] Arthur's modesty prevented him from ever being photographed wearing the complete set. Together with his Victoria Cross and Bar they were consigned to a drawer in the dining-room sideboard.

Once the Treaty of Versailles was signed in June, 1919, (and the irony of Boer leaders Smuts and Botha being signatories was not lost on Arthur) he succumbed to requests from Calcutta to return there and set off from Marshalls on 16 January, 1920. Winter was always the best time to arrive in India, before the onset of the hot weather. His reappearance at Garden Reach was met with a shower of congratulations from railway employees and fellow polo-players alike; he found that his club, the Bengal in Calcutta, had commissioned a portrait of him by the artist Lance Calkin. In April, 1922, the reluctant hero was persuaded to attend its unveiling, at the same time as that of the Club's War Memorial, by Lord Ronaldshay, the Governor of Bengal. One story had it that Arthur in fact failed to turn up and had to be led in, while friends posted themselves at the doors in case he tried to 'escape'.[4] The painting, considered to be 'a splendid likeness of Dr Leake,' was hung in the Club's Reading Room, and Arthur was described by His Excellency as 'one of the bravest of the brave'.[5]

In residence once again at his old address, 14 Garden Reach, Arthur's daily life continued as before, almost as if it had not been interrupted by the Great War, except in one respect: he was no longer a member of the Bengal Nagpur Railway Volunteers. To mark his past service with the unit he was given another medal, the India Volunteer Force Decoration. His junior colleague from before the War, Vivian St John Croly, was now the Battalion

Medical Officer, but Arthur rather welcomed this development as it gave him more time to indulge his other interests, especially tracking and shooting wildlife. There were several acquaintanceships to renew and he developed a particularly close friendship with Charles and Winifred Carroll. Charles, who had been on the staff of the BNR since 1901, had risen steadily through the ranks of middle management to become one of the Railway's Superintendents in 1919.[6] He had also been a member of the Railway Volunteers alongside Arthur since before the War, so they knew one another very well. He and his wife were most solicitous of the comfort of their newly-returned neighbour, helping him to settle back into his bungalow and providing him with meals and companionship until he was re-established.

He was able to share with the Carrolls his many anxieties about the family back home at Marshalls. These years after the War were marked by an inevitable deterioration in the health and fortunes of the hitherto robust and energetic Martin-Leakes. it was a cliché, but true, that age was catching up with Arthur's brothers and sisters; of the seven still surviving, not one had married, and there were no direct heirs to the Marshalls estate. Arthur's father had left it in trust for his wife, and then it was to proceed down through the family, beginning with Steenie, the eldest son. No special provision had been made for Georgiana and Isabella, their father no doubt assuming that they would marry and be taken care of. In the event they remained spinsters and still lived at Marshalls where their brothers, following the sense of familial duty imbued in them since birth, entered into an unspoken agreement to look after them. The sisters in return kept house for the brothers and their mother, a perfect arrangement all round. Alterations were always being carried out on the house: in 1923 the old verandah at the rear was pulled down and a new one built, and in 1933 the lighting system was converted to electricity and was connected to the North Metropolitan Electric Supply Company. Old stables were replaced by a new brick garage.[7]

Brother Frank's well-being received a nasty jolt soon after Arthur had returned to India. He had taken a shore job at Portsmouth as Assistant to the Director of Naval Ordnance, and, returning there on his motorcycle one day in May, 1920, he collided with a car at Hatfield. He suffered serious head injuries. The effects of his old injury sustained when *Pathfinder* was sunk at the beginning of the War now reappeared and Frank seemed to age quickly, though he was actually only fifty-one. In March the next year he was appointed Naval Aide de Camp to the King and was awarded a Good Service Pension. In the summer an eminent American, Admiral W. S. Sims, who had commanded the United States naval forces in Europe during the War, visited Britain and Frank was officially attached to his party. Admiral Sims was to receive an honorary degree at Cambridge, and the opportunity was taken to invite him and his wife to Marshalls. Here Mrs Simms was presented with a bouquet of flowers by two little girls of the Church of England Waifs and Strays Society, and was 'loudly cheered by the inhabitants of the village'.[8] The American Distinguished Service Medal was bestowed on Frank. But he was now eager to leave the Service; promotion to the rank of Rear Admiral in September, 1921, paved the way, and he requested permission to retire 'in order to facilitate the promotion of younger officers', and did so on 19 November.[9] On the occasion of George V's fifty-seventh birthday in June, 1922, he was made a Companion of the Order of the Bath. When Arthur arrived home on leave that summer he was shocked to find that Frank was practically an invalid, confined to Marshalls and unable to ride his beloved motorcycle.

Apart from the concern he felt about Frank's health, Arthur's main preoccupation during this leave was his journey to Glasgow on 25 July to be presented with the Gold Medal 'For Distinguished Merit' by the British Medical Association. Though awarded to him in 1915, this medal could not be conferred on him until now.[10] Hating public attention as he did, Arthur viewed the event as a dreadful ordeal, and was glad to escape back to India and comparative obscurity. Letters of congratulations pursued him, however, from those who had again seen his name in the newspapers; one came from Baden-Powell and another from the Committee of University College Hospital.[11] The BNR Board of Directors presented him with an Address expressing, on behalf of all Railway employees:

> 'Congratulations and admiration of your record of service in various parts of the world, and in particular of your achievements under war conditions, and to assure you that the Staff of the Bengal-Nagpur Railway are very proud of the fact that they may count you on the Staff and most gratified that the British Medical Association has conferred upon you the highest honour at their disposal.'[12]

Frank's decline affected Mrs Martin-Leake badly, and on 15 February, 1924, she died peacefully in her ninetieth year, surrounded by her family, all except Arthur who was in India. It was a great blow to lose his 'Dearest Mammy', recipient of hundreds of his letters over the years. Sittie and Bella sent him press-cuttings about her death, including a fulsome obituary in the *Hertfordshire Mercury*:

> 'The late Mrs Martin-Leake possessed the old-world charm of manners and courtly grace that characterized the Victorian age. She was generally beloved and had a beautiful conception of happy Christian life with its crowning gift of ineffable and

glorious immortality. . . . Any duty she undertook was always faithfully fulfilled and the poor, in any matter affecting their interests, had no kinder or more sympathetic advocate. In her own parish she added to many cottage homes, and her wise counsel and advice so often sought could hardly have been more efficacious.'[13]

The funeral service was at High Cross, the former vicar Mr Overton officiating. Then a motor hearse took the coffin to Thorpe-le-Soken, followed by a stream of motor coaches, and Isabel was laid to rest with her husband Stephen and son Theodore in the family vault in the churchyard. She was the last Martin-Leake to be buried at Thorpe, all ties with Thorpe Hall having been severed when it was bought by General Byng in 1913. Arthur had to grieve alone thousands of miles away from the woman he had cared for most. Her will left him the sum of one hundred pounds, the same as to all of her children. In her memory the oak reredos at Thorpe Church was extended, and was re-dedicated on 29 September, 1926.

Frank, promoted Vice-Admiral on the Retired List in October, 1926, declined quickly after the death of his mother and died peacefully at Marshalls on 21 January, 1928, at the age of fifty-eight. His former Commanding Officer Sir Lewis Bayley declared that:

'No officer of or near his standing was so highly respected and more universally liked in the Navy than he was. . . . During his service as Chief of Staff in Queenstown, he made a great reputation and friendship amongst the United States officers and men owing to his selfless tact and constant willingness to help all ranks and ratings of whatever nationality. No-one ever carried out better the role laid down by St Paul, "In honour preferring one another".'[14]

Frank was the first of his generation to be buried at High Cross, in a new family plot in the north-eastern corner of the churchyard. Mr Overton returned once more to his old parish to conduct the service. A few months later Frank's brothers and sisters installed a bell in the High Cross church tower.[15] Again, Arthur was in India when his brother died.

Whenever his railway duties allowed, his favourite recreational activity was, without doubt, the tracking and shooting of wild animals. The scrubland or 'jungle' areas stretching for hundreds of miles on each side of the BNR tracks teemed with wildlife of every kind, and Arthur's skills soon became legendary all the way from Calcutta to Nagpur. In August, 1926, he wrote an account of his pursuit of a rogue elephant which 'appeared to have been a firm believer in the German methods of frightfulness for conquering and holding territory'. The huge animal had killed nine people during the previous few years and had trampled crops and villages. Eventually, with the help of two native trackers, Arthur cornered it and positioned himself for the kill:

'At last a clear view of the head was obtained. He sank down slowly to the shot and other shots were given to make certain that he would never rise again. What a sight to behold! A huge black mass looking like an enormous rounded trap boulder sticking up in the forest. A jet of blood was coming from the uppermost earhole and rising at least eighteen inches high. The blood was flowing like water from a hosepipe and forming a stream on the ground. The only sound to be heard was the splashing of the blood. Much to the relief of all, the gigantic heart was ceasing to work; there was not enough blood to keep it ¬oing. The trackers began to talk loud and fast; it brought one '‚ack to earth and to the knowledge that there was yet a hard day's work ahead to cut out the tusks and cut off the feet.'[16]

He decided to collect his experiences together in a handbook for would-be hunters, and with a colleague, BNR Chief Engineer R. D. T. Alexander he made a series of *shikari* excursions to gather material. The book, illustrated by Arthur's line drawings and photographs, was published in April, 1932.[17] All the major animals of India and Burma were included. Their footprints had been photographed, as had examples of the r stuffed and mounted heads. Lists of recommended camping equipment were complete to the smallest detail, and included Coal Tar soap, toilet paper, canvas bath, tin opener, wine glasses and teapot. 'Be comfortable,' admonished the authors, 'even in war there is no object or merit in suffering more privation or discomfort than necessary.'[18] Essential medical supplies were Keating's powder (for fleas), Lysol (for ticks), Flit (for mosquitoes), aspirin, cascara and quinine. The well-equipped *shikari* must wear jodhpurs with puttees and soft leather 'mosquito' boots. Food and drink were of the utmost importance: dry rations such as Ryvita biscuits, Quaker Oats, Golden Syrup, tins of sardines, butter, marmalade and fruit, and Kia-ora squashes were all vital. At the end of the day a meal beside the camp fire was the well-earned reward of the hunter, whose trophies would include much that was edible:

'Concerning the edible parts of the big game, some of us no doubt look back, possibly with an excusable smacking of the lips, to various Home Leaves before the war, when we partook of oysters, sole and Porterhouse steak at Gow's in the Strand, a cut from the joint at Simpson's a little further along, dinner at the Carlton, and supper (preferably with a fair companion) at the Savoy. Wonderful as these feasts of Lucullus certainly were, can they for real enjoyment compare with a well-cooked dinner in the jungle off the product of one's very own efforts? Can the finest turtle soup of a Guildhall banquet bear comparison with the soup made from the tail of a bison tracked from early morn throughout the heat of a mid-May day in the Central Provinces and eventually brought to bag?'[19]

The authors advised that elephant flesh was good to eat, but the tongue and trunk were not recommended, being as tough as rubber tyres. Parts of the Indian bear would be good in a shortcrust pie, and birds like snipe and peafowl made admirable curries. To wash all this down, the *shikari* must not forget to take with him plentiful supplies of beer, vermouth, gin, whisky and brandy.[20]

First Aid notes were supplied by Arthur, who pointed out that a 'tiger maul' is nearly always fatal because the wounds will always be serious in themselves, and the tiger's teeth and claws are likely to introduce blood-poisoning. Snakebite, panther attacks, dysentery and cholera all merited the author's attention. The preservation of trophies (including the boiling of skulls and the skinning of tigers) was carefully described, as were the mounting of heads and the use of elephants' feet as umbrella stands.

Arthur's other great interest during the 1920s was flying. Ever since his attempt in September, 1916, to join the Royal Flying Corps he had been fascinated with the aeroplane, and when the Bengal Flying Club was founded in Calcutta in December, 1927, he was one of the first to join. Its Headquarters was the old British Artillery Mess, and by 1929 Arthur was one of eighteen Europeans and two Indians to hold a pilot's licence. He saw at once that an aeroplane would be a wonderful aid to tracking wildlife, and soon bought himself a Gypsy Moth, Number VT AAC. He was photographed standing proudly beside it at Calcutta's Dum Dum Aerodrome, on the east side of the city. Aeroplanes were soon seen to have commercial potential and by 1930, via Imperial Airways, it was possible to fly home to England in seven days, via Hyderabad, Karachi, Baghdad, Cairo, Athens, Belgrade, Vienna, Nuremberg and Cologne, and thence to Croydon. The cost of a one-way ticket was £121.[21]

In November, 1929, a pressing invitation arrived at 14 Garden Reach from the Secretary to the Prince of Wales, requesting Arthur to attend a dinner to be given in London by the Prince for holders of the Victoria Cross. Arthur refused to go; such functions had always been anathema to him.[22] But the next month he was delighted to receive a visit from Steenie and Dick, who had been invited by Sir Trevredyn Wynne, now Managing Director of the BNR, to accompany his on his Cold Weather inspection of the whole BNR network. The Martin-Leakes were still convinced that Wynne had defrauded them over the building of the Roopnaryan Bridge north-west of Calcutta, but enjoyed the trip and were fascinated to see how much the railway had developed since they worked on it thirty years previously. They were gratified to find that their own engineering handiwork still stood.

Arthur entertained them in his bungalow at Garden Reach, but at their ages they found the smoky atmosphere of the area almost too much to bear. He offered them a trip in his aeroplane, but they could not summon up the courage to accept: 'unlike the Doctor we thought ourselves too old for new ventures.' He took them frequently to the Bengal Club and gave them beer 'at irregular hours', and they all attended the annual Fancy Dress Ball at the Railway's Garden Reach Club. After a two-day *shikar* in the Chilka Lake district they were presented with the Freedom of the Railway. Then 'the Engineers' went home.[23]

Whether they had any suspicions about forthcoming events in Arthur's private life is not known, but it seems likely that he kept his intentions to himself. Soon after Dick and Steenie returned to England their sister Bella died, on 5 April, 1930. She was fifty-nine years old and had never recovered from the blood-poisoning and general weakness that had developed during her work in the Great War. She was buried with Frank at High Cross.

Within weeks, Arthur telegraphed that he was coming home with astounding news: he was about to be married!

The lady in question was Winifred Carroll. She had been widowed in July, 1929, when her husband Charles had died while they were on Home Leave in London. Apparently he succumbed to cancer which was exacerbated by a long-standing weakness caused by the Indian climate. He was only fifty-two and his widow was forty-five. They had been near-neighbours of Arthur at Garden Reach, and now Arthur found himself repaying his debt to them by comforting Winifred. She had a mother living in Hove and several brothers and sisters in England, but returned to India, alone, very soon after Charles' death – to be with Arthur? One can only speculate. Her husband's will, published a few weeks after his death, left her the sum of £10,310, enough to provide for a moderately comfortable lifestyle.[24]

Throughout Arthur's story it has been impossible to avoid the conclusion that he was a misogynist. He disliked nurses, hated 'Railway Wives', disapproved of suffragettes and had no time at all for vicars' wives and village do-gooders. His brothers felt the same. The only woman they had any real respect for was their mother, closely followed by their sisters, and it may be that Arthur was unconsciously trying to replace his lost mother.

But Winifred was something different. She and Arthur had much in common. She loved India. She even loved going on *shikar*, having been brought up in the Central Provinces where her father, William A. Nedham, was a senior civil servant. She and Arthur each made notable contributions to the *B.N.R. Magazine*, a journal published monthly since 1823. As soon as the Girl Guide movement was founded by Baden-Powell in 1910 Winifred had taken up the cause with enthusiasm, and energetically promoted it among the children of BNR employees. She wrote a report on the girls' activities for each issue of the magazine. For his part, Arthur was developing a reputation as a talented artist, and drew monthly cartoons of his fellow BNR officials – cartoons that were not caricatures but simply a gentle means of poking fun at friends and colleagues. His co-authored book on *shikar* was illustrated with his sensitive drawings of wild animals. He still lived just a few doors away from Winifred at Garden Reach and an 'understanding' rapidly developed between them.

Fourteen months after Charles Carroll's death, in September, 1930, they announced their engagement in India. The *BNR Magazine* was sure that all of its readers would be 'greatly thrilled at the news.'[25] Before the announcement was made they were on their way to England, displaying an almost obsessive desire for secrecy. The story of the 'romance' broke in England on 26 September,[26] when Arthur was already at Marshalls and Winifred was staying with her mother in Hove. Georgiana's reaction to Arthur's stupefying announcement is still remembered in High Cross:

'But you can't! Marshalls people don't marry!'

But in this, as in so many other matters, once Arthur had made his mind up he would not be swayed. The wedding took place very quietly, at Christ Church, Westminster, on Wednesday 1 October, 1930. Even the verger was sworn to secrecy and none of the family was present.[27] Arthur had a great dread of the press finding out; there was still a lively interest in the activities of the first, and only living, man to be awarded the Victoria Cross and Bar. He brought a somewhat nervous Winifred to visit Marshalls after the wedding, and photographs were taken to mark the occasion. One print, of Winifred, Arthur and the family's Austin 7 car, she captioned in her album: 'My first visit to Marshalls as a member of the family'.[28] One can imagine how daunting the prospect of that first visit must have been, the first outsider to enter the Marshalls family since Arthur's mother Isabel in 1859.

They began the long journey back to India in the middle of November, travelling by train to Marseilles first, then boarding the P. & O. ship *Maloja* for the voyage through the Suez Canal and on to Bombay, where they arrived on 5 December. Three days later Arthur was back at work, travelling up and down the BNR lines checking that all was well in his territory. Winifred was installed in the doctor's personal carriage and enjoyed tracking and shooting with him whenever it could be managed. For the next year she went everywhere with him as he researched in the jungle for his forthcoming book on *shikar*. She rode on elephants, helped set up camp from the state of Assam to the Central Provinces; she was photographed many times by Arthur, with native bearers, or posing with the results of a shoot, or simply relaxing in picturesque surroundings. Sometimes they were accompanied by R. D. T. Alexander, Arthur's co-author, and his wife; as the men were not too skilled in the culinary art, together with two other ladies Winifred experimented with camp cooking at home, and a rather charming tribute was paid to them when the book was published in April, 1932:

'We have called to our aid certain lady friends in the persons of Mrs W. J. Anthony, Mrs A. Martin-Leake and Mrs R. Mac-Gregor Innes, to assist in this matter, and we owe them our thanks for much help and useful advice.'[29]

The couple instituted a rifle-shooting competition among the Girl Guides of the Railway, the winner to be presented with the 'Leake Challenge Cup'. Winifred went up in Arthur's aeroplane for the first time in December, 1930, and enjoyed it so much that she took frequent flights after that. At home in Garden Reach they found a mutual liking for small dogs as pets, and a particular favourite of them both was a terrier, Billy William.

But all was not well. In the late summer of 1932 they spent a Home Leave in England; back in India a few weeks later a deep unhappiness had overtaken Winifred. There are very few clues as to its cause. She does not seem to have felt neglected or lonely; she loved India and much preferred to live there than anywhere else; she had her own interests as well as a wide circle of BNR friends and acquaintances that she shared with her husband; financially they were very comfortably placed. But on the negative side, it is known that she had recurrent bouts of illness, possibly of malaria, and the hot weather certainly affected her physical well-being. Unlike many other Britons in India, there was no possibility of Arthur escaping to the cooler temperatures in the hill country, and there is no evidence that Winifred ever went away alone; her photograph album contains only snaps of their joint activities. She was 'a woman of a certain age', forty-eight years old. Did she suddenly realize that life was passing her by, that she would never have children, and perhaps that Arthur would never understand her feelings? His lack of sympathy for womankind had, rather sadly for Winifred, been demonstrated many times in the past.

Whatever the underlying reasons, something made Winifred wild or desperate on Friday 14 October, 1932. She and Arthur were staying, in their railway saloon carriage, at Chandia Road Station in the Central Provinces.

In the small hours of the morning, she killed herself. Exactly how is not known.

She was buried the same day, without inquest or post mortem. The grave was in a tiny churchyard adjacent to Saint Augustine's Church at Bilaspur, the nearest town of any size, and the burial certificate, completed and signed by Mr H. E. McClanaghan, the lay-reader who recited the Burial Service over poor Winifred, stated baldly that the cause of death was 'Suicide while temporarily insane at Chandia Road Railway Station'.[30] Two days later a stark notice of death appeared in the columns of *The Times* in London, giving no details of the cause of death or of any memorial service, and placing the event, wrongly, in Calcutta. A subsequent report stated that she had been 'found dead in Camp where she had accompanied her husband on a shooting expedition.'[31]

For the first time in his life, Arthur had met with something that he just could not face. He immediately took ship for England, arriving there on 11 November. He sought refuge at Marshalls, but the press soon found him. A *Daily Mail* journalist turned up on the doorstep expecting to interview Stephen about the news from India; instead, he was surprised to come face to face with Arthur himself. The newspaper's offices had received conflicting reports about the tragedy and asked Arthur to clear up what its headlines called 'THE MYSTERY OF VC's WIFE – DEATH REPORTED TWICE.' The story from its Bombay office was that she had been found dead in camp, murdered by an unknown assailant, and that her body had been removed to Calcutta.

Arthur's reaction to the journalist's questions was fully reported:

'I arrived back in England only on Friday. My wife died over a month ago of natural causes in a special train in which I was travelling through the Central Provinces in the normal course of my duties. The illness from which she died was the result of a prolonged association with tropical diseases into which she had come into contact while travelling through India in my company.

'I was present when she died, and there is no truth whatever in the story that she met her death as a result of foul play. There is no accounting for the rumours that get about in India. My wife has been dead for a month. The fact was announced in both the Indian and British newspapers, and I should have thought that the matter would have ended there so far as the public was concerned.'[32]

In this way, with a statement that was carefully but firmly phrased, Arthur sought to divert attention from Winifred's suicide. One can understand why, given the climate of opinion in the early 1930s, he would not wish the stigma of a suicide to attach itself to his family. In later years even members of other branches of the family did not know what had happened. For a reserved and retiring man like Arthur the intrusion by the press into his private life must have been even more painful than for most people. The *Daily Mail* seems to have accepted his story, however, and the matter was dropped. The newspaper reported at the end of Arthur's statement that it was, in fact, another Englishwoman who had been murdered; coincidentally she was also the wife of a BNR official, Major Locke.

To give Arthur all due credit, he did not shrink from returning to India, (though at fifty-eight years old he could easily have taken the easy option and retired from the Railway), where he had to face friends and colleagues who had known them both. Naturally there will have been gossip, but the *BNR Magazine* tackled the subject sensitively:

> 'For years both our Chief Medical Officer and his wife have been more than just acquaintances on the Railway; they have both endeared themselves to our hearts by their charming dispositions and their ready sympathy at all times. . . . The news that she has passed to the Great Beyond made all of us feel that we had lost one of our own. To our old friend, Doctor Martin-Leake, every heart on the BNR goes out in a deep and poignant sympathy. Words are of little avail on such occasions, but we feel we voice the feelings of every man and woman on the BNR when we say we wish we could take a portion of his great grief on our own shoulders.'[33]

Winifred was never mentioned in the *Magazine* again.

In the summer of 1933 alarming news arrived in the mail from High Cross. Across the lane from the house, Marshalls Farm had caught fire and was burnt to the ground. Fortunately the rebuilding cost of £1,820 was covered by insurance, but Arthur was aware that his brothers were getting on in years and were finding it difficult to cope with unexpected incidents of this kind. At the same time Steenie decided to undertake some minor road-widening works in Marshalls Lane, and to build two semi-detached houses near the farm, to provide homes for elderly Marshalls staff.[34]

By 1936 Arthur had decided to retire and return home as soon as was practicable; he was granted the usual long pre-retirement leave, during which he flew from Dum Dum Airport in an aircraft of the Royal Dutch Mail to Nyasaland and Portuguese East Africa for a safari lasting several weeks. In the company of a guide known as 'One Shot Araujo' he shot many small animals, two bull elephants and two buffalo; 'One Shot' bagged three lions and a leopard.[35] But Arthur found this kind of hunting 'rather too easy and over-organized', compared with the rigours and demands of Indian *shikar*.[36]

Finally, on 1 October, 1937, he left Calcutta for the last time. His Railway colleagues were denied the opprtunity of giving him a farewell party or any retirement presents. He allowed the *BNR Magazine* photographer to record his departure from Dum Dum, but that was all. The *Magazine* could only mark the occasion with several column inches that resembled an obituary:

> 'On the 1st October last there slipped quietly from our midst (we can think of no more effective way of describing his departure) Arthur Martin-Leake, VC, Chief Medical Officer of the Railway since 1st January, 1904. (Can any officer of any railway show a longer record of service as the Head of a Department?) The manner of Dr Leake's departure seemed so in keeping with his nature that we feel sure he would not have wished it otherwise. Quiet, dignified, unobtrusive (many would say 'shy', but we think 'disliking publicity' to be nearer the mark) and, above all, patient to a degree (as many of our poorer brethren when in trouble will testify), he has left behind him a record of service which we believe contains many a lesson which even the best of us can take to heart with advantage. By his service to mankind (especially to the humbler fraternity); by his fame as a shikari; by his contempt of the word 'danger'; by his high degree of physical fitness; by his skill as an aviator; by his humility and retiring disposition, he seems to have given us all a real lead. . . . While we wish him everything of the best, we hardly like to add 'and a well-earned rest', because we cannot see him taking it!'[37]

There was no reference at all to Winifred.

Arthur soon established himself back at Marshalls. He spent his time reading, gardening, occasionally flying in a borrowed machine. High Cross residents still remember his flight over the village on his way to Cambridge. He photographed Marshalls from the air, delighted to be able to pick out Sittie's sheets blowing on the washing line. Steenie and Dick had built a miniature railway, with an engine large enough to pull excited local children along a track laid in a small circle in the garden. Arthur bought himself a motorcycle, something he had always wanted to own, but which now seemed a doubly sensible mode of travel if petrol supplies were to be curtailed by reason of war. For the storm-clouds were gathering over Europe once again, and when war was declared on Germany on 3 September, 1939, the Marshalls household was as prepared as it could be, with a more than adequate vegetable garden and a larder filled with Georgiana's pickles and jams. She had a wonderful time as Evacuation Billeting Officer for the village, dashing about on her bicycle and organizing everyone.

At their ages there was little point in Steenie, Dick, Willie and Arthur offering themselves to the Army, but the announcement of the formation of the Local Defence Volunteers (LDV) in May, 1940, was seen by them as a heaven-sent opportunity. Steenie and Arthur immediately set up an Air Raid Precautions Post at the White Horse public house in High Cross, and here one or other of them organized the other members of the village's 'Dad's Army', fire-watching, manning the telephone or practising rescue techniques in anticipation of bombing from the sky. Arthur taught First Aid classes at Puckeridge, and so efficient was his mobile unit that it won many prizes in inter-unit competitions. Sittie told the *Evening Standard* that "he runs the unit and digs for victory with undiminished energy."[38] The course of the Battle of Britain in the skies about southern England was followed with great interest, especially by Arthur who had kept his pilot's licence up to date, but at its height Steenie's health gave way and he died at Marshalls on 7 September, 1940. He was buried with Frank and Bella at High Cross, and Arthur had to carry on in the Home Guard alone.

His part of Hertfordshire suffered occasional air-raids and he could certainly see the glow from the London Blitz in the night sky to the south. The Marshalls household suffered the same privations as every other family, although in the country there were more opportunities for obtaining useful extras like eggs and butter. As for clothes rationing, it is unlikely that the family was much affected. Even Sittie had always gone around the village in old clothes. "My sister's a bloody tramp," Frank used to say.

When war ended again in 1945 High Cross celebrated VE Day, as did the rest of the country. But the remaining Martin-Leakes were now elderly. A visiting child recalled that the house seemed to be "full of little old men".[39] The household had been severely reduced during the war as gardeners and other staff had had to leave, so that peacetime found no resident staff, just a daily woman, and later a visiting nurse if anyone was ill. Sittie had to enter a nursing home. She was eighty-two years old and her brothers could not give her the care she needed. On 8 February, 1947, in bitter winter weather, Willie died at home, aged eighty-one. He had occupied his last years in writing a biography of each member of the family, in the process compiling some very complex family trees, but only survived long enough to complete the life stories of Theodore and Frank. Only Arthur was fit enough to attend his lonely funeral at High Cross.[40]

Two years later, on 23 January, 1949, Sittie died; Arthur and Dick decided on cremation for her but her ashes were interred in the High Cross church-yard. A small group of villagers were at the graveside, remembering no doubt the days when Georgiana dashed about the countryside in an ancient motor-car, endangering residents and wildlife alike, or when she supervised the decoration of the church or the installation of its new organ. Dick had become virtually housebound, though he was able in fine weather to potter about in the garden. Four months after his sister's death he collapsed with a heart attack and died on the Marshalls lawn, beneath the venerable mulberry tree so beloved by their mother. Once again Arthur made his solitary way to the churchyard as the ashes of his last brother were laid to rest.[41]

So he was alone, the last of his generation. From time to time two cousins, Dorothy and Margery, came to stay, but basically he lived a bachelor's existence. He was visited by one or two younger relatives of the next generation, like Hugh Martin-Leake and his wife Sybil, and in the process it seems that his attitude towards women mellowed considerably. There was no telephone at the house during his lifetime, and certainly no television set. The Royal Army Medical Corps kept in touch with him, repeatedly asking him to attend dinners at their Central Mess or to visit the Depot at Crookham, but every invitation was politely refused. When asked about the Victoria Cross and Bar he said:

'I feel a bit of a fraud about all that; so many other chaps deserved it just as much.'[42]

They named a ward after him at the Queen Alexandra Hospital at Millbank, London, and the cars of 16 Field Ambulance bore the names 'Martin-Leake' and 'Chavasse'. Visiting children might be allowed to see and touch the Cross and Bar, but Arthur would never tell them how he came to have them.[43] He became quite an accomplished cook, and was described in the kitchen by a medical friend "wearing a surgical coat, cooking herrings with his cheeks well floured and a cigarette in his mouth".[44] After going up to Cambridge on his motor-cycle to see Hugh and Sybil, and finding them away from home, he left a splendid game pie on their doorstep – he had shot the pheasant and made the pie himself. He expressed great indignation when Ministry of Transport officials refused to renew his motorcycle licence when he was seventy-five.[45] He enjoyed gardening, painted in water-colour and began to draw a series of illustrations for another book on *shikar*, but it was never published.

And now his own health began to let him down, a sad condition for a man who throughout his life had been so keen on physical fitness and activity. A troublesome cough led him to seek medical advice; the results of the tests were no surprise. He had been a life-long smoker, and although the link between cigarette smoking and lung cancer was not yet formally established, as a doctor he cannot have been unaware of it. King George VI's death in

February, 1952, made the illness a national talking-point anyway. In October that year Arthur wrote to an old South African Constabulary friend:

'My senile troubles have been coming to the fore these days. If I had been a King they would say there was a structural alteration in the lung. Being a commoner, the medical profession call it a neoplasm; the man in the street calls it a ruddy cancer. I think I like the latter best, it is at least straightforward. I can still get about locally and do light jobs.

'I often think of the days gone by when you pulled me out of awkward places. I hope you are very fit and have none of the troubles of advancing age.'[46]

He tried to reduce the mental and physical pain with brandy, and survived until June the next year; in his last weeks he was delighted to receive the Queen Elizabeth II Coronation Medal; he had been just as pleased to have the George V Silver Jubilee Medal in 1935, and the George VI Coronation Medal in 1937. He presented one of his tiger skins and a leopard skin to the RAMC, and was glad to learn that the latter would be worn in the Coronation procession.[47] He also donated an ebony-headed cane to be carried by the Regimental Sergeant-Major, and a khaki jacket.[48] Reports of the conquest of Mount Everest excited him enormously, just the kind of exploit he understood, 'because it was there'. But now his illness was reaching an acute stage, though he still told no-one in his family just how serious it was.

On Monday 22 June, 1953, at the age of seventy-nine, he was found, collapsed, in a pool of blood on the Marshalls bathroom floor. His little terrier Waif, the last of a long line of Martin-Leake dogs, was nearby. Arthur never regained consciousness. His body was cremated on the morning of 26 June and his funeral in the little church at High Cross later the same day was attended by his cousins John and Hugh and a few more-distant relatives. The Director-General Army Medical Services was represented by Major-General E. E. J. Barnsley, and a party of young non-commissioned officers from the Corps filed past the grave in the corner of the churchyard.

So the ashes of Lieutenant-Colonel Arthur Martin-Leake, VC & Bar, RAMC, were laid to rest in the village he loved, after a short and simple service of which he would surely have approved, with 'no flowers or mourning, by request.'[49] The British Medical Journal's obituary summed him up:

'He was a great man, a simple man, and a character to admire and to love.'[50]

Postscript

In the Essex village of Thorpe-le-Soken after the First World War, Viscount and Lady Byng took up residence at Thorpe Hall, albeit briefly. He was rewarded, for his services during the war, with a peerage and a grant of £30,000, and chose the title Baron Byng of Vimy and Thorpe-le-Soken. The French Commune of Vimy presented him with a young silver birch sapling grown on the famous ridge, and its graceful lines may still be seen in the gardens at Thorpe Hall. Lady Byng undertook extensive landscaping works, and an extension to the Hall was completed in 1926. But Byng was destined not to live at the hall for any length of time; in 1921 he became a popular choice as Governor-General of Canada, and in 1928 was appointed Commissioner of the London Metropolitan Police. He died at Thorpe in 1935 and was buried at Beaumont-cum-Moze, a few miles from the Hall. Lady Byng continued to live there until her death in 1949. Three years later the house was bought by Sir George Nelson of English Electric, to serve as the 'Lady Nelson Convalescent Home' for male employees of the company. Today it stands empty. The gardens are well cared for, but the house is a shadow of its former glory, an example of the inexorable decline of many minor English country houses.

The executors of Arthur's estate asked the RAMC to accept the care of Waif, Arthur's little terrier, and he was looked after by the Regimental Police until he died a few years later. The estate totalled £110,320[1] including Marshalls. Arthur's medals were bequeathed to the RAMC, and at a ceremony in June, 1955, they were handed into 'the perpetual keeping' of the Corps following a drumhead service at the Queen Elizabeth II Barracks at Crookham. Two Chelsea Pensioners, who had known Arthur on active service, were present. Queen Elizabeth the Queen Mother, Colonel-in-Chief of the Corps, sent the following message:

> 'I have heard with the greatest interest of the ceremony you are holding today. The supreme gallantry and courage of Colonel Martin-Leake, of which these medals are an abiding symbol, will, I know, be an inspiration to the Corps. I am sure that these historic medals will be treasured by all ranks, not only for

themselves but as a symbol of that devotion to duty for which you have for so long been famed.'[2]

Waif was close by:

'He slept in his kennel outside the main guardroom throughout the parade. The ageing dog is said to be a little uncertain in temper these days, and although on normal days he makes his round of the barracks to greet old friends, it was thought wiser to confine him to the kennel for this occasion.'[3]

It was decided, in order that the medals would be seen by the greatest possible number of members of the Corps, that they would be displayed at the Depot at Aldershot, and at the Headquarters Mess at Millbank in London on Regimental Guest Nights and other special occasions.

Marshalls remained in the Martin-Leake family for another twenty years, lived in by Arthur's second cousin John. When he died in 1973, the house was auctioned, exactly 200 years after it came into the family, and the contents were sold in a separate sale. Thus many of Arthur's personal mementoes were dispersed – a tigerskin rug for eighty pounds, and an Indian hearthrug for four; a pair of elephants' feet adapted as jardinieres made seventy pounds while an 'important' pair of large elephant tusks went for £480; Arthur's eighteenth-century mahogany bookcase from his study raised £1,900, but his mother's cane invalid carriage fetched only three pounds.

In 1986 it became apparent that the grave in High Cross churchyard was in need of some maintenance and refurbishment. This was undertaken by men of the RAMC, and permission was obtained to erect a memorial plaque to Arthur beneath the west window of the church. At a ceremony on 13 June that year the plaque was dedicated by the Bishop of St Albans, the Right Reverend John Taylor, in the presence of members of the family and of the RAMC, whose senior representative was Surgeon-General Sir Cameron Moffat KBE, QHS. A reception was held at Marshalls, where Arthur Martin-Leake's story had begun 112 years before

References

Key to References

BNR	Bengal-Nagpur Railway
ERO	Essex Record Office
HRO	Hertfordshire Record Office
ML Papers	Martin-Leake Papers in private hands
PRO	Public Record Office
SAC	South African Constabulary
UCH	University College Hospital
WCCMA	Wellcome Centre: Contemporary Medical Archives

Family References

AML	Arthur Martin-Leake
BML	Bella Martin-Leake (sister)
FML	Francis Martin-Leake (brother)
GML	Georgiana Martin-Leake (sister)
IML	Isabel Martin-Leake (mother)
RML	Richard Martin-Leake (brother)
SML	Stephen Martin-Leake (brother)
WML	William Martin-Leake (brother)

1. *An Illustrious Inheritance*
   1. S. Martin-Leake, *The Life of Sir John Leake*, 1750, Navy Records Society 1919, Vol. II, pp. 422–3.
   2. W. Martin-Leake, Manuscript, ML Papers.
   3. S. Martin-Leake, *op. cit.*
   4. WML, Manuscript, M L Papers.
   5. Ibid.
   6. SML Typescript, HRO, 1933.
   7. Martin-Leake Papers, HRO.
   8. R. Tricker, *Brief History of the Church of St John the Evangelist, High Cross*, 1990.
   9. E. A. Wood, *A History of Thorpe-le-Soken to the Year 1890*, T.C. Webb, 1975, p. 116.

10. S. Martin-Leake, Manuscript, n.d. ERO.
11. ML Papers, ERO.
12. *Herts Mercury* 23.2.1924.

2. *'Mammy Makes a Lovely Widow'*
   1. Charterhouse Archives: *The Carthusian*, 1879.
   2. ML Papers.
   3. Ibid.
   4. Ibid.
   5. Ibid.
   6. Ibid.
   7. Ibid.
   8. Ibid.
   9. AML to IML 5.3.1900, HRO.
   10. J. Field, *The King's Nurseries: The Story of Westminster School*, James & James, London, 1987, passim.
   11. Field, *op. cit.*, pp. 67–68.
   12. Westminster School: *'The Elizabethan'*, Vol. VI Number 1, February 1889.
   13. ML Papers
   14. ML Papers.
   15. RML to IML, 22.11.1890, ML Papers.
   16. WML, Manuscript, ML Papers.
   17. *Pioneers of the Planting Enterprise in Ceylon No. 9*, 'W. Martin-Leake Esq.', Ferguson, Colombo 1897.
   18. Radley College: Archive.
   19. ML Papers, HRO.
   20. *Times*, 4.3.1893.
   21. ML Papers, HRO.
   22. BML to SML, 15.3.1893, ML Papers.
   23. RML to IML 5.4.1893, ML Papers.

3. *'Ride Straight, Shoot Straight, and Keep Straight!'*
   1. RML to IML 26.4.1893, ML Papers.
   2. Radley College Archives; ML Papers.
   3. WML to IML, 25.4.1895, ML Papers.
   4. UCH Archive: Student Records, 1893–99.
   5. S. Paget, *Sir Victor Horsley*, Constable, London 1919, p. 158.
   6. *Lancet* 29.7.1916, p202.
   7. *British Medical Journal* 29.7.1916, p. 16.
   8. General Medical Council: Register
   9. UCH Student Records, 1893–1899.

10. AML to IML 1.10.1899, HRO
11. AML to IML, 1.10.1899.
12. *Notes* on West Herts. Infirmary, HRO.
13. Patients' Record Book, 1899, West Herts Infirmary, HRO.
14. WML to IML 27,8.1885, ML Papers.
15. *Times*, 11.10.1899.
16. *Times*, 13.10.1899.
17. J.D. Sainsbury, *Hertfordshire Yeomanry and Artillery: Uniforms, Arms and Equipment.* Vol. 1. Herts Yeomanry & Artillery Historical Trust, 1980, pp. 22–23.
18. West Herts. Infirmary House Committee Minute Book, HRO.
19. *Herts Mercury*, 10.2.1900
20. AML to IML, 11.1.1900, HRO.
21. Sainsbury *loc.cit.*
22. *Herts Advertiser*, 3.2.1900.
23. AML to IML, 17.1.1900, HRO.
24. AML to IML 24.1.1900, HRO.
25. AML to IML 1.2.1900, HRO.
26. *Herts Mercury*, 3.2.1900.
27. Ibid.
28. *Herts Mercury* ibid.
29. ibid.
30. *Herts Mercury* 10.2.1900.
31. Menu Cards, HRO D/E YO 2/9 & 10.
32. *Herts Mercury* 10.2.1900.
33. Ibid.
34. Ibid.
35. AML to IML 12.2.1900, HRO.
36. AML to IML 16.2.1900, HRO.
37. AML to IML 20.2.1900, HRO.
38. *Herts Mercury* 10.3.1900.
39. AML to IML 1.3.1900, HRO.
40. *Herts Mercury*, loc. cit.

4. *'Where Do All The Boers Come From?'*
   1. AML to IML 5.3.1900 HRO.
   2. AML to IML 5.3. & 9.3. 1900, HRO.
   3. AML to IML 5.3.1900, HRO.
   4. AML to IML 27.3.1900, HRO.
   5. AML to IML 9.3.1900, HRO.
   6. AML to IML 27.3.1900, HRO.
   7. AML to IML 2.4.1900, HRO.

8. Ibid.
9. *Times* 7.4.1900.
10. Ibid.
11. Ibid.
12. Ibid.
13. Brian Roberts: *Those Bloody Women*, John Murray 1991, p. 5.
14. AML to IML 18.4.1900, HRO.
15. Ibid.
16. WML to IML 5.4.1900, HRO.
17. WML to IML 17.5.1900, HRO.
18. T. Pakenham, *The Boer War*, Futura 1982, p. 179.
19. AML to IML 29.4.1900, HRO.
20. AML to IML 8.5. 1900, HRO.
21. AML to IML 16.5.1900, HRO.
22. AML to IML 25.5.1900, HRO.
23. AML to IML 19.6.1900, HRO.
24. Michael Barthorp, *The Anglo-Boer Wars*, Blandford 1991, p. 129.
25. Ibid.
26. AML to IML July 1900, HRO.
27. AML to IML 2.8.1900, 8.8.1900, 7.9.1900, HRO.
28. AML to IML 25.8.1900, HRO.
29. P.W.L. Broke-Smith, 'The History of Early British Aeronautics', *Journal of the Institute of Royal Engineers* Offprint, n.d. p. 23.
30. AML to IML 7.9.1900 & 18.9.1900, HRO.
31. WML to IML, 8.11.1900, HRO.
32. AML to IML 18.9.1900, HRO.
33. J.D. Sainsbury, *Hertfordshire's Soldiers*, Herts. Local History Council 1969, p. 22.
34. AML to IML 18.10.1900, HRO.
35. *Jubilee Scrapbook of the RAMC 1898–1948.* Gale & Polden 1948, pp. 14–15.

5. *'The Hat and Legging Brigade'*
    1. AML to IML 1.11.1900, HRO.
    2. AML to IML 6.11.1900, HRO.
    3. AML to IML 21.11.1900, HRO.
    4. L.S. Amery (Ed.), *The Times History of the War in South Africa*, Sampson 1900–1909, Vol. VI p. 503.
    5. AML to IML 21.11.1900, HRO
    6. AML to IML 31.12.1900, HRO.
    7. AML to IML 18.12.1900, HRO.
    8. AML to IML 27.11.1900, HRO.

9. AML to IML 18.12.1900, HRO.
10. S. Martin-Leake, 'The Roopnarayan Bridge', in *Proceedings of the Institute of Civil Engineers*, Paper Number 3275, December 1902.
11. AML to IML 31.12.1900, HRO.
12. FML to IML 3.11.1900, HRO.
13. FML to IML 16.2.1901, HRO.
14. AML to IML 31.12.1900, HRO.
15. AML to IML 14.4.1901 and 3.5.1901, HRO.
16. WML to IML, Jan. 1901, ML Papers.
17. AML to IML 27.1.1901 & 7.3.1901, HRO.
18. FML to IML 10.3.1901, HRO.
19. AML to IML 31.12.1900, HRO.
20. AML to IML 8.1.1901, HRO.
21. AML to IML 27/28.1.1901, HRO.
22. AML to IML 12.2.1901, HRO.
23. AML to IML 16.2.1901 HRO.
24. WML to IML 21.1.1901 and 20.3.1901, HRO.
25. AML to IML 28.2.1901, HRO.
26. L.S. Amery, *op. cit.*, p. 537.
27. D.A. Lane, 'The South African Constabulary', *Nongqai*, Johannesburg, August, 1950, pp. 906–7.
28. *Daily Graphic* 20.2.1902.
29. Ibid.
30. Lane, op.cit., p. 911.
31. D.A. Lane, *Nongqai*, Johannesburg, September 1950, p. 1035.
32. AML to IML 17.5.1901, HRO.
33. AML to IML 24.5.1901, HRO.
34. AML to IML 22.8.1901, HRO.
35. AML to IML 1.6.1901, HRO.
36. AML to IML 8.6.1901, HRO.
37. AML to IML 11.7/5.8.1901, HRO.
38. AML to IML 20.8.1901, HRO.
39. AML to IML 24.9.1901, HRO.
40. AML to IML 1.10.1901, HRO.
41. For a full description, see B. Roberts, *Those Bloody Women: Three Heroines of the Boer War*, John Murray, 1991.
42. WML to IML 23.7.1901, ML Papers
43. AML to IML 29.12.1901, HRO.
44. AML to IML 22.1.1902, HRO.
45. AML to IML 4.2.1902, HRO.

6. *'And Then He Refused Water'*

1. G.H. Cullis to R.J. Franklin 24.8.1960, WCCMA, RAMC 801/15.
2. J.S. Nicolson, 'Remarks', 15.2.1902, typescript, ML Papers.
3. *Times*, 12.2.1902.
4. Proceedings of Board of Officers, SAC, Roodekop, 12.2.1902, PRO/ WO/32 4990.
5. Cullis to Franklin, loc.cit.
6. Proceedings of Board of Officers, loc.cit.
7. Nicolson, op.cit.
8. *South African Field Force Casualty List Jan–May 1902*, J.B. Hayward 1902, p. 86.
9. Medical Report on A. Martin-Leake, PMO's Office, Johannesburg, 12.3.1902. WCCMA, RAMC/303.
10. *Times*, 12.2.1902.
11. AML to IML 20.2.1902, HRO.
12. FML to IML 15.3.1902, HRO.
13. WML to IML 14.3.1902, HRO.
14. WML to IML 23.4.1902, HRO.
15. M. Barthorp, *The Anglo-Boer Wars*, Blandford 1987, p. 166.
16. PRO WO/32 4990.
17. Ibid.
18. Ibid.
19. Ibid.
20. Ibid.
21. PRO/32 4990.
22. Ibid, 4.5.1902.
23. *London Gazette*, 13.5.1902.
24. *Herts Mercury* 17.5.1902.
25. *People*, 25.5.1902.
26. S. Paget, *Sir Victor Horsley*, Constable 1919, p. 168.
27. *London Illustrated News* 24.5.1902.
28. WML Senior to IML 14.5.1902, HRO.
29. WML Senior to AML 14.5.1902, HRO.
30. F. Russell Reynolds to AML, 15.5.1902, HRO.
31. William Ralph Martin-Leake to AML 15.5.1902, HRO.
32. WML to AML 21.5.1902, HRO.
33. RML to AML 14.5.1902, HRO.
34. FML to IML, 12–18.6.1902, HRO.
35. Mrs F. Joy to IML 14.5.1902, HRO.
36. T.F. Halsey to AML 22.5.1902, HRO.
37. Captain of Westminster to AML, 29.5.1902, HRO.
38. James Gow to IML 15.5.1902, HRO.

39. *Times* 18.12.1902.
40. L. Fuller to AML 15.5.1902, HRO.
41. C. Bolton to AML 15.5.1902, HRO.
42. WML to IML 16.4.1902, HRO.
43. H. Nicolson: *King George V*, Constable 1952, pp. 80–81.
44. I.S. Uys, *For Valour, The History of South Africa's Victoria Cross Heroes*, Uys 1973, p. 188.
45. R. Miller to AML, 3.7.1903, HRO.
46. Contract between BNR and AML, 28.7.1903, HRO.
47. Colonial Office to AML 6.5.1905, HRO.
48. AML to Colonial Office, 23.12.1903, HRO.
49. Proceedings of Medical Board on AML, Calcutta, 7.11.1904, HRO.

7. *'The City of Dreadful Night'*
  1. AML to IML 7.1.1904, HRO.
  2. AML to IML 8.1.1904, HRO.
  3. AML to IML 17.1.1904, HRO.
  4. R.D. Connell, *Travel in India*, Bengal-Nagpur Railway 1916, p. 130.
  5. Connell, *op. cit.*, pp21–24.
  6. AML to IML 27.1.1904, HRO.
  7. G. Moorhouse: *Calcutta*, Penguin 1983, p. 228.
  8. AML to IML 30.1.1904, HRO.
  9. AML to IML 4.2.1904, HRO.
  10. AML to IML 11.2.1904, HRO.
  11. AML to IML 16.3.1904, HRO.
  12. AML to IML 2.3.1904, HR.
  13. AML to IML 16.3.1904, HRO.
  14. AML to IML 19.5.1904, HRO.
  15. AML to IML 2.3.1904, HRO.
  16. AML to IML 19.5.1904, HRO.
  17. A Martin-Leake and R.T.D. Alexander: *Some Signposts to Shikar*, Granyer, 1932, p. 101.
  18. AML to IML 9.6.1904, HRO
  19. AML to IML 25.5.1904, HRO.
  20. AML to IML 18.5.1905, HRO.
  21. AML to IML 16.6.1904, HRO.
  22. C. Allen, ed., *Plain Tales From the Raj*, Futura 1988 p. 146.
  23. AML to IML 7.7.1904, HRO.
  24. C. Allen: *op. cit.*, p. 46.
  25. AML to IML 17.11. 1904, HRO.
  26. AML to IML 24.11.1904, HRO.
  27. WML Manuscript, ML Papers.

28. War Office to IML 6.6.1907, ML Papers.
29. ML Papers.
30. *Hertfordshire Mercury* 6.7.1907.
31. GML, letter 4.7.1907, HRO.
32. Indian Army List, Army HQ, India, passim.
33. AML to IML 11.1.1904, HRO.
34. AML to IML 18.5.1905, HRO.
35. AML to IML 2.1.1908 WCCMA RAMC 801/15.
36. R. Ticker, *A Brief History of St. John the Evangelist, High Cross,* 1990, p. 4.

8. *'Quite the Worst Country that I Have Ever Seen'*
   1. *Times*, 8.10.1912.
   2. *Times*, 10.10.1912.
   3. B. Oliver, *The British Red Cross in Action*, Faber 1966, p. 218.
   4. *Times*, 17.10.1912.
   5. Oliver, *loc.cit.*
   6. Oliver, *op.cit*, p. 219.
   7. AML to IML 19.10.1912, HRO.
   8. *Daily Telegraph* 18.10.1912.
   9. Ibid.
   10. AML to IML, 19.10.1912, HRO.
   11. Ibid.
   12. *Daily Telegraph* 29.10.1912.
   13. *Daily Telegraph* 30.2.1915.
   14. AML to IML 25.10.1912, HRO.
   15. AML to IML 26.10.1912, HRO.
   16. AML to IML 29.10.1912, HRO.
   17. AML to IML 31.10.1912, HRO.
   18. AML to IML 29.10.1912, HRO.
   19. AML to IML 7.11.1912, ML Papers.
   20. Ibid.
   21. Ibid.
   22. Ibid.
   23. AML Diary 8.11.1912, typescript, ML Papers.
   24. Ibid.
   25. Ibid.
   26. Ibid.
   27. AML Diary 10.11.1912, typescript, ML Papers.
   28. Ibid.
   29. Ibid.
   30. Ibid.

31. Ibid.
32. AML Diary 11.11.1912, typescript, ML Papers.
33. AML Diary 12.11.1912, typescript, ML Papers.
34. AML to IML 24.11.1912, HRO.
35. Ibid.
36. AML to IML 25.11.1912, HRO.
37. AML to IML 2.12.1912, HRO.
38. AML to IML 8.12.1912, HRO.
39. Ibid.
40. Ibid.
41. AML to IML 12.1.1913, HRO.
42. *Times* 15.1.1913.
43. *Times* 19.2.1913.
44. *Times*, 15.5.1913.
45. Oliver, *op. cit.*, p. 223.

9. *'A Uniform Does Everything Now'*
    1. J. Williams: *Byng of Vimy*, Leo Cooper 1983, pp. 60–61.
    2. AML to IML 23.7.19.14, HRO.
    3. I.S. Uys: *For Valour: The History of South Africa's VC Heroes'*, Uys, 1973 p. 185.
    4. AML to IML 22.8.1914, HRO.
    5. AML to IML 28.8.1914, HRO.
    6. AML to IML 30.8. 1914, HRO.
    7. AML to IML 28.10.1914 HRO.
    8. *British Medical Journal* 8.3.1919.
    9. W.G. Macpherson: *Official History of the War – Medical Services General History Vol. II*, HMSO 1923, p. 16.
    10. *Times* 6.9.1914.
    11. *Times History of the War*, Vol. II London 1915, p. 15.
    12. FML to IML 8.9.1914, ML Papers
    13. Lady Beatty to IML 7.9.1914 HRO.
    14. A. Fripp to IML, 11.9.1914, HRO.
    15. *Times History of the War* Vol. IV, London 1915, p. 45.
    16. PRO WO/95 1337.
    17. Ibid.
    18. Ibid.
    19. Ibid.
    20. Ibid.

10. *'A Very Gallant Fellow'*
    1. PRO WO/95 1337.
    2. AML to IML 26.10.1914, HRO.

3. Ibid.
4. J. Giles, *The Western Front Then and Now*, After the Battle 1992, p. 72.
5. AML to IML, September 1914, WCCMA RAMC/267.
6. AML to IML 28.10.1914, HRO.
7. AML to IML 3.11.1914, HRO.
8. AML to IML 4.11.1914, HRO.
9. AML to IML 6.11.1914, HRO.
10. AML to IML 9.11.1914, HRO.
11. Pte. D. Wolfe, Tape Recording Number 914/915, Liddle Collection, University of Leeds, 1993.
12. PRO WO/95 1337.
13. *Times*, 2.11.1914.
14. AML to IML 9.11.1914, HRO.
15. *British Medical Journal*, Obituary, 29.7.1916.
16. AML to IML 18.11.1914, HRO.
17. Ibid.
18. AML to IML 14.12.1914, HRO.
19. AML to IML 18.12.1914, HRO.
20. R. Tanner to AML 9.12.1914, HRO.
21. AML to IML 23.12.1914, HRO.
22. AML to IML 26.12.1914, HRO.
23. AML to IML 29.12.1914, HRO.
24. AML to IML 10.1.1915, HRO.
25. AML to IML 3.1.1915, HRO.
26. AML to IML 10.1.1915, HRO.
27. AML to IML 13.1.1915, HRO.
28. AML to IML 18.1.1915, HRO.
29. AML to IML 21.1.1915, HRO.
30. AML to IML 10.2.1915, HRO.
31. AML to IML 14/17.2.1915, HRO.
32. AML to IML 20.2.1915, HRO.
33. *London Gazette* 18.2.1915.
34. *London Gazette* 17.2.1915.
35. PRO WO/32 4991.
36. PRO WO/32 4991.
37. See M.J. Crook, *The Evolution of the Victoria Cross*, Ogilvy Trust 1975.
38. PRO WO/32 4991.
39. PRO WO/32 4991.
40. E.A. James, *A Record of the Battles and Engagements of the British Armies in France and Flanders, 1914–1918*, Gale & Polden, Aldershot 1924, p. 5.

41. Edward Lugard to J.C.C. Daunt V.C., 3.3.1863, PRO WO32/4991.
42. *Daily Telegraph* 22.5.1915.
43. *Herts Mercury* 27.2.1915.
44. *Daily Mail* 26.2.1915.
45. *Daily Mail* 11.3.1915.
46. Ibid.
47. FML to IML 9/14.7.1915, ML Papers.
48. FML to Mrs Rose Trent, 8.8.1915, ML Papers.
49. *London Gazette* 4.3.1915.
50. *Town Topics* 6.3.1915.
51. *Morning Post* 9.3.1915.
52. AML to William Martin-Leake Senior 4.3.1915, ML Papers.
53. *Lancet* 27.2.1915.
54. *Tatler* 24.2.1915.
55. *Herts Mercury* 27.2.1915.
56. *The Indiaman*, 26.2.1915.
57. AML to IML 2–7.3.1915, HRO.

11. *'The Germans Must be Squashed'*

1. AML to IML 10.3.1915, HRO.
2. AML to IML 23.3.1915, HRO.
3. FML to IML 15.6.1915, ML Papers.
4. PRO WO/95 1337.
5. AML to IML 23.3.1915, HRO.
6. AML to IML 30.3.1915, HRO.
7. H. Nicolson: *King George V*, Constable 1952, p. 262.
8. AML to IML 7.4.1915, HRO.
9. AML to IML 7.4.1915, HRO.
10. AML to IML 19.4.1915, HR.
11. AML to IML 28.4.–2.5.1915, HRO.
12. Ibid.
13. PRO WO/95 1377.
14. AML to IML 21.5.1915, HRO.
15. AML to IML 27.5.1915, HRO.
16. PRO WO/95 1337.
17. AML to IML 2.6.1915, HRO.
18. AML to IML 24–26.6.1915, HRO.
19. AML to IML 2.6.1915, HRO.
20. PRO WO/32 4992.
21. FML to IML 9.7.1915, ML Papers.
22. AML to IML 8.7.1915, HRO.
23. Telegram 21.7.1915 WCCMA RAMC/801/15.

24. AML to William Martin -Leake Senior, 29.7.1915, ML Papers.
25. IML to Louisa Martin-Leake 27.7.1915 M-L Papers.
26. *British Medical Journal* 25.1.1919.
27. AML to IML 1.8.1915, HRO.
28. *Times History of the War*, Vol. VIII, p. 320.
29. AML to IML 2.8.1915, HRO.
30. AML to IML 15.8.1915, HRO.
31. PRO WO/95 3771.
32. AML to IML 15.8.1915, HRO.
33. AML to IML 4.11.1915, HRO.
34. *London Gazette*, 29.11.1915.

12. '*A Bally Awful Muddle*'
    1. AML to IML 18.12.1914 HRO.
    2. J. Berry et al, *The Story of a British Red Cross Unit in Serbia*, Churchill, London, 1916, p. 9.
    3. Berry, *op.cit*, pp. 124–5.
    4. C. Falls, *Official History of the War: Military Operations – Macedonia*, HMSO 1933, p. 36.
    5. *Times*, 19.10.1915.
    6. *Times*, 1.11.1915.
    7. *Times*, 2.11.1915.
    8. AML to IML 1.12.1915, HRO.
    9. AML to IML 4.12.1915, HRO.
    10. AML to IML 7–10.12.1915, HRO.
    11. M. Krippner, *The Quality of Mercy*, David & Charles 1980, p. 111.
    12. L.F. Waring: *Servia*, Williams & Norgate 1917, pp. 244–5.
    13. AML to IML 18.12.1915, HRO.
    14. AML to IML 27.12.1915, HRO.
    15. AML to IML 15.1.1916, HRO.
    16. AML to IML 16.1.1916, HRO.
    17. AML to IML 29.1.1916, HRO.
    18. AML to IML 2.2.1916, HRO.
    19. *Times*, 2.2.1916.
    20. AML to IML 7.2.1916, HRO.
    21. AML to IML 19.2.1916, HRO.
    22. W.G. Macpherson and T.J. Mitchell, *Official History of the War, Medical Services*. HMSO 1924, Vol. IV, p. 101.
    23. AML to IML 2.2.1916, HRO.
    24. IML to WML 1.1.1916, ML Papers.
    25. IML to WML 25.4.1916, ML Papers.
    26. WML to IML no date, ML papers.

13. *'I am no Soldier . . .'*
   1. AML to IML 27.3.1916, HRO.
   2. MacPherson: *Official History (Medical Services) Vol. II*, pp. 42–49.
   3. AML to IML 29.6.1916, HRO.
   4. AML to IML 28.7.1916, HRO.
   5. AML to IML 18.8.1916, HRO.
   6. L.W. Bills: *A Medal for Life*, Spellmount 1990, p. 66.
   7. AML to Sir M. Holt, 3.1.1917, WCCMA RAMC/267.
   8. AML to IML 17.11.1916, HRO.
   9. AML to IML 16.12.1916, HRO.
   10. G.H. Swindell, *Diary*, WCCMA RAMC/80/115.
   11. P. Gosse, *Army Medical Services Magazine*, Vol. 4 Autumn, 1953, pp. 106–7.
   12. AML to IML 24.12.1916, HRO.
   13. AML to IML 6.1.1917, HRO.
   14. AML to IML 10.1.1917, HRO.
   15. AML to IML 10.3.1917, HRO.
   16. AML to IML 13.3.1917, HRO.
   17. AML to IML 18.3.1917, HRO.
   18. PRO WO/95 1931.
   19. PRO WO/95 1931.
   20. AML to IML 28.3.1917, HRO.
   21. *London Gazette* 22.6.1917.
   22. AML to IML 31.3.1917, HRO.
   23. J. Nicholls, *Cheerful Sacrifice: the Battle of Arras 1917*, Leo Cooper 1990, p. 69.
   24. PRO WO/95 1931.
   25. Ibid.
   26. AML to IML 15.4.1917, HRO.
   27. Ibid., 26.4.1917.
   28. Ibid., 28.4.1917.
   29. AML to IML 20.5.1917, HRO.
   30. PRO WO/95 1931.
   31. AML to IML 24.5.1917, HRO.
   32. Ibid.
   33. E.S. Turner, *Dear Old Blighty*, Michael Joseph, 1980, p. 237.
   34. WCCMA RAMC 801/15.
   35. AML to IML 14.6.1917, HRO.
   36. PRO WO/95 1931.

14. *'War is a Fearful Waste'*
   1. PRO WO/95 1931.
   2. Ibid.

3. Colston, loc. cit.
4. AML to IML 25.6.1917, HRO.
5. AML to IML 17.7.1917, HRO.
6. AML to IML 28.6.1917, HRO.
7. PRO WO/95 1931.
8. Ibid.
9. L. Macdonald, *They Called It Passchendaele*, Michael Joseph 1978, p. 73.
10. PRO WO/95 1931.
11. AML to IML 17.7.1917, HRO.
12. L. Macdonald: *op. cit.*, p. 87.
13. PRO WO/95 1931.
14. M. Gilbert: *Churchill, A Life*, Heinemann 1992, p. 320.
15. AML to IML 28.7.1917, HRO.
16. War Diary, ADMS 55th Division, PRO WO/95 2912.
17. PRO WO/95 1931.
18. AML to IML 1.8.1917, HRO.
19. J.R. Colston, *Diary*, WCCMA, RAMC 801/15.
20. A. Clayton: *Chavasse: Double VC*, Leo Cooper 1992, Chapter 14.
21. J.A.C. Colston to 'Mr Peel', 1956, WCCMA, RAC 801/15.
22. AML to IML 13.8.1917, HRO.
23. AML to IML 4.8.1917, HRO.
24. PRO WO/95 1931.
25. AML to IML 7/9.8.1917, HRO.
26. AML to IML 19.9.1917, HRO.
27. AML to IML 23.10.1917, HRO.
28. PRO WO/95 1931.
29. AML to IML 26.12.1917, HRO.
30. *British Medical Journal* 19.1.1918.
31. AML to IML 16.1.1918, HRO.
32. Ibid.
33. AML to IML 9.2.1918, HRO.
34. AML to IML 16.3.1917, HRO.
35. AML to IML 26.3.1918, HRO.
36. *London Gazette*, 13.4.1918.
37. AML to IML 13.2.1918, HRO.
38. AML to IML 28.2.1918, HRO.
39. AML to IML 3.3.1918, HRO.
40. AML to IML 9/17.4.1918, HRO.
41. AML to IML 31.3.1918, HRO.
42. AML to IML 13.5.1918, HRO.
43. AML to IML 23.5.1918, HRO.

44. *London Gazette* 25.5.1918.
45. AML to IML 2.6.1918, HRO.
46. Fairley Capt. G.D., RAMC, *Diary*, Liddle Collection, University of Leeds.
47. AML to IML 13.6.1918, HRO.
48. AML to IML 18/24.6.1918, HRO.
49. AML to IML 9.7.1918, HRO.
50. AML to IML 1.8.1918, HRO.
51. AML to IML 7/12.8.1918, HRO.
52. AML to IML 28.8.1918, HRO.

15. *'A Simple Man*
   1. IML to WML 20/8/1916, ML Papers.
   2. FML to IML 11.11.1918, ML Papers.
   3. I. Uys: *For Valour, The History of South Africa's Victoria Cross Heroes*, Uys 1973, p. 188.
   4. *Evening News* 6.10.1930.
   5. *The Statesman*, Calcutta, 1.4.1921.
   6. *BNR Magazine*, August 1929.
   7. SML: *'Marshalls'*, ML Papers, HRO.
   8. *Herts Mercury* 4.6.1921.
   9. *Times* 1.12.1921.
   10. *British Medical Journal* 29.7.1922.
   11. WCCMA RAMC/267.
   12. *BNR Magazine*, December, 1937.
   13. *Herts Mercury* 23.2.1924.
   14. *Times* 27.1.1928.
   15. R. Tricker, *Brief History & Guide to the Church of St John the Evangelist, High Cross*, 1990.
   16. AML: 'The Death of a Rogue', *BNR Magazine*, September 1926.
   17. A. Martin-Leake VC, VD and R.D.T. Alexander DSO, OBE, TD: *Some Signposts to Shikar*. Grenyer, Calcutta, 1932.
   18. Martin-Leake and Alexander, op.cit., p. 2.
   19. Ibid., p. 14.
   20. Ibid., p. 17.
   21. *Indian State Railways Magazine*, December, 1930.
   22. *Daily Express*, 11.11.1929.
   23. *BNR Magazine*, November-December 1930.
   24. *Times*, 28.8.1929.
   25. *BNR Magazine*, November, 1930.
   26. *Evening News* 26.9.1930.
   27. *Evening News* 6.10.1930.

28. Winifred Martin-Leake, Album, WCCMA/RAMC.
29. A. Martin-Leake and R.D.T. Alexander, *op.cit.*, p. 16.
30. Indian Ecclesiastical Records held at British Library, India Office Collection.
31. *Times*, 14.11.1932.
32. *Daily Mail*, 14.11.1932.
33. *BNR Magazine*, November, 1932.
34. Miscellaneous ML Papers, HRO.
35. *African World*, 26.11.1936.
36. *Army Medical Services Magazine*, October, 1949.
37. *BNR Magazine*, December, 1937.
38. *Evening Standard*, 28.6.1944.
39. Interview 1992.
40. *Herts Mercury*, 14.2.1947.
41. *Herts Mercury*, 13.5.1949.
42. *Army Medical Services Magazine*, Autumn, 1953.
43. Told to the author, 1992.
44. *British Medical Journal*, 4.7.1953.
45. *Army Medical Services Magazine*, October, 1949.
46. AML to Lt-Gen Sir Matthew Fell, 21.10.1952, WCCMA.
47. *Army Medical Services Magazine*, October, 1953.
48. Ibid., October, 1955.
49. *Times*, 24.6.1953.
50. *British Medical Journal*, 4.7.1953.

Postscript
1. *Times*, 27.5.1954.
2. *Army Medical Services Magazine*, October, 1955.
3. *Aldershot News*, 27.6.1955.
4. Marshalls, Auction of Contents, Catalogue, Phillips Son and Neale, September 1973.

Sources

Newspapers, Journals and Registers

African World
Aldershot News
Daily Express
Daily Graphic
Daily Mail
Daily Telegraph
Evening News
Herts Advertiser
Herts Mercury
Indiaman
London Gazette
London Illustrated News
Morning Post
The People
The Statesman
The Times
Tatler
Town Topics

Army Medical Services Magazine
Bengal-Nagpur Railway Magazine
British Medical Journal
Indian State Railways Magazine
Lancet
Nongquai (South Africa)
Proceedings of the Institute of Civil Engineers
Royal Engineers Journal
The Elizabethan (Westminster School)

Army List
Commonwealth War Graves Commission, Memorial and Cemetery Registers
Indian Army List

General Medical Council Register
Officers Died in the Great War (HMSO 1919)
South African Field Force Casualty List (J.B. Hayward 1902)

Unpublished Sources

Martin-Leake Papers in private hands
Martin-Leake Papers, Hertfordshire Record Office, Hertford
Martin-Leake Papers, Essex Record Office, Chelmsford
Miscellaneous Papers, Imperial War Museum
Miscellaneous Papers, the Liddle Collection, University of Leeds
Parish Registers, High Cross, Herts., and Thorpe-le-Soken, Essex
Records of Herts. Imperial Yeomanry, Herts. Record Office
Unit War Diaries 1914–1918, Public Record Office
Royal Army Medical Corps Papers, Contemporary Medical Archives Centre,
    Wellcome Institute for the History of Medicine
West Herts. Infantry Records, Herts. Record Office
Archives of Charterhouse, Radley College and Westminster School
Indian Ecclesiastical Records, British Library
University College Hospital Archives

Select Bibliography

Allen, C. (ed.) *Plain Tales from the Raj*, Futura, 1988.

Amery, L.S. (ed.) *The Times History of the War in South Africa*, Sampson, 1900–1909.

Becke, A.F. *Official History of the Great War: Military Operations Macedonia*, HMSO, 1933–35.

Crook, M.J. *The Evolution of the Victoria Cross*, Ogilvy Trust,1975.

Field, J. *The King's Nurseries: the Story of Westminster School*, James and James, 1987.

Edmonds, J.E. (ed.) *Official History of the Great War: Military Operations, France and Belgium*, HMSO, 1922–49.

McLaughlin, R. *The Royal Army Medical Corps*, Leo Cooper, 1972.

Macpherson, W.G. et al. *Official History of the Great War: Medical Services Vols I–IV*, HMSO 1928–31.

Nicholls, J. *Cheerful Sacrifice: the Battles of Arras 1917*, Leo Cooper 1990.

Oliver, B. *The British Red Cross in Action*, Faber, 1966.

Sainsbury, J.D. *Hertfordshire Yeomanry and Artillery: Uniforms, Arms and Equipment, Vol I*, Herts Yeomanry Historical Trust, 1980.

Sainsbury, J.D. *Hertfordshire's Soldiers*, Herts Local History Council, 1969.

Uys, I.S. *For Valour, the History of South Africa's Victoria Cross Heroes*, Uys, 1973.

Index